1 MONTH OF
FREE
READING

at

www.ForgottenBooks.com

By purchasing this book you are eligible for one month membership to ForgottenBooks.com, giving you unlimited access to our entire collection of over 1,000,000 titles via our web site and mobile apps.

To claim your free month visit:

www.forgottenbooks.com/free597688

ISBN 978-0-483-59292-6
PIBN 10597688

W O R K S

OF THE

A U T H O R

OF THE

N I G H T - T H O U G H T S.

IN THREE VOLUMES.

REVISED AND CORRECTED BY HIMSELF.

V O L. I.

A NEW EDITION.

L O N D O N:

inted for J. Dodsley, C. Dilly, T. Cadell, J. Nichols,
G. G. J. and J. Robinson, H. Baldwin, F. and C.
Rivington, J. Sewell, W. Otridge and Son, Ogilvy
and Speare, S. Bladon, Hookham and Carpenter, and
S. Hayes.

M.DCC.XCII.

ADVERTISEMENT

OF THE

AUTHOR.

I THINK the following pieces in * four volumes to be the moſt excuſeable of all that I have formerly written; and I wiſh leſs apology was needful for theſe. As there is no recalling what is got abroad, the pieces here republiſhed I have reviſed and correEted, and rendered them as pardonable, as it was in my power to do.

---

* The firſt edition was in four volumes, but is now comprized in three.

CONTENTS of VOL. I.

CONTENTS of VOL. II.

✦✦✦✦✦✦✦✦✦✦✦

V O L. III.

A POEM

A POEM

ON THE

LAST DAY.

IN THREE BOOKS.

Venit fumma dies. — — Virg.

V E R S E S

TO THE

A U T H O R.

NOW let the *Atheift* tremble; Thou alone
Canft bid his confcious heart the Godhead own.
Whom fhalt thou not reform? O thou haft feen,
How God defcends to judge the fouls of men.
Thou heard'ft the fentence how the guilty mourn,
Driv'n out from God, and never to return.

Yet more, behold ten thoufand thunders fall,
And fudden vengeance wrap the flaming ball:
When nature funk, when every bolt was hurl'd,
Thou faw'ft the boundlefs ruins of the world.

When guilty *Sodom* felt the burning rain,
And fulphur fell on the devoted plain;
The *patriarch* thus, the fiery tempeft paft,
With pious horror view'd the defart wafte;
The reftlefs fmoke ftill wav'd its curls around,
For ever rifing from the glowing ground.

But tell me, oh! what heav'nly pleafure tell,
To think fo greatly, and defcribe fo well!
How waft thou pleas'd the wond'rous theme to try,
And find the thought of man could rife fo high?

Beyond

Beyond this world the labour to purfue,
And open all ETERNITY to view?
   But thou art beft delighted to rehearfe
Heav'n's holy dictates in exalted verfe:
O thou haft power the harden'd heart to warm,
To grieve, to raife, to terrify, to charm;
To fix the foul on God; to teach the mind
To know the dignity of human-kind;
By ftricter rules well-govern'd life to fcan,
And practife o'er the angel in the man.

Magd. Coll.   T. WARTON.
Oxon.

To a LADY, with the LAST DAY.

MADAM,

HERE, sacred truths, in lofty numbers told,
  The prospect of a future state unfold:
The realms of night to mortal view display,
And the glad regions of eternal day.
This daring author scorns, by vulgar ways
Of guilty wit, to merit worthless praise.
Full of her glorious theme, his tow'ring muse,
With gen'rous zeal, a nobler fame pursues:
Religion's cause her ravish'd heart inspires,
And with a thousand bright ideas fires;
Transports her quick, impatient, piercing eye,
O'er the strait limits of *mortality*,
To boundless orbs, and bids her fearless soar,
Where only MILTON gain'd renown before;
Where various scenes alternately excite
Amazement, pity, terror, and delight.
  Thus did the muses sing in early times,
Ere skill'd to flatter vice, and varnish crimes:
Their lyres were tun'd to Virtue's sons alone,
And the chaste poet, and the priest, were one.
But now, forgetful of their infant state,
They sooth the wanton pleasures of the great:
And from the press, and the licentious stage,
With luscious poison taint the thoughtless age;
Deceitful charms attract our wond'ring eyes,
And specious ruin unsuspected lies.

So

So the rich foil of *India*'s blooming fhores,
Adorn'd with lavifh nature's choiceft ftores,
Where ferpents lurk, by flow'rs conceal'd from fight,
Hides fatal danger under gay delight.
 Thefe purer thoughts from grofs alloys refin'd,
With heav'nly raptures elevate the mind :
Not fram'd to raife a giddy fhort-liv'd joy,
Whofe falfe allurements, while they pleafe, deftroy ;
But blifs refembling that of faints above,
Sprung from the vifion of th' Almighty Love:
Firm, folid blifs, for ever great and new,
The more 'tis known, the more admir'd like you;
Like you, fair nymph, in whom united meet
Endearing fweetnefs, unaffeincluded wit,
And all the glories of your fparkling race,
While inward virtues heighten ev'ry grace.
By thefe fecur'd, you will with pleafure read
Of future judgment, and the rifing dead;
Of time's grand period, heav'n and earth o'ertbrown;
And gafping nature's laft tremendous groan.
Thefe, when the ftars and fun fhall be no more,
Shall beauty to your ravag'd form reftore :
Then fhall you fhine with an immortal ray,
Improv'd by death, and brighten'd by decay.

Pemb. Coll.
. Oxon.

T. TRISTRAM.

To the AUTHOR,

On his LAST DAY and UNIVERSAL PASSION.

AND muſt it be as thou haſt ſung,
    Celeſtial bard, ſeraphic YOUNG?
Will there no trace, no point be found
Of all this ſpaciôus glorious round?
Yon lamps of light, muſt they decay?
On nature's ſelf, deſtruction prey?
Then fame, the moſt immortal thing
Ev'n thou canſt hope, is on the wing.
Shall NEWTON's Syſtem be admir'd,
When time and motion are expir'd?
Shall ſouls be curious to explore
Who rul'd an orb that is no more?
Or ſhall they quote the pictur'd age,
From POPE's and Thy corrective page,
When vice and virtue loſe their name
In deathleſs joy, or endleſs ſhame?
While wears away the grand machine,
The works of genius ſhall be ſeen:
Beyond, what laurels can there be,
For HOMER, HORACE, POPE, or THEE?
Thro' life we chaſe, with fond purſuit,
What mocks our hope, like *Sodom's* fruit:
And ſure, thy plan was well deſign'd,
To cure this madneſs of the mind;

Firſt,

Firſt, beyond time our thoughts to raiſe;
Then laſh our love of tranſient praiſe.
In both, we own thy doctrine juſt;
And fame's a breath, and men are duſt.

1736.　　　　　　　　J. Bancks.

THE

THE
LAST DAY.

BOOK I.

Ipse pater, media nimborum in nocte, corusca
Fulmina molitur dextra. Quo maxima motu
Terra tremit: fugêre feræ! et mortalia corda
Per gentes humilis stravit pavor.   VIRG.

WHILE others sing the fortune of the Great;
    Empire and Arms, and all the pomp of State;
With *Britain*'s Hero * set their souls on fire,
And grow immortal as his deeds inspire;
I draw a deeper scene: a scene that yields
A louder trumpet, and more dreadful fields;
The world alarm'd, both earth and heav'n o'erthrown,
And gasping nature's last tremendous groan;
Death's antient sceptre broke, the teeming tomb,
The righteous Judge, and man's eternal doom.

* The Duke of MARLBOROUGH.

'Twixt

'Twixt joy and pain I view the bold defign,
And afk my anxious heart, if it be mine.
Whatever great or dreadful has been done
Within the fight of confcious ftars or fun,
Is far beneath my daring : I look down
On all the fplendors of the *Britifh* crown.
This globe is for my verfe a narrow bound ;
Attend me, all the glorious worlds around !
O ! all ye angels, howfoe'er disjoin'd,
Of every various order, place, and kind,
Hear, and affift, a feeble mortal's lays ;
'Tis your *Eternal King* I ftrive to praife.
   But chiefly Thou, great Ruler ! Lord of all !
Before whofe throne archangels proftrate fall ;
If at thy nod, from difcord, and from night,
Sprang beauty, and yon fparkling worlds of light,
Exalt e'en me ; all inward tumults quell ;
The clouds and darknefs of my mind difpel ;
To my great fubject Thou my breaft infpire,
And raife my lab'ring foul with equal fire.
   Man, bear thy brow aloft, view every grace
In God's great offspring, beauteous nature's face :
See fpring's gay bloom ; fee golden autumn's ftore ;
See how earth fmiles, and hear old ocean roar.
Leviathans but heave their cumb'rous mail,
It makes a tide, and wind-bound navies fail.
Here, forefts rife, the mountain's awful pride ;
Here, rivers meafure climes, and worlds divide ;
There, vallies fraught with gold's refplendent feeds,
Hold kings, and kingdoms fortunes, in their beds :
There, to the fkies, afpiring hills afcend,
And into diftant lands their fhades extend.
View cities, armies, fleets ; of fleets the pride,
See *Europe's* law, in *Albion's* channel ride.

View

View the whole earth's vaſt landſkip unconfin'd,
Or view in *Britain* all her glories join'd.

 Then let the firmament thy wonder raiſe;
'Twill raiſe thy wonder, but tranſcend thy praiſe.
How far from eaſt to weſt ? The lab'ring eye
Can ſcarce the diſtant azure bounds deſcry :
Wide theatre! where tempeſts play at large,
And God's right-hand can all its wrath diſcharge.
Mark how thoſe radiant lamps inflame the pole,
Call forth the ſeaſons, and the year controul :
They ſhine thro' time, with an unalter'd ray :
See This grand period riſe, and That decay :
So *vaſt*, this world's a grain; yet myriads grace;
With golden pomp, the throng'd ethereal ſpace ;
So *bright*, with ſuch a wealth of glory ſtor'd,
'Twere ſin in heathens not to have ador'd.

 How great, how firm, how ſacred, all appears !
How worthy an immortal round of years !
Yet all muſt drop, as autumn's ficklieſt grain,
And earth and firmament be ſought in vain :
The tract forgot where *conſtellations* ſhone,
Or where the S T U A R T S fill'd an awful throne :
Time ſhall be ſlain, all *nature* be deſtroy'd,
Nor leave an atom in the mighty void.

 Sooner, or later, in ſome future date,
(A dreadful ſecret in the book of fate !)
This hour, for aught all human wiſdom knows,
Or when ten thouſand harveſts more have roſe ;
When ſcenes are chang'd on this revolving earth,
Old empires fall, and give new empires birth ;
While other *Bourbons* rule in other lands,
And (if man's ſin forbids not) other A N N E S ;
While the ſtill buſy world is treading o'er
The paths they trod five thouſand years before,
Thoughtleſs

Thoughtlefs as thofe who *now* life's mazes run,
Of earth diffolv'd, or an extinguifh'd fun;
(Ye fublunary worlds, awake, awake!
Ye rulers of the nation, hear, and fhake!)
Thick clouds of darknefs fhall arife on day;
In fudden night all earth's dominions lay;
Impetuous winds the fcatter'd forefts rend;
Eternal mountains, like their cedars, bend;
The valleys yawn, the troubled ocean roar,
And break the bondage of his wonted fhore;
A fanguine ftain the filver moon o'erfpread;
Darknefs the circle of the fun invade;
From inmoft heav'n inceffant thunders roll,
And the ftrong echo bound from pole to pole.

When, lo, a mighty trump, one half conceal'd
In clouds, one half to mortal eye reveal'd,
Shall pour a dreadful note; the piercing call
Shall rattle in the centre of the ball;
Th' extended circuit of creation fhake,
The living die with fear, the dead awake.

Oh pow'rful blaft! to which no equal found
Did e'er the frighted ear of nature wound,
Tho' rival clarions have been ftrain'd on high,
And kindled wars immortal thro' the fky,
Tho' God's whole enginery difcharg'd, and all
The rebel Angels bellow'd in their fall.

Have angels finn'd? and fhall not man beware?
How fhall a fon of earth decline the fnare?
Not folded arms, and flacknefs of the mind,
Can promife for the fafety of mankind:
None are fupinely good: thro' care and pain,
And various arts, the fteep afcent we gain.
This is the fcene of combat, not of reft,
Man's is laborious happinefs at beft;

On

On this fide death his dangers never ceafe,
His joys are joys of conqueft, not of peace.
   If then, obfequious to the will of fate,
And bending to the terms of human ftate,
When guilty joys invite us to their arms,
When beauty fmiles, or grandeur fpreads her charms,
The confcious foul would *this* great fcene difplay,
Call down th' immortal hofts in dread array,
The *trumpet* found, the Chriftian banner fpread,
And raife from filent graves the trembling dead;
Such deep impreffion would the picture make,
No pow'r on earth her firm refolve could fhake;
Engag'd with angels fhe would greatly ftand,
And look regardlefs down on fea and land;
Not proffer'd worlds her ardour could reftrain,
And death might fhake his threat'ning lance in vain!
Her certain conqueft would endear the fight,
And danger ferve but to exalt delight.
   Inftructed thus to fhun the fatal fpring,
Whence flow the terrors of that *day* I fing;
More boldly we our labours may purfue,
And all the dreadful image fet to view.
   The fparkling eye, the fleek and painted breaft,
The burnifh'd fcale, curl'd train, and rifing creft,
All that is lovely in the noxious fnake,
Provokes our fear, and bids us flee the brake:
The fting once drawn, his guiltlefs beauties rife
In pleafing luftre, and detain our eyes;
We view with joy, what once did horror move,
And ftrong averfion foftens into love.
   Say then, my mufe, whom difmal fcenes delight,
Frequent at tombs, and in the realms of night;
Say, melancholy maid, if bold to dare
The laft extremes of terror and defpair;

Oh

Oh fay, what change on earth, what heart in man,
This blackeft moment fince the world began.
　Ah mournful turn! the blifsful earth, who late
At leifure on her axle roll'd in ftate;
While thoufand golden planets knew no reft,
Still onward in their circling journey preft;
A grateful change of feafons fome to bring,
And fweet viciffitude of fall and fpring:
Some thro' vaft oceans to conduct the keel,
And fome thofe watry worlds to fink, or fwell:
Around her fome their fplendors to difplay,
And gild her globe with tributary day:
This world fo great, of joy the bright abode,
Heav'n's darling child, and fav'rite of her God,
Now looks an exile from her Father's care,
Deliver'd o'er to darknefs and defpair.
No fun in radiant glory fhines on high;
No light, but from the terrors of the fky:
Fall'n are her mountains, her fam'd rivers loft,
And all into a fecond chaos toft:
One univerfal ruin fpreads abroad;
Nothing is fafe beneath the throne of God.
　Such, earth, thy fate: what then canft thou afford
To comfort and fupport thy guilty lord?
Man, haughty lord of all beneath the moon,
How muft he bend his foul's ambition down?
Proftrate, the reptile own, and difavow
His boafted ftature, and affuming brow?
Claim kindred with the clay, and curfe his form,
That fpeaks diftinction from his fifter worm?
What dreadful pangs the trembling heart invade?
Lord, why doft thou forfake, whom thou haft made?
Who can fuftain thy anger? who can ftand
Beneath the terrors of thy lifted hand?

It flies the reach of thought; oh save me, Pow'r
Of pow'rs supreme, in that tremendous hour!
Thou who beneath the frown of fate haft stood,
And in thy dreadful agony sweat blood;
Thou, who for me, thro' every throbbing vein,
Haft felt the keeneft edge of mortal pain;
Whom death led captive through the realms below,
And taught thofe horrid myfteries of woe;
Defend me, O my God! Oh save me, Pow'r
Of pow'rs supreme, in that tremendous hour!

From eaft to weft they fly, from pole to line,
Imploring shelter from the wrath divine;
Beg flames to wrap, or whelming feas to fweep,
Or rocks to yawn, compaffionately deep:
Seas caft the monfter forth to meet his doom,
And rocks but prifon up for wrath to come.

So fares a traitor to an earthly crown;
While death fits threat'ning in his prince's frown,
His heart's difmay'd; and now his fears command,
To change his native for a diftant land:
Swift orders fly, the king's fevere decree
Stands in the channel, and locks up the fea;
The port he feeks, obedient to her lord,
Hurls back the rebel to his lifted fword.

But why this idle toil to paint *that* day?
This time elaborately thrown away?
Words all in vain pant after the diftrefs,
The height of eloquence would make it lefs;
Heav'ns! how the *good* man trembles!—
And is there a *Laft Day?* and muft there come
A fure, a fix'd, inexorable doom?
Ambition fwell, and, thy proud fails to fhow,
Take all the winds that *vanity* can blow;
Wealth on a golden mountain blazing ftand,
And reach an *India* forth in either hand;

Spread

Spread all thy purple clufters, tempting *vine*,
And thou, more dreaded foe, bright *beauty*, fhine;
Shine all; in all your charms together rife;
That all, in all your charms, I may defpife,
While I mount upward on a ftrong defire,
Borne, like *Elijah*, in a car of fire.

In hopes of glory to be quite involv'd!
To fmile at death! to long to be diffolv'd!
From our decays a pleafure to receive!
And kindle into tranfport at a grave!
What equals *this* ? And fhall the victor now
Boaft the proud laurels on his loaded brow?
Religion! Oh thou cherub, heav'nly bright!
Oh joys unmix'd, and fathomlefs delight!
Thou, Thou art all; nor find I in the whole
Creation aught, but God and my own foul.

For ever then, my foul, thy God adore,
Nor let the brute creation praife him more.
Shall things inanimate my conduct blame,
And flufh my confcious cheek with fpreading fhame?
They all for him purfue, or quit, their end;
The mounting flames their burning pow'r fufpend;
In folid heaps th' unfrozen billows ftand,
To reft and filence aw'd by his command:
Nay, the dire monfters that infeft the flood,
By nature dreadful, and athirft for blood,
His will can calm, their favage tempers bind,
And turn to mild protectors of mankind.
Did not the prophet this great truth maintain
In the deep chambers of the gloomy main;
When darknefs round him all her horrors fpread,
And the loud ocean bellow'd o'er his head?
When now the thunder roars, the light'ning flies,
And all the warring winds tumultuous rife;

When

When now the foaming furges, toft on high,
Difclofe the fands beneath, and touch the fky;
When death draws near, the mariners aghaft,
Look back with terror on their actions paft;
Their courage fickens into deep difmay,
Their hearts, through fear and anguifh, melt away;
Nor tears, nor pray'rs, the tempeft can appeafe;
Now they devote their treafure to the feas;
Unload their fhatter'd barque, tho' richly fraught,
And think the hopes of life are cheaply bought
With gems and gold; but oh, the ftorm fo high!
Nor gems nor gold the hopes of life can buy.

   The trembling prophet then, themfelves to fave,
They headlong plunge into the briny wave;
Down he defcends, and, booming o'er his head,
The billows clofe; he's number'd with the dead.
(Hear, O ye juft! attend, ye virtuous few!
And the bright paths of piety purfue)
Lo! the great Ruler of the world, from high,
Looks fmiling down with a propitious eye,
Covers his fervant with his gracious hand,
And bids tempeftuous nature filent ftand;
Commands the peaceful waters to give place,
Or kindly fold him in a foft embrace:
He bridles in the monfters of the deep:
The bridled monfters awful diftance keep:
Forget their hunger, while they view their prey;
And guiltlefs gaze, and round the ftranger play.

   But ftill arife new wonders; nature's Lord
Sends forth into the deep his pow'rful word,
And calls the great leviathan: the great
Leviathan attends in all his ftate;
Exults for joy, and, with a mighty bound,
Makes the fea fhake, and heav'n and earth refound;

Blackens the waters with the rifing fand,
And drives vaſt billows to the diſtant land.

    As yawns an earthquake, when impriſon'd air
Struggles for vent, and lays the centre bare,
The whale expands his jaws enormous ſize;
The prophet views the cavern with ſurprize;
Meaſures his monſtrous teeth, afar deſcry'd,
And rolls his wond'ring eyes from ſide to ſide:
Then takes poſſeſſion of the ſpacious ſeat,
And ſails ſecure within the dark retreat

    Now is he pleas'd the northern blaſt to hear,
And hangs on liquid mountains, void of fear;
Or falls immers'd into the depths below,
Where the dead ſilent waters never flow;
To the foundations of the hills convey'd,
Dwells in the ſhelving mountain's dreadful ſhade:
Where plummet never reach'd, he draws his breath,
And glides ſerenely thro' the paths of death.

    Two wond'rous days and nights thro' coral groves,
Thro' labyrinths of rocks and ſands, he roves:
When the third morning with its level rays
The mountains gilds, and on the billows plays,
It ſees the king of waters riſe and pour
His ſacred gueſt uninjur'd on the ſhore:
A type of that great bleſſing, which the muſe
In her next labour ardently purſues.

THE

THE

L A S T D A Y.

B O O K II.

—————'Εκ γαίης ἐλπίζομεν ἐς φά⊙· ἐλθεῖν.
Δείψαν ἀποιχομένων· ὀπίσω δὲ Θεοὶ τελέθονlαι.

PHOCYL.

i. e.

——— *We hope, that the departed will rife again from the*
duſt : after which, like the gods, they will be im-
mortal.

NOW Man awakes, and from his ſilent bed,
　　Where he has ſlept for ages, lifts his head;
Shakes off the ſlumber of ten thouſand years,
And on the borders of new worlds appears.
Whate'er the bold, the raſh, adventure coſt,
In wide ETERNITY I dare be loſt.
The muſe is wont in narrow bounds to ſing,
To *teach the ſwain*, or *celebrate the king*.
I graſp the whole, no more to parts confin'd,
I lift my voice, and ſing to *human kind:*

I ſing

I fing to men and angels; angels join,
While fuch the theme, their facred fongs with mine.
　Again the trumpet's intermitted found
Rolls the wide circuit of creation round,
An univerfal concourfe to prepare
Of all that ever breath'd the vital air:
In fome wide field, which active whirlwinds fweep,
Drive cities, forefts, mountains, to the deep,
To fmooth and lengthen out th' unbounded fpace,
And fpread an area for all human race.
　Now monuments prove faithful to their truft,
And render back their long committed duft.
Now charnels rattle; fcatter'd limbs, and all
The various bones, obfequious to the call,
Self-mov'd, advance; the neck perhaps to meet
The diftant head; the diftant legs the feet.
Dreadful to view, fee through the dufky fky
Fragments of bodies in confufion fly,
To diftant regions journeying, there to claim
Deferted members, and compleat the frame.
　When the world bow'd to *Rome*'s almighty fword,
Rome bow'd to Pompey, and confefs'd her lord.
Yet one day loft, this deity below
Became the fcorn and pity of his foe.
His blood a traitor's facrifice was made,
And fmok'd indignant on a ruffian's blade.
No trumpet's found, no gafping army's yell,
Bid, with due horror, his great foul farewel.
Obfcure his fall! all welt'ring in his gore,
His trunk was caft to perifh on the fhore!
While Julius frown'd the bloody monfter dead,
Who brought the world in his great rival's head.
This fever'd head and trunk fhall join once more,
Tho' realms now rife between, and oceans roar.

　　　　　　　　　　　　　　The

The trumpet's found each fragrant mote fhall hear,
Or fix'd in earth, or if afloat in air,
Obey the fignal wafted in the wind,
And not one fleeping atom lag behind.

So fwarming bees, that on a fummer's day
In airy rings, and wild meanders play,
Charm'd with the brazen found, their wand'rings end,
And, gently circling, on a bough defcend.

The body thus renew'd, the confcious foul,
Which has perhaps been flutt'ring near the pole,
Or midft the burning planets wond'ring ftray'd,
Or hover'd o'er where her pale corpfe was laid;
Or rather coafted on her final ftate,
And fear'd or wifh'd for, her appointed fate :
This foul, returning with a conftant flame,
Now weds for ever her immortal frame.
Life, which ran down before, fo high is wound,
The fprings maintain an everlafting round.

Thus a frail model of the work defign'd
Firft takes a copy of the builder's mind,
Before the ftructure firm with lafting oak,
And marble bowels of the folid rock,
Turns the ftrong arch, and bids the columns rife,
And bear the lofty palace to the fkies ;
The wrongs of time enabled to furpafs,
With bars of adamant, and ribs of brafs.

That antient, facred, and illuftrious * dome,
Where foon or late fair *Albion*'s heroes come,
From camps, and courts, tho' great, or wife, or juft,
To feed the worm, and moulder into duft ;
That folemn manfion of the royal dead,
Where paffing flaves o'er fleeping monarchs tread,

* *Weftminfter Abbey.*

C 3

Now populous o'erflows : a num'rous race
Of rifing kings fill all th' extended fpace :
A life well fpent, not the victorious fword,
Awards the crown, and ftiles the greater lord.

  Nor monuments alone, and burial-earth,
Labours with man to this his fecond birth ;
But where gay palaces in pomp arife,
And gilded theatres invade the fkies,
Nations fhall wake, whofe unrefpected bones
Support the pride of their luxurious fons.
The moft magnificent and coftly dome
Is but an upper chamber to a tomb.
No fpot on earth but has fupply'd a grave,
And human fkulls the fpacious ocean pave.
All's full of man ; and at this dreadful turn,
The fwarm fhall iffue, and the hive fhall burn.

  Not all at once, nor in like manner, rife :
Some lift with pain their flow unwilling eyes :
Shrink backward from the terror of the light,
And blefs the grave, and call for lafting night.
Others, whofe long-attempted virtue ftood
Fix'd as a rock, and broke the rufhing flood,
Whofe firm refolve, nor beauty could melt down,
Nor raging tyrants from their pofture frown ;
Such, in this day of horrors, fhall be feen
To face the thunders with a godlike mien ;
The planets drop, their thoughts are fixt above ;
The centre fhakes, their hearts difdain to move :
An earth diffolving, and a heav'n thrown wide,
A yawning gulph, and fiends on every fide,
Serene they view, impatient of delay,
And blefs the dawn of everlafting day.

  Here, *greatnefs* proftrate falls ; there, *ftrength* gives place;
Here, *lazars* fmile ; there, beauty hides her face.

Chriftians,

Chriſtians, and *Jews*, and *Turks*, and *Pagans* ſtand,
A blended throng, one undiſtinguiſh'd band.
Some who, perhaps, by mutual wounds expir'd,
With zeal for their diſtinct perſuaſions fir'd,
In mutual friendſhip their long ſlumber break,
And hand in hand their Saviour's love partake.

But none are fluſh'd with brighter joy, or, warm
With juſter confidence, enjoy the ſtorm,
Than thoſe, whoſe pious bounties, unconfin'd,
Have made them public fathers of mankind.
In that illuſtrious rank, what ſhining light
With ſuch diſtinguiſh'd glory fills my ſight?
Bend down, my grateful muſe, that homage ſhow,
Which to ſuch worthies thou art proud to owe.
WICKHAM! Fox! CHICHLEY! hail, illuſtrious * names,
Who to far diſtant times diſpenſe your beams;
Beneath your ſhades, and near your chryſtal ſprings,
I firſt preſum'd to touch the trembling ſtrings.
All hail, thrice honour'd! 'Twas your great renown
To bleſs a people, and oblige a crown.
And now you riſe, eternally to ſhine,
Eternally to drink the rays divine.

Indulgent God! Oh how ſhall mortal raiſe
His ſoul to due returns of grateful praiſe,
For bounty ſo profuſe to human kind,
Thy wond'rous gift of an eternal mind?
Shall I, who, ſome few years ago, was leſs
Than worm, or mite, or ſhadow can expreſs,
Was Nothing; ſhall I live, when ev'ry fire
And ev'ry ſtar ſhall languiſh and expire?
When earth's no more, ſhall I ſurvive above,
And thro' the radiant files of angels move?

* *Founders of* New-College, Corpus Chriſti, *and* All Souls, *in* Oxford; *of all which the author was a member.*

Or,

Or, as before the throne of God I ftand,
See new worlds rolling from His fpacious hand,
Where our adventures fhall perhaps be taught,
As we now tell how Michael fung or fought?
All that has being in full concert join,
And celebrate the depths of *Love divine!*

But oh! before this blifsful ftate, before
Th' afpiring foul this wond'rous height can foar,
The Judge, defcending, thunders from afar,
And all mankind is fummon'd to the Bar.

This mighty fcene I next prefume to draw:
Attend, great Anna, with religious awe.
Expect not here the known fuccefsful arts
To win attention, and command our hearts:
Fiction, be far away; let no machine
Defcending here, no fabled God, be feen;
Behold the God of *Gods* indeed defcend,
And worlds unnumber'd his approach attend!

Lo! the wide theatre, whofe ample fpace
Muft entertain the whole of human race,
At heav'n's all-pow'rful edict is prepar'd,
And fenc'd around with an immortal guard.
Tribes, provinces, dominions, worlds, o'erflow
The mighty plain, and deluge all below:
And ev'ry age, and nation, pours along;
Nimrod and Bourbon mingle in the throng:
Adam falutes his youngeft fon; no fign,
Of all thofe ages, which their births disjoin.

How empty learning, and how vain is art,
But as it mends the life, and guides the heart!
What volumes have been fwell'd, what time been fpent,
To fix a hero's birth day, or defcent!
What joy muft it now yield, what rapture raife,
To fee the glorious race of ancient days!

Tᴏ

To greet thofe worthies, who perhaps have ftood
Illuftrious on record before the flood !
Alas ! a nearer care your foul demands,
Cæsar un-noted in your prefence ftands.

How vaft the concourfe ! not in uumber more
The waves that break on the refounding fhore,
The leaves that tremble in the fhady grove,
The lamps that gild the fpangled vaults above :
Thofe overwhelming armies, whofe command
Said to one empire, *Fall*; another *Stand* :
Whofe rear lay wrapt in night, while breaking awn
Rous'd the broad front, and call'd the battle on :
Great Xerxes' world in arms, proud *Cannæ*'s field,
Where *Carthage* taught victorious *Rome* to yield,
(Another blow had broke the fates decree,
And earth had wanted her fourth monarchy)
Immortal *Blenheim*, fam'd *Ramillia's* hoft,
They All are here, and here they All are loft :
Their millions fwell to be difcern'd in vain,
Loft as a billow in th' unbounded main.

This echoing voice now rends the yielding air,
For judgment, judgment, fons of men, prepare !
Earth fhakes anew ; I hear her groans profound ;
And hell through all her trembling realms refound.

Whoe'er thou art, thou greateft pow'r of earth,
Bleft with moft equal planets at thy birth ;
Whofe valour drew the moft fuccefsful fword,
Moft realms united in one common lord ;
Who, on the day of triumph, faidft, Be thine
The fkies, Jehovah, all this world is mine :
Dare not to lift thine eye—Alas ! my mufe,
How art thou loft ! what numbers canft thou chufe ?

A fudden blufh inflames the waving fky,
And now the crimfon curtains open fly ;

Lo !

Lo! far within, and far above all height,
Where heav'n's great Sov'reign reigns in worlds of light,
Whence nature He informs, and with one ray
Shot from his eye, does all her works survey,
Creates, supports, confounds! Where *time*, and *place*,
Matter, and *form*, and *fortune*, *life*, and *grace*,
Wait humbly at the footstool of their God,
And move obedient at his awful nod;
Whence he beholds us vagrant emmets crawl
At random on this air-suspended ball
(Speck of creation) : if he pour one breath,
The bubble breaks, and 'tis eternal death.
　　Thence issuing I behold (but mortal sight
Sustains not such a rushing sea of light!)
I see, on an empyreal flying throne
Sublimely rais'd, Heav'n's everlasting Son;
Crown'd with that majesty, which form'd the world,
And the grand rebel flaming downward hurl'd.
Virtue, dominion, praise, omnipotence,
Support the train of their triumphant prince.
A zone, beyond the thought of angels bright,
Around him, like the zodiac, winds its light.
Night shades the solemn arches of his brows,
And in his cheek the purple morning glows.
Where-e'er serene, he turns propitious eyes,
Or we expect, or find, a paradise :
But if resentment reddens their mild beams,
The *Eden* kindles, and the world's in flames.
On one hand, *knowledge* shines in purest light;
On one, the sword of *justice* fiercely bright.
Now bend the knee in sport, present the reed;
Now tell the scourg'd Impostor he shall bleed!
　　Thus glorious thro' the courts of heav'n, the source
Of life and death eternal bends his course;

　　　　　　　　　　　Loud

Loud thunders round him roll, and lightnings play;
Th' angelic hoft is rang'd in bright array:
Some touch the ftring, fome ftrike the founding fhell,
And mingling voices in rich concert fwell;
Voices feraphic; bleft with fuch a ftrain,
Could *Satan* hear, he were a god again.

    Triumphant King of GLORY! Soul of Blifs!
What a ftupendous turn of fate is this!
O! whither art thou rais'd above the fcorn
And indigence of *him* in *Bethlem* born;
A needlefs, helplefs, unaccounted, gueft,
And but a fecond to the fodder'd beaft!
How chang'd from *him*, who meekly proftrate laid,
Vouchfaf'd to wafh the feet himfelf had made!
From *him* who was betray'd, forfook, deny'd,
Wept, languifh'd, pray'd, bled, thirfted, groan'd, and dy'd;
Hung pierc'd and bare, infulted by the foe,
All heav'n in tears above, earth unconcern'd below!

    And was't enough to bid the Sun retire?
Why did not Nature at thy groan expire?
I fee, I hear, I feel, the pangs divine;
The world is vanifh'd,—I am wholly thine.

    Miftaken CAIAPHAS! Ah! which blafphem'd;
Thou, or thy Pris'ner? which fhall be condemn'd?
Well might'ft thou rend thy garments, well exclaim;
Deep are the horrors of eternal flame!
But God is good! 'Tis wond'rous all! Ev'n He
Thou gav'ft to death, fhame, torture, dy'd for Thee.

    Now the defcending triumph ftops its flight
From earth full twice a planetary height.
There all the clouds condens'd, two columns raife
Diftinct with orient veins, and golden blaze.
One fix'd on earth, and one in fea, and round
Its ample foot the fwelling billows found.

                             Thefe

Thefe an immeafurable arch fupport,
The grand tribunal of this awful court.
Sheets of bright azure, from the pureft fky,
Stream from the chryftal arch, and round the columns fly.
Death, wrapt in chains, low at the bafis lies,
And on the point of his own arrow dies.

Here high enthron'd th' eternal Judge is plac'd,
With all the grandeur of his Godhead grac'd;
Stars on his robes in beauteous order meet,
And the fun burns beneath his awful feet.

Now an archangel eminently bright,
From off his filver ftaff of wond'rous height,
Unfurls the *Chriftian* flag, which waving flies,
And fhuts and opens more than half the fkies:
The Crofs fo ftrong a red, it fheds a ftain,
Where-e'er it floats, on earth, and air, and main;
Flufhes the hill, and fets on fire the wood,
And turns the deep-dy'd ocean into blood.

Oh formidable GLORY! dreadful bright!
Refulgent torture to the guilty fight.
Ah turn, unwary mufe, nor dare reveal
What horrid thoughts with the polluted dwell.
Say not, (to make the *Sun* fhrink in his beam)
Dare not affirm, they wifh it all a dream;
Wifh, or their fouls may with their limbs decay,
Or GOD be fpoil'd of his eternal fway.
But rather, if thou know'ft the means, unfold
How they with tranfport might the fcene behold.

Ah how! but by Repentance, by a mind
Quick, and fevere its own offence to find?
By tears, and groans, and never-ceafing care,
And all the pious violence of Pray'r?
Thus then, with fervency till now unknown,
I caft my heart before th' eternal throne,

In this great temple, which the skies surround,
For homage to its Lord, a narrow bound.

"O Thou! whose balance does the mountains weigh,
"Whose will the wild tumultuous seas obey,
"Whose breath can turn those wat'ry worlds to flame,
"That flame to tempest, and that tempest tame;
"Earth's meanest son, all trembling, prostrate falls,
"And on the boundless of thy goodness calls.

"Oh! give the winds all past offence to sweep,
"To scatter wide, or bury in the deep:
"Thy pow'r, my weakness, may I ever see,
"And wholly dedicate my soul to Thee:
"Reign o'er my will; my passions ebb and flow
"At thy command, nor human motive know!
"If anger boil, let anger be my praise,
"And sin the graceful indignation raise.
"My love be warm to succour the distress'd,
"And lift the burden from the soul opprefs'd.
"Oh may my understanding ever read
"This glorious volume, which Thy wisdom made!
"Who decks the maiden Spring with flow'ry pride?
"Who calls forth Summer, like a sparkling bride?
"Who joys the mother Autumn's bed to crown?
"And bids old Winter lay her honours down?
"Not the Great OTTOMAN, or Greater CZAR,
"Not *Europe's* arbitress of peace and war.
"May sea and land, and earth and heav'n be join'd,
"To bring th' eternal Author to my mind!
"When oceans roar, or awful thunders roll,
"May thoughts of Thy dread vengeance shake my soul!
"When earth's in bloom, or planets proudly shine,
"Adore, my heart, the MAJESTY *Divine!*

"Thro' ev'ry scene of life, or peace, or war,
"Plenty, or want, Thy glory be my care!

"Shine

" Shine we in arms ? or fing beneath our vine ?
" Thine is the vintage, and the conqueft Thine :
" Thy pleafure points the fhaft, and bends the bow;
" The clufter blafts, or bids it brightly glow :
" 'Tis thou that lead'ft our pow'rful armies forth,
" And giv'ft Great ANNE *Thy* fceptre o'er the north.
　" Grant I may ever, at the *Morning-Ray*,
" Open with Pray'r the confecrated day;
" Tune Thy great praife, and bid my foul arife,
" And with the mounting fun afcend the fkies :
" As that advances, let my zeal improve,
" And glow with ardour of confummate love ;
" Nor ceafe at eve, but with the *Setting Sun*
" My endlefs worfhip fhall be ftill begun.
　" And, oh ! permit the gloom of folemn night
" To facred thought may forcibly invite.
" When this world's fhut, and awful planets rife,
" Call on our minds, and raife them to the fkies ;
" Compofe our fouls with a lefs dazzling fight,
" And fhew all nature in a milder light ;
" How every boifterous thought in calms fubfides !
" How the fmooth'd fpirit into goodnefs glides !
" O how divine ! to tread the milky way,
" To the bright palace of the Lord of day ;
" His court admire, or for his favour fue,
" Or leagues of friendfhip with his faints renew ;
" Pleas'd to look down, and fee the *World* afleep,
" While I long vigils to its *Founder* keep !
　" Can'ft Thou not fhake the centre ? Oh ! controul,
" Subdue by force, the rebel in my foul :
" Thou, who canft ftill the raging of the flood,
" Reftrain the various tumults of my blood ;
" Teach me, with equal firmnefs, to fuftain
" Alluring pleafure, and affaulting pain.
　　　　　　　　　　　　" O may

" O may I pant for Thee in each defire !
" And with ftrong faith foment the holy fire !
" Stretch out my foul in hope, and grafp the prize,
" Which in *Eternity*'s deep bofom lies !
" At the *Great Day* of recompence behold,
" Devoid of fear, the *fatal Book* unfold !
" Then wafted upward to the blifsful feat,
" From age to age, my grateful fong repeat ;
" My Light, my Life, my God, my *Saviour* fee,
" And rival angels in the praife of THEE."

THE

LAST DAY.

BOOK III.

Effe quoque in fatis reminifcitur, affore tempus,
Quo mare, quo tellus, correptaque regia cæli
Ardeat; & mundi moles operofa laboret. OVID. MET.

THE book unfolding; the refplendent feat
  Of faints and angels; the tremendous fate
Of guilty fouls; the gloomy realms of woe;
And all the horrors of the world below;
I next prefume to fing: What yet remains
Demands my laft, but moft exalted ftrains.
And let the *Mufe* or now affect the fky,
Or in inglorious fhades for ever lie.
She kindles, fhe's inflam'd fo near the goal;
She mounts, fhe gains upon the ftarry pole;
The world grows lefs as fhe purfues her flight,
And the fun darkens to her diftant fight.
Heav'n op'ning, all its facred pomp difplays,
And overwhelms her with the rufhing blaze!

The

The triumph rings ! archangels shout around !
And echoing nature lengthens out the sound !
   Ten thousand trumpets *now* at once advance ;
Now deepest silence lulls the vast expanse :
So deep the silence, and so strong the blast,
As nature dy'd, when she had groan'd her last.
Nor man, nor angel, moves ; the Judge on high
Looks round, and with his glory fills the sky :
Then on the fatal book his hand he lays,
Which high to view supporting seraphs raise ;
In solemn form the rituals are prepar'd,
The seal is broken, and a groan is heard.
And thou, my soul, (oh fall to sudden pray'r,
And let the thought sink deep !) shalt thou be there ?
   See on the left (for by the great command
The throng divided falls on either hand ;)
How weak, how pale, how haggard, how obscene,
What more than death in ev'ry face and mien !
With what distress, and glarings of affright,
They shock the heart, and turn away the sight !
In gloomy orbs their trembling eye-balls roll,
And tell the horrid secrets of the soul.
Each gesture mourns, each look is black with care,
And ev'ry groan is loaden with despair.
Reader, if guilty, spare the muse, and find
A truer image pictur'd in thy mind.
   Should'st thou behold thy brother, father, wife,
And all the soft companions of thy life,
Whose blended int'rests levell'd at one aim,
Whose mix'd desires sent up one common flame,
Divided far ; thy wretched Self alone
Cast on the left, of all whom thou hast known ;
How would it wound ! What millions wouldst thou give
For One more trial, One more day to live !

VOL. I.   D   Flung

Flung back in time an hour, a moment's fpace,
To grafp with eagernefs the means of Grace; .
Contend for mercy with a pious rage,
And in that moment to redeem an age ?
Drive back the tide, fufpend a ftorm in air,
Arreft the *Sun !*—but ftill of *this* defpair.

    Mark, on the right, how amiable a grace !
Their Maker's image frefh in ev'ry face !
What purple bloom my ravifh'd foul admires,
And their eyes fparkling with immortal fires !
Triumphant beauty ! charms that rife above
This world, and in bleft angels kindle love !
To the Great Judge with holy pride they turn,
And dare behold th' Almighty's anger burn;
Its flafh fuftain, againft its terror rife,
And on the dread tribunal fix their eyes.
Are thefe the forms that moulder'd in the duft ?
Oh the tranfcendent glory of the juft !
Yet ftill fome thin remains of fear and doubt,
Th' infected brightnefs of their joy pollute.

    Thus the chafte bridegroom, when the prieft draws nigh,
Beholds his blefling with a trembling eye,
Feels doubtful paffions throb in every vein,
And in his cheeks are mingled joy and pain,
Left ftill fome intervening chance fhould rife,
Leap forth at once, and fnatch the golden prize;
Inflame his woe, by bringing it fo late,
And ftab him in the crifis of his fate.

    Since ADAM's family, from firft to laft,
Now into one diftinct furvey is caft;
Look round, vain-glorious mufe, and you whoe'er
Devote yourfelves to fame, and think her fair;
Look round, and feek the lights of human race,
Whofe fhining acts *time*'s brighteft annals grace;

Who

Who founded fects; crowns conquer'd, or refign'd;
Gave names to nations; or fam'd empires join'd;
Who rais'd the vale, and laid the mountain low;
And taught obedient rivers where to flow;
Who with vaft fleets, as with a mighty chain,
Could bind the madnefs of the roaring main:
All loft? all undiftinguifh'd? no where found?
How will this truth in Bou r bon's palace found?
  That hour, on which th' Almighty King on high
From all eternity has fix'd his eye,
Whether his right-hand favour'd, or annoy'd,
Continu'd, alter'd, threaten'd, or deftroy'd;
Southern or eaftern fceptre downward hurl'd,
Gave north or weft dominion o'er the world;
The point of time, for which the world was built,
For which the blood of God himfelf was fpilt,
That dreadful moment is arriv'd.
  Aloft, the feats of blifs their pomp difplay
Brighter than brightnefs, this diftinguifh'd day;
Lefs glorious, when of old th' eternal Son
From realms of night return'd with trophies won:
Thro' heav'n's high gates, when he triumphant rode,
And fhouting angels hail'd the Victor God.
Horrors, *beneath*, darknefs in darknefs, hell
Of hell, where torments behind torments dwell;
A furnace formidable, deep, and wide,
O'er-boiling with a mad fulphureous tide,
Expands its jaws, moft dreadful to furvey,
And roars outrageous for the deftin'd prey.
The fons of light fcarce unappall'd look down,
And nearer prefs heav'n's everlafting throne.
  Such is the fcene; and one fhort moment's fpace
Concludes the hopes and fears of human race.
Proceed who dares!—I tremble as I write;
The whole creation fwims before my fight:

I fee, I fee, the Judge's frowning brow;
Say not, 'tis diftant; I behold it *now*;
I faint, my tardy blood forgets to flow,
My foul recoils at the ftupendous woe;
That woe, thofe pangs, which from the *guilty* breaft,
In thefe, or words like thefe, fhall be expreft.

   " Who burft the barriers of my peaceful grave?
" Ah! cruel death, that would no longer fave,
" But grudg'd me e'en that narrow dark abode,
" And caft me out into the wrath of God;
" Where fhrieks, the roaring flame, the rattling chain,
" And all the dreadful eloquence of pain,
" Our only fong; black fire's malignant light,
" The fole refrefhment of the blafted fight.
" Muft all thofe pow'rs, heav'n gave me to fupply
" My foul with pleafure, and bring in my joy,
" Rife up in arms againft me, join the foe,
" *Senfe, reafon, memory*, increafe my woe?
" And fhall my voice, ordain'd on hymns to dwell,
" Corrupt to groans, and blow the fires of hell?
" Oh! muft I look with terror on my gain,
" And with *exiftence* only meafure *pain?*
" What! no reprieve, no leaft indulgence giv'n,
" No beam of hope, from any point of heav'n!
" Ah Mercy! Mercy! art thou dead above?
" Is Love extinguifh'd in the Source of Love?
   " Bold that I am, did heav'n ftoop down to hell?
" Th' expiring Lord of life my ranfom feal?
" Have I not been induftrious to provoke?
" From his embraces obftinately bróke?
" Purfu'd, and panted for his mortal hate,
" Earn'd my deftruction, labour'd out my fate?
" And dare I on extinguifh'd Love exclaim?
" Take, take full vengeance, rouze the flack'ning flame;

                              " Juft

" Juft is my lot—but oh ! muft it tranfcend
" The reach of time, defpair a diftant end ?
" With dreadful growth fhoot forward, and arife,
" Where thought can't follow, and bold fancy dies ?
   " *NEVER !* where falls the foul at that dread found ?
" Down an abyfs how dark, and how profound ?
" Down, down, (I ftill am falling, horrid pain !)
" Ten thoufand thoufand fathoms ftill remain ;
" My plunge but ftill begun—And this for fin ?
" Could I offend, if I had never been,
" But ftill increas'd the fenfelefs happy mafs,
" Flow'd in the ftream, or fhiver'd in the grafs ?
   " Father of mercies ! why from filent earth
" Did'ft thou awake, and curfe me into birth ?
" Tear me from quiet, ravifh me from night,
" And make a thanklefs prefent of thy light ?
" Pufh into being a reverfe of Thee,
" And animate a clod with mifery ?
   " The beafts are happy ; they come forth, and keep
" Short watch on earth, and then lie down to fleep.
" Pain is for man ; and oh ! how vaft a pain
" For crimes, which made the Godhead bleed in vain !
" Annull'd his groans, as far as in them lay,
" And flung his agonies, and death, away !
" As our dire punifhment for ever ftrong,
" Our conftitution too for ever young.
" Curs'd with returns of vigour, ftill the fame
" Pow'rful to bear, and fatisfy the flame :
" Still to be caught, and ftill to be purfu'd !
" To perifh ftill, and ftill to be renew'd !
   " And this, *My Help ! My God !* at thy decree ?
" Nature is chang'd, and *hell* fhould *fuccour* me.
" And can'ft Thou then look down from perfect blifs,
" And fee me plunging in the dark abyfs ?

" Calling

" Calling Thee Father, in a fea of fire ?
" Or pouring blafphemies at Thy defire ?
" With mortals anguifh wilt Thou raife *Thy* name,
" And by my pangs omnipotence proclaim ?
  " Thou, who canft tofs the planets to and fro,
" Contract not Thy great vengeance to my woe ;
" Crufh worlds ; in hotter flames fall'n angels lay ;
" On me Almighty wrath is caft away.
" Call back Thy thunders, Lord, hold in Thy rage,
" Nor with a fpeck of wretchednefs engage :
" Forget me quite, nor ftoop a worm to blame ;
" But lofe me in the greatnefs of Thy name.
" Thou art all Love, all Mercy, all Divine,
" And fhall I make thofe glories ceafe to fhine ?
" Shall finful man grow great by his offence,
" And from its courfe turn back Omnipotence ?
  " Forbid it ! and oh ! grant, Great *God*, at leaft
" This one, this flender, almoft *no* requeft ;
" When I have wept a thoufand lives away,
" When torment is grown weary of its prey,
" When I have rav'd ten thoufand years in fire,
" Ten thoufand thoufand, let me then expire."
  Deep anguifh ! but too late ; the hopelefs foul
Bound to the bottom of the burning pool,
Though loth, and ever loud blafpheming, owns
He's juftly doom'd to pour eternal groans ;
Enclos'd with horrors, and transfix'd with pain,
Rolling in vengeance, ftruggling with his chain :
To talk to fiery tempefts ; to implore
The raging flame to give its burnings o'er ;
To tofs, to writhe, to pant beneath his load,
And bear the weight of an offended God.
  The favour'd of their Judge, in triumph move
To take poffeffion of their thrones above ;

                                        Satan's

Satan's accurs'd defertion to fupply,
And fill the vacant ftations of the fky;
Again to kindle long-extinguifh'd rays,
And with new lights dilate the heav'nly blaze;
To crop the rofes of immortal youth,
And drink the fountain-head of facred truth;
To fwim in feas of blifs, to ftrike the ftring,
And lift the voice to their Almighty KING;
To lofe eternity in grateful lays,
And fill heav'n's wide circumference with praife.

But I attempt the wond'rous height in vain,
And leave unfinifh'd the too lofty ftrain:
What boldly I begin, let others end;
My ftrength exhaufted, fainting I defcend,
And chufe a lefs, but no ignoble, theme,
Diffolving elements, and worlds, in flame.

The fatal period, the great hour, is come,
And nature fhrinks at her approaching doom;
Loud peals of thunder give the fign, and all
Heav'n's terrors in array furround the ball;
Sharp lightnings with the meteors blaze confpire,
And, darted downward, fet the world on fire;
Black rifing clouds the thicken'd *Æther* choke,
And fpiry flames dart through the rolling fmoke,
With keen vibrations cut the fullen night,
And ftrike the darken'd fky with dreadful light;
From heav'n's four regions, with immortal force,
Angels drive on the wind's impetuous courfe,
T' enrage the flame: It fpreads, it foars on high,
Swells in the ftorm, and billows through the fky:
Here winding pyramids of fire afcend,
Cities and defarts in one ruin blend;
Here blazing volumes wafted, overwhelm
The fpacious face of a far diftant realm;

There, undermin'd, down rush eternal hills,
The neighb'ring vales the vast destruction fills.
   Hear'st thou that dreadful crack? that sound which broke
Like peals of thunder, and the centre shook?
What wonders must that groan of nature tell?
Oylmpus there, and mightier *Atlas*, fell;
Which seem'd above the reach of fate to stand,
A tow'ring monument of God's right hand;
Now dust and smoke, whose brow, so lately, spread
O'er shelter'd countries its diffusive shade.
   Shew me that celebrated spot, where all
The various rulers of the fever'd ball
Have humbly sought wealth, honour, and redress,
That land which heav'n seem'd diligent to bless,
Once call'd *Britannia* : Can her glories end?
And can't surrounding seas her realms defend?
Alas! in flames behold surrounding seas!
Like oil, their waters but augment the blaze.
   Some angel say, Where ran proud *Asia*'s bound?
Or where with fruits was fair *Europa* crown'd?
Where stretch'd waste *Lybia?* Where did *India*'s shore
Sparkle in diamonds, and her golden ore?
Each lost in each, their mingling kingdoms glow,
And all dissolv'd, one fiery deluge flow:
Thus earth's contending monarchies are join'd,
And a full period of ambition find.
   And now whate'er or swims, or walks, or flies,
Inhabitants of sea, or earth, or skies;
All on whom ADAM's wisdom fix'd a name,
All plunge, and perish in the conqu'ring flame.
   This globe alone would but defraud the fire,
Starve its devouring rage: the flakes aspire,
And catch the clouds, and make the heav'ns their prey;
The sun, the moon, the stars, all melt away;
All,

All, all is loft; no monument, no fign,
Where once fo proudly blaz'd the gay machine.
So bubbles on the foaming ftream expire,
So fparks that fcatter from the kindling fire;
The devaftations of One dreadful hour
The Great Creator's Six days work devour.
A mighty, mighty ruin! yet One *foul*
Has more to boaft, and far outweighs the whole;
Exalted in fuperior excellence,
Cafts down to nothing, fuch a vaft expence.
Have you not feen th' eternal mountains nod,
An earth diffolving, a defcending God?
What ftrange furprizes through all nature ran?
For whom thefe revolutions, but for Man?
For him, Omnipotence new meafures takes,
For him, through all eternity, awakes;
Pours on him gifts fufficient to fupply
Heav'n's lofs, and with frefh glories fill the fky.

 Think deeply then, O Man, how *great* thou art;
Pay thyfelf homage with a trembling heart;
What angels guard, no longer dare negleft,
Slighting thyfelf, affront not God's refpeft.
Enter the facred temple of thy breaft,
And gaze, and wander there, a ravifh'd gueft;
Gaze on thofe hidden treafures thou fhalt find,
Wander thro' all the glories of thy mind.
Of perfeft knowledge, fee, the dawning light
Foretels a noon moft exquifitely bright!
Here, fprings of endlefs joy are breaking forth!
There, buds the promife of celeftial worth!
Worth, which muft ripen in a happier clime,
And brighter *Sun*, beyond the bounds of time.
Thou, *Minor*, canft not guefs thy vaft eftate,
What ftores, on foreign coafts, thy landing wait;

Lofe not thy claim, let virtue's path be trod;
Thus glad all heav'n, and pleafe that bounteous God,
Who, to light thee to pleafures, hung on high
Yon radiant orb, proud regent of the fky:
That fervice done, its beams fhall fade away,
And God fhine forth in one *Eternal* Day.

THE

THE
FORCE of RELIGION;

OR,

VANQUISH'D LOVE.

POEM.

IN TWO BOOKS.

Gratior & pulchro veniens in corpore virtus. VIRG.

THE

FORCE of RELIGION;

OR,

VANQUISH'D LOVE.

BOOK I.

—— *Ad cœlum ardentia lumina tollens,*
Lumina; nam teneras arcebant vincula palmas.

VIRG.

FROM lofty themes, from thoughts that foar'd on high,
And open'd wond'rous fcenes above the fky,
My mufe defcend: Indulge my fond defire;
With fofter thoughts my melting foul infpire,
And fmooth my numbers to a female's praife:
A partial world will liften to my lays,
While ANNA reigns, and fets a female name
Unrival'd in the glorious lifts of fame.
   Hear, ye fair daughters of this happy land,
Whofe radiant eyes the vanquifh'd world command,
Virtue is Beauty: But when charms of mind
With elegance of outward form are join'd;
When *youth* makes fuch bright objects ftill more bright,
And *fortune* fets them in the ftrongeft light;

'Tis

'Tis all of heav'n that we below may view,
And all, but Adoration, is your due.
　　Fam'd female virtue did this ifle adorn,
Ere *Ormond*, or her glorious QUEEN, was born:
When now *Maria*'s pow'rful arms prevail'd,
And haughty DUDLEY's bold ambition fail'd,
The beauteous daughter of great SUFFOLK's race,
In blooming youth adorn'd with every grace;
Who gain'd a crown by treafon not her own,
And innocently fill'd another's throne;
Hurl'd from the fummit of imperial ftate,
With equal mind fuftain'd the ftroke of fate.
　　But how will GUILFORD, her far dearer part,
With manly reafon fortify his heart?
At once fhe longs, and is afraid, to *know :*
Now fwift fhe moves, and now advances flow,
To find her lord; and, finding, paffes by,
Silent with fear, nor dares fhe meet his eye;
Left that, unafk'd, in fpeechlefs grief, difclofe
The mournful fecret of his inward woes.
Thus, after ficknefs, doubtful of her face,
·The melancholy virgin fhuns the glafs.
　　At length, with troubled thought, but look ferene,
And forrow foften'd by her heav'nly mien,
She clafps her lord, brave, beautiful, and young,
While tender accents melt upon her tongue;
Gentle, and fweet, as vernal Zephyr blows,
Fanning the lily, or the blooming rofe.
　　" Grieve not, my lord; a crown indeed is loft;
" What far outfhines a crown, we ftill may boaft;
" A mind compos'd; a mind that can difdain
" A fruitlefs forrow for a lofs fo vain.
" Nothing is lofs that virtue can improve
" To wealth eternal; and return above;

　　　　　　　　　　　　　" Above,

" Above, where no diftinction fhall be known
" 'Twixt him whom ftorms have fhaken from a throne,
" And him, who, bafking in the fmiles of fate,
" Shone forth in all the fplendor of the great:
" Nor can I find the diff'rence here below;
" I lately was a Queen; I ftill am fo,
" While Guilford's Wife: Thee rather I *obey*,
" Than o'er mankind extend imperial fway.
" When we lie down in fome obfcure retreat,
" Incens'd Maria may her rage forget;
" And I to death my duty will improve,
" And what you mifs in empire, add in love—
" Your godlike foul is open'd in your look,
" And I have faintly your great meaning fpoke,
" For this alone I'm pleas'd I wore the crown,
" To find with what content we lay it down.
" Heroes may win, but 'tis a heav'nly race
" Can *quit* a throne with a becoming grace."
    Thus fpoke the faireft of her fex, and cheer'd
Her drooping lord; whofe boding bofom fear'd
A darker cloud of ills would burft, and fhed
Severer vengeance on her guiltlefs head:
Too juft, alas, the terrors which he felt!
For; lo! a guard!—Forgive him, if he melt—
How fharp her pangs, when fever'd from his fide,
The moft fincerely lov'd, and loving bride,
In fpace confin'd, the mufe forbears to tell;
Deep was her anguifh, but fhe bore it well.
His pain was equal, but his virtue lefs;
He thought in grief there could be no excefs.
Penfive he fat, o'ercaft with gloomy care,
And often fondly clafp'd his abfent fair;
Now, filent, wander'd through his rooms of ftate,
And ficken'd at the pomp, and tax'd his fate;

Which

Which thus adorn'd, in all her shining store,
A splendid wretch, magnificently poor.
Now on the bridal-bed his eyes were cast,
And anguish fed on his enjoyments past;
Each recollected pleasure made him smart,
And ev'ry transport stabb'd him to the heart.

That happy moon, which summon'd to delight,
That moon which shone on his dear nuptial night,
Which saw him fold her yet untasted charms
(Deny'd to princes) in his longing arms;
Now sees the transient blessing fleet away,
Empire and Love! the vision of a day.

Thus, in the *British* clime, a summer-storm
Will oft the smiling face of heav'n deform;
The winds with violence at once descend,
Sweep flow'rs and fruits, and make the forest bend;
A sudden winter, while the sun is near,
O'ercomes the season, and inverts the year.

But whither is the captive borne away,
The beauteous captive, from the chearful day?
The scene is chang'd indeed; before her eyes
Ill-boding looks and unknown horrors rise:
For pomp and splendor, for her guard and crown,
A gloomy dungeon, and a keeper's frown:
Black thoughts, each morn, invade the *Lover*'s breast,
Each night, a ruffian locks the *Queen* to rest.

Ah mournful change, if judg'd by vulgar minds!
But SUFFOLK's daughter its advantage finds.
Religion's force divine is best display'd
In deep desertion of all human aid:
To succour in extremes, is her delight,
And chear the heart, when terror strikes the fight.
We, disbelieving our own senses, gaze,
And wonder what a mortal's heart can raise

To

To triumph o'er misfortunes, fmile in grief,
And comfort thofe who come to bring relief:
We gaze; and as we gaze, wealth, fame, decay,
And all the world's vain glories fade away.

Againft her cares fhe rais'd a dauntlefs mind,
And with an ardent heart, but moft refign'd,
Deep in the dreadful gloom, with pious heat,
Amid the filence of her dark retreat,
Addrefs'd her God—" Almighty Pow'r Divine!
" 'Tis thine to raife, and to deprefs, is Thine;
" With honour to light up the name unknown,
" Or to put out the luftre of a throne.
" In my fhort fpan both fortunes I have prov'd,
" And though with ill frail nature will be mov'd,
" I'll bear it well: (O ftrengthen me to bear!)
" And if my piety may claim thy care;
" If I remember'd, in youth's giddy heat,
" And tumult of a court, a Future State;
" O favour, when thy mercy I implore
" For *one* who never guilty fceptre bore!
" 'Twas I receiv'd the crown; my lord is free;
" If it muft fall, let vengeance fall on me.
" Let him furvive, his country's name to raife,
" And in a guilty land to fpeak Thy praife!
" O may th' indulgence of a *father's* love,
" Pour'd forth on me, be doubled from above!
" If *thefe* are fafe, I'll think my pray'rs fucceed,
" And blefs thy tender mercies, whilft I bleed."
'Twas now the mournful eve before that day
In which the queen to her full wrath gave way;
Thro' rigid juftice, rufh'd into offence,
And drank in zeal the blood of innocence:
The fun went down in clouds, and feem'd to mourn
The fad neceffity of his return;

The hollow wind, and melancholy rain,
Or did, or was imagin'd to, complain :
The tapers caſt an inauſpicious light;
Stars there were none, and doubly dark the night.

    Sweet innocence in chains can take her reſt;
Soft ſlumber gently creeping through her breaſt,
She ſinks ; and in her ſleep is re-inthron'd,
Mock'd by a gaudy dream, and vainly crown'd.
She views her fleets and armies, ſeas and land,
And ſtretches wide her ſhadow of command :
With royal purple is her viſion hung ;
By phantom hoſts are ſhouts of conqueſt rung ;
Low at her feet the ſuppliant rival lies ;
Our priſoner mourns her fate, and bids her riſe.

    Now level beams upon the waters play'd,
Glanc'd on the hills, and weſtward caſt the ſhade ;
The buſy trades in city had began
To ſound, and ſpeak the painful life of man.
In tyrants breaſts the thoughts of vengeance rouze,
And the fond bridegroom turns him to his ſpouſe.
At this firſt birth of light, while morning breaks,
Our ſpouſeleſs bride, our widow'd wife, awakes ;
Awakes, and ſmiles ; nor night's impoſture blames ;
Her *real* pomps were little more than dreams ;
A ſhort-liv'd blaze, a light'ning quickly o'er,
That dy'd in birth, that ſhone, and were no more :
She turns her ſide, and ſoon reſumes a ſtate
Of mind, well ſuited to her alter'd fate,
Serene, though ſerious ; when dread tidings come
(Ah wretched GUILFORD !) of her inſtant doom.
Sun, hide thy beams ; in clouds as black as night
Thy face involve ; be guiltleſs of the ſight ;
Or haſte more ſwiftly to the weſtern main ;
Nor let her blood the conſcious day-light ſtain !

                                  Oh!

Oh! how fevere! to fall fo new a bride,
Yet blufhing from the prieft, in youthful pride;
When time had juft matur'd each perfect grace,
And open'd all the wonders of her face!
To leave her GUILFORD dead to all relief,
Fond of his woe, and obftinate in grief.
Unhappy fair! whatever fancy drew,
(Vain promis'd bleffings) vanifh from her view;
No train of chearful days, endearing nights,
No fweet domeftic joys, and chafte delights;
Pleafures that bloffom e'en from doubts and fears;
And blifs and rapture rifing out of *cares :*
No little GUILFORD, with paternal grace,
Lull'd on her knee, or fmiling in her face;
Who, when her *deareft father* fhall return,
From pouring tears on her untimely urn,
Might comfort to his filver hairs impart,
And fill her place in his indulgent heart:
As where fruits fall, quick-rifing bloffoms fmile,
And the blefs'd *Indian* of his care beguile.
  In vain thefe various reafons jointly prefs,
To blacken death, and heighten her diftrefs;
She, through th' encircling terrors, darts her fight
To the blefs'd regions of eternal light,
And fills her foul with peace: To weeping friends
Her *father,* and her *lord,* fhe recommends;
Unmov'd herfelf: Her foes her air furvey,
And rage to fee their malice thrown away.
She foars; now nought on earth detains her care——
But GUILFORD; who ftill ftruggles for his fhare.
Still will his form importunately rife,
Clog and retard her tranfport to the fkies;
As trembling flames now take a feeble flight,
Now catch the brand with a returning light,

Thus

Thus her foul onward from the feats above,
Falls fondly back, and kindles into love:
At length fhe conquers in the doubtful field;
That Heav'n fhe feeks will be her GUILFORD's fhield.
Now death is welcome; his approach is flow;
'Tis tedious longer to expect the blow.

Oh! mortals, fhort of fight, who think the paft
O'erblown misfortune ftill fhall prove the laft:
Alas! misfortunes travel in a train,
And oft in life form one perpetual chain;
Fear buries fear, and ills on ills attend,
'Till life and forrow meet one common end.

She thinks that fhe has nought but death to fear,
And death is conquer'd. Worfe than death is near:
Her rigid trials are not yet complete;
The news arrives of her great father's fate.
She fees his hoary head, all white with age,
A victim to th' offended monarch's rage.
How great the mercy, had fhe breath'd her laft,
Ere the dire fentence on her father paft!

A fonder parent nature never knew;
And as his age increas'd, his fondnefs grew.
A parent's love ne'er better was beftow'd;
The pious daughter in her heart o'erflow'd.
And can fhe from all weaknefs ftill refrain?
And ftill the firmnefs of her foul maintain?
Impoffible! a figh will force its way;
One patient tear her *mortal* birth betray;
She fighs and weeps! but fo fhe weeps and fighs,
As filent dews defcend, and vapours rife.

Celeftial *Patience!* how doft thou defeat
The foe's proud menace, and elude his hate!
While *Paffion* takes his part, betrays our peace;
To death and torture fwells each flight difgrace;

By

By not oppofing, thou doft ills deftroy,
And wear thy conquer'd forrows into joy.

   Now *fhe* revolves within her anxious mind,
What woe ftill lingers in referve behind.
Griefs rife on griefs, and fhe can fee no bound,
While nature lafts, and can receive a wound.
The fword is drawn; The queen to rage inclin'd,
By mercy, nor by piety, confin'd.
What mercy can the *Zealot*'s heart affuage,
Whofe piety itfelf converts to rage ?
She thought, and figh'd. And now the blood began
To leave her beauteous cheek all cold and wan.
New forrow dimm'd the luftre of her eye,
And on her cheek the fading rofes die.
Alas ! fhould GUILFORD too—When now fhe's brought
To that dire view, that *precipice* of thought,
While there fhe trembling ftands, nor dares look down,
Nor can recede, till heav'n's decrees are known ;
Cure of all ills, till now, her lord appears—
But not to chear her heart, and dry her tears !
Not now, as ufual, like the rifing day,
To chafe the fhadows, and the damps away :
But, like a gloomy ftorm, at once to fweep
And plunge her to the bottom of the deep.
Black were his robes, dejeéted was his air,
His voice was frozen by his cold defpair ;
Slow, like a ghoft, he mov'd with folemn pace ;
A dying palenefs fat upon his face.
Back fhe recoil'd, fhe fmote her lovely breaft,
Her eyes the anguifh of her heart confefs'd ;
Struck to the foul, fhe ftagger'd with the wound,
And funk, a breathlefs image, to the ground.

   Thus the fair lily, when the fky's o'ercaft,
At firft but fhudders in the feeble blaft ;

But when the winds and weighty rains defcend,
The fair and upright ftem is forc'd to bend ;
Till broke at length, its fnowy leaves are fhed,
And ftrew with dying fweets their native bed.

THE
FORCE of RELIGION;
.OR,
VANQUISH'D LOVE.

·BOOK II.

Hic pietatis honos ? fic nos in fceptra reponis ?   VIRG.

HER GUILFORD clafps her, beautiful in death,
And with a kifs recalls her fleeting breath,
To tapers thus, which by a blaft expire,
A lighted taper, touch'd, reftores the fire :
She rear'd her fwimming eye, and faw the light,
And GUILFORD too, or fhe had loath'd the fight :
Her *father*'s death fhe bore, defpis'd her *own*,
But now fhe muft, fhe will, have leave to groan :
Ah! GUILFORD, fhe began, and would have fpoke;
But fobs rufh'd in, and ev'ry accent broke :
Reafon itfelf, as gufts of paffion blew,
Was ruffled in the tempeft, and withdrew.
  So the youth loft his *image* in the well,
When tears upon the yielding furface fell :

The

The scatter'd features slid into decay,
And spreading circles drove his face away.

   To touch the soft affections, and controul
The manly temper of the bravest soul,
What with afflicted beauty can compare,
And drops of love distilling from the fair?
It melts us down; our pains delight bestow;
And we with fondness languish o'er our woe.

   This GUILFORD prov'd; and, with excess of pain,
And pleasure too, did to his bosom strain
The weeping fair: Sunk deep in soft desire,
Indulg'd his love, and nurs'd the raging fire:
Then tore himself away; and, standing wide,
As fearing a relapse of fondness, cry'd,
With ill-dissembled grief; " My life, forbear!
" You wound your GUILFORD with each cruel tear:
" Did you not chide my grief? Repress your own;
" Nor want compassion for *yourself* alone:
" Have you beheld, how, from the distant main,
" The thronging waves roll on, a num'rous train,
" And foam, and bellow, till they reach the shore;
" There burst their noisy pride, and are no more?
" Thus the successive flows of human race,
" Chas'd by the coming, the preceding, chase;
" They found, and swell, their haughty heads they rear;
" Then fall, and flatten, break, and disappear.
" Life is a forfeit we must shortly pay;
" And where's the mighty lucre of a day?
" Why should you mourn *my* fate? 'Tis most unkind;
" Your *own* you bore with an unshaken mind:
" And which, can you imagine, was the dart
" That drank most blood, sunk deepest in my heart?
" I cannot live without you; and my doom
" I meet with joy, to share one common tomb.—

                                         " And

" And are again your tears profuſely ſpilt !
" Oh ! then, my kindneſs blackens to my guilt ;
" It foils itſelf, if it recall your pain ;—
" Life of my life, I beg you to refrain !
" The load which fate impoſes, you increaſe ;
" And help MARIA to deſtroy my peace."
  But, oh ! againſt himſelf his labour turn'd ;
The more He comforted, the more She mourn'd :
Compaſſion ſwells our grief ; words ſoft and kind
But ſooth our weakneſs, and diſſolve the mind :
Her ſorrow flow'd in ſtreams ; nor Her's alone,
While That he blam'd, he yielded to his own.
Where are the ſmiles ſhe wore, when ſhe, ſo late,
Hail'd him great partner of the regal ſtate ;
When orient gems around her temples blaz'd,
And bending nations on the glory gaz'd ?
  'Tis now the _Queen_'s command, they both retreat,
To weep with dignity, and mourn in ſtate :
She forms the _decent_ miſery with joy,
And loads with pomp the wretch ſhe would deſtroy.
A ſpacious hall is hung with black ; all light
Shut out, and noon-day darken'd into night.
From the mid-roof a lamp depends on high,
Like a dim creſcent in a clouded ſky :
It ſheds a quiv'ring melancholy gloom,
Which only ſhews the darkneſs of the room.
A ſhining ax is on the table laid ;
A dreadful ſight ! and glitters through the ſhade.
  In this ſad ſcene the lovers are confin'd ;
A ſcene of terrors, to a guilty mind !
A ſcene, that would have damp'd with riſing cares,
And quite extinguiſh'd, every love but theirs.
What can they do ? They fix their mournful eyes——
Then GUILFORD, thus abruptly ; " I deſpiſe

" An

" An empire loft; I fling away the crown;
" Numbers have laid that bright delufion down;
" But where's the CHARLES, or DIOCLESIAN where,
" Could quit the blooming, wedded, weeping fair?
" Oh! to dwell ever on thy lip! to ftand
" In full poffeffion of thy fnowy hand!
" And, thro' th' unclouded chryftal of thine eye,
" The heav'nly treafures of thy mind to fpy!
" Till rapture reafon happily deftroys,
" And my foul wanders through immortal joys!
" Give me the world, and afk me, Where's my blifs?
" I clafp thee to my breaft, and anfwer, *This*.
" And fhall the grave"—He groans, and can no more;
But all her charms in filence traces o'er;
Her lip, her cheek, and eye, to wonder wrought;
And, wond'ring, fees, in fad *prefaging* thought,
From that fair neck, that world of beauty fall,
And roll along the duft, a ghaftly ball!

  Oh! let thofe *tremble*, who are greatly blefs'd!
For who, but GUILFORD, could be thus diftrefs'd?
Come hither, all you Happy, all you Great,
From flow'ry meadows, and from rooms of ftate;
Nor think I call, your pleafures to deftroy,
But to refine, and to exalt your joy:
Weep not; but, fmiling, fix your ardent care
On nobler titles than the *Brave* or *Fair*.

  Was ever fuch a mournful, moving, fight?
See, if you can, by that dull, trembling, light:
Now they embrace; and, mix'd with bitter woe,
Like *Ifis* and her *Thames*, one ftream they flow:
Now they ftart wide; fix'd in benumbing care,
They ftiffen into ftatues of defpair:
Now, tenderly fevere, and fiercely kind,
They rufh at once; they fling their cares behind,

                        And

And clasp, as if to death; new vows repeat;
And, quite wrapp'd up in love, forget their fate.
A short delusion! for the raging pain
Returns; and their poor hearts must bleed again.
　　Mean time, the QUEEN new cruelty decreed;
But, ill content that they should *only* bleed,
A priest is sent; who, with insidious art,
Instills his poison into SUFFOLK's heart;
And GUILFORD drank it: Hanging on the breast,
He from his childhood was with *Rome* possest.
When now the ministers of death draw nigh,
And in her dearest lord she first must die,
The subtle priest, who long had watch'd to find
The most unguarded passes of her mind,
Bespoke her thus: " Grieve not; 'tis in your pow'r
" Your lord to rescue from this fatal hour."
Her bosom pants; she draws her breath with pain;
A sudden horror thrills through every vein;
Life seems suspended, on his words intent;
And her soul trembles for the great event.
　　The priest proceeds: " Embrace the faith of *Rome,*
" And ward your own, your lord's, and father's doom."
Ye blessed spirits! now your charge sustain;
The past was ease; now *first* she suffers pain.
Must she pronounce her father's death? must she
Bid GUILFORD bleed?—It must not, cannot, be.
It *cannot* be! But 'tis the Christian's praise,
Above impossibilities to raise
The weakness of our nature; and deride
Of vain philosophy the boasted pride.
What though our feeble sinews scarce impart
A moment's swiftness to the feather'd dart;
Though tainted air our vig'rous *youth* can break,
And a chill blast the hardy *warrior* shake,

　　　　　　　　　　　　　　Yet

Yet are we ftrong: Hear the loud tempeft roar
From eaft to weft, and call us weak no more;
The light'ning's unrefifted force proclaims
Our might; and thunders raife our humble names;
'Tis *our* JEHOVAH fills the heav'ns; as long
As He fhall reign Almighty, We are ftrong:
We, by devotion, *borrow* from his throne;
And almoft make Omnipotence our own:
We force the gates of heav'n, by fervent pray'r;
And call forth triumph out of *man*'s defpair.

    Our lovely mourner, kneeling, lifts her eyes
And bleeding heart, in filence, to the fkies,
Devoutly fad—Then, bright'ning, like the day,
When fudden winds fweep fcatter'd clouds away,
Shining in majefty, till now unknown,
And breathing life and fpirit·fcarce her own;
She, rifing, fpeaks: " If thefe the terms——"

    Here, GUILFORD, cruel GUILFORD, (barb'rous man!
Is this thy love?) as fwift as light'ning ran;
O'erwhelm'd her with tempeftuous forrow fraught,
And ftifled, in its birth, the mighty thought;
Then burfting frefh into a flood of tears,
Fierce, refolute, delirious with his fears;
His fears for her *alone:* He beat his breaft,
And thus the fervour of his foul expreft:
" O! let thy thought o'er our paft converfe rove,
" And fhew one moment uninflam'd with love!
" Oh! if thy kindnefs can no longer laft,
" In pity to thyfelf, forget the paft!
" Elfe wilt thou never, void of fhame and fear,
" Pronounce *his* doom, whom thou haft held fo dear:
" Thou who haft took me to thy arms, and fwore
" Empires were vile, and Fate could give no more;

                                            " That

" That to *continue*, was its utmoſt pow'r,
" And make the future like the preſent hour.
" Now call a ruffian; bid his cruel ſword
" Lay wide the boſom of thy worthleſs lord;
" Transfix his heart (ſince you its love diſclaim),
" And ſtain his honour with a *Traitor*'s name.
" *This* might perhaps be borne without remorſe;
" But ſure a *father*'s pangs will have their force!
" Shall his good age, ſo near its journey's end,
" Through cruel torment to the grave deſcend?
" His ſhallow blood all iſſue at a wound,
" Waſh a ſlave's feet, and ſmoak upon the ground?
" But he to you has ever been ſevere;
" Then take your vengeance"—SUFFOLK now drew near;
Bending beneath the burden of his care;
His robes neglected, and his head was bare;
Decrepid winter, in the yearly ring,
Thus ſlowly creeps, to meet the blooming ſpring:
Downward he caſt a melancholy look;
Thrice turn'd, to hide his grief; then faintly ſpoke,
" Now deep in years, and forward in decay,
" That ax can only rob *me* of a day;
" For *thee*, my ſoul's deſire! I can't refrain;
" And ſhall my tears, my *laſt* tears, flow in vain?
" When you ſhall know a mother's tender name,
" My heart's diſtreſs no longer will you blame."
At this, afar his burſting groans were heard;
The tears ran trickling down his ſilver beard:
He ſnatch'd her hand, which to his lips he preſt,
And bid her plant a dagger in his breaſt;
Then, ſinking, call'd her piety unjuſt,
And ſoil'd his hoary temples in the duſt.
    Hard-hearted men! will you no mercy know?
Has the *Queen* brib'd you to diſtreſs her foe?

O weak

O weak deferters to misfortune's part,
By falfe affection thus to pierce her heart!
When fhe had foar'd, to let your arrows fly,
And fetch her bleeding from the middle fky!
And can her virtue, fpringing from the ground,
Her flight recover, and difdain the wound,
When cleaving love, and human intereft, bind
The broken force of her afpiring mind;
As round the gen'rous eagle, which in vain
Exerts her ftrength, the ferpent wreaths his train,
Her ftruggling wings entangles, curling plies
His pois'nous tail, and ftings her as fhe flies!
    While yet the blow's firft dreadful weight fhe feels,
And with its force her refolution reels;
Large doors, unfolding with a mournful found,
To view difcover welt'ring on the ground,
Three headlefs trunks, of thofe whofe arms maintain'd,
And in her wars immortal glory gain'd:
The lifted ax affur'd her ready doom,
And filent mourners fadden'd all the room.
Shall I proceed; or here break off my tale;
Nor truths, to ftagger human faith, reveal?
    She met this utmoft malice of her fate
With Chriftian dignity, and pious ftate:
The beating ftorm's propitious rage fhe bleft,
And all the *martyr* triumph'd in her breaft:
Her *lord* and *father*, for a moment's fpace,
She ftrictly folded in her foft embrace!
Then thus fhe fpoke, while angels heard on high,
And fudden gladnefs fmil'd along the fky:
    " Your over-fondnefs has not mov'd my hate;
" I am well pleas'd you make my death fo *great*;
" I joy I cannot fave you; and have giv'n
" Two lives, much *dearer* than my own, to heav'n,

" If

" If fo the queen decrees * :—But I have caufe
" To hope my blood will fatisfy the laws ;
" And there is mercy ftill, for you, in ftore:
" With me the bitternefs of death is o'er.
" He fhot his fting in *that* farewell-embrace ;
" And all, that is to come, is joy and peace.
" Then let miftaken forrow be fuppreft,
" Nor feem to envy my approaching reft."
Then, turning to the minifters of fate,
She, fmiling, fays, " My victory complete :
" And tell your *Queen*, I thank her for the blow,
" And grieve my gratitude I cannot fhow :
" A poor return I leave in *England*'s crown,
" For everlafting pleafure, and renown :
" Her guilt alone allays this happy hour ;
" Her guilt,—the *only* vengeance in her pow'r."
    Not *Rome*, untouch'd with forrow, heard her fate;
And fierce MARIA pity'd her too late.

        * Here fhe embraces them.

L O V E

PREFACE.

THESE Satires have been favourably received at home and abroad. I am not confcious of the leaft malevolence to any particular perfon through all the charaders; though fome perfons may be fo felfifh, as to engrofs a general application to themfelves. A writer in polite letters fhould be content with reputation; the private amufement he finds in his compofitions; the good influence they have on his feverer ftudies; that admiffion they give him to his fuperiors; and the poffible good effect they may have on the public; or elfe he fhould join to his politenefs fome more lucrative qualification.

But it is poffible, that Satire may not do much good: Men may rife in their affections to their follies, as they do to their friends, when they are abufed by others: It is much *to be feared*, that mifconduct will never be chafed out of the world by *Satire*; all therefore that is to be faid for it, is, that mifconduct will *certainly* be never chafed out of the world by Satire, if no Satires are written: Nor is

that

that term unapplicable to graver compofitions. *Ethics,* Heathen and Chriſtian, and the Scriptures themſelves, are, in a great meaſure, a *Satire* on the weakneſs and iniquity of men; and ſome part of that Satire is in verſe too: Nay, in the firſt Ages, Philoſophy and Poetry were the ſame thing; wiſdom wore no other dreſs: So that, I hope, theſe Satires will be the more eaſily pardoned that misfortune by the ſevere. Nay, *Hiſtorians* themſelves may be conſidered as Satiriſts, and Satiriſts moſt ſevere; ſince ſuch are moſt human actions, that to *relate,* is to *expoſe* them.

No man can converſe much in the world, but, at what he meets with, he muſt either be inſenſible, or grieve, or be angry, or ſmile. Some paſſion (if we are not impaſſive) muſt be moved; for the general conduct of mankind is by no means a thing *indifferent* to a reaſonable and virtuous man. Now to ſmile at it, and turn it into ridicule, I think moſt eligible; as it hurts ourſelves leaſt, and gives vice and folly the greateſt offence: And that for *this* reaſon; becauſe what men aim at by them, is, generally, public opinion and eſteem; which truth is the ſubject of the following Satires; and joins them together, as ſeveral branches from the ſame root: An unity of deſign, which has not, I think, in a ſet of ſatires, been attempted before.

Laughing

Laughing at the mifconduct of the world, will, in a great meafure, eafe us of any more difagreeable paffion about it. One paffion is more effectually driven out by another, than by reafon; whatever fome may teach:. For to reafon we owe our paffions:. Had we not reafon, we fhould not be offended at what we find amifs: And the *Caufe* feems not to be the natural cure of any *Effect*.

Moreover, *Laughing Satire* bids the faireft for fuccefs: The world is too proud to be fond of a ferious tutor; and when an Author is in a paffion, the laugh, generally, as in converfation, turns againft him. This kind of Satire only has any delicacy in it. Of this delicacy *Horace* is the beft mafter: He appears in good humour while he cenfures; and therefore his cenfure has the more weight, as fuppofed to proceed from judgment, not from paffion. *Juvenal* is ever in a paffion: He has little valuable but his eloquence and morality: The laft of which I have had in my eye; but rather for emulation, than imitation, through my whole work.

But though I comparatively condemn *Juvenal*, in part of the fixth Satire (where the occafion moft required it), I endeavoured to touch on his manner; but was forced to quit it foon, as difagreeable to the writer, and reader too. *Boileau* has joined *both* the *Roman* Satirifts with great fuccefs; but has too much

of

of *Juvenal* in his very serious Satire on Woman, which should have been the gayest of all. . An excellent critic of our own commends *Boileau*'s closeness, or, as he calls it, *Preſſneſs*, particularly; whereas, it appears to me, that repetition is his fault, if any fault should be imputed to him.

There are some prose Satyrists of the greatest delicacy and wit; the last of which can never, or should never, succeed without the former. An Author without it, betrays too great a contempt for mankind, and opinion of himself; which are bad advocates for reputation and success. What a difference is there between the *Merit*, if not the *Wit*, of *Cervantes* and *Rabelais?* The last has a particular art of throwing a great deal of genius and learning into frolic and jest; but the genius and the scholar is all you can admire; you want the gentleman to converse with in him: he is like a criminal who receives his life for some services; you commend, but you pardon too. Indecency offends our pride, as men; and our unaffected taste, as judges of compoſition: Nature has wisely formed us with an averſion to it; and he that succeeds in spite of it, is, * *aliena venia, quam sua providentia tutior.*

Such wits, like falſe oracles of old (which were wits and cheats), should set up for reputation among

* Val. Max.

the

the *weak*, in some *Bæotia*, which was the land of ora-
cles; for the *wise* will hold them in contempt. Some
wits, too, like oracles, deal in *ambiguities*; but not
with equal success: For though ambiguities are the
first excellence of an impostor, they are the *last* of a
wit.

Some satirical wits and humourists, like their father
Lucian, laugh at every thing indiscriminately; which
betrays such a poverty of wit, as cannot afford to
part with any thing; and such a want of virtue, as to
postpone it to a jest. Such writers encourage vice
and folly, which they pretend to combat, by setting
them on an equal foot with better things: And while
they labour to bring every thing into contempt, how
can they expect their own parts should escape? Some
French writers particularly, are guilty of this in mat-
ters of the last consequence; and some of our own.
They that are for lessening the true dignity of man-
kind, are not sure of being successful, but with
regard to *one individual* in it. It is this conduct that
justly makes a *Wit* a term of reproach.

Which puts me in mind of *Plato*'s fable of the birth
of *Love*; one of the prettiest fables of all antiquity;
which will hold likewise with regard to modern
Poetry. *Love*, says he, is the son of the goddess
Poverty, and the god of *Riches*: He has from his
father his daring genius; his elevation of thought;

his

his building caftles in the air; his prodigality; his negleft of things ferious and ufeful; his vain opinion of his own merit; and his affeftation of preference and diftinction: From his *mother* he inherits his indigence, which makes him a conftant beggar of favours; that importunity with which he begs; his flattery; his fervility; his fear of being defpifed, which is infeparable from him. This addition may be made; *viz.* That *Poetry*, like *Love*, is a little fubjeft to *blindnefs*, which makes her miftake her way to preferments and honours; that fhe has her fatirical *quiver*; and, laftly, that fhe retains a dutiful admiration of her *father's* family; but divides her favours, and generally lives with her *mother's* relations.

However, this is not *neceffity*, but *choice:* Were Wifdom her governefs, fhe might have much more of the father than the mother; efpecially in fuch an age as this, which fhews a due paffion for her charms.

SATIRE.

SATIRE I.

TO HIS GRACE

THE DUKE OF DORSET.

——*Tanto major Famæ fitis eft, quam Virtutis.*   Juv. Sat. 10.

✦✦✦✦✦✦✦✦✦✦✦✦

MY verfe is Satire; DORSET, lend your ear,
And *patronize* a mufe you cannot *fear*.
To poets facred is a DORSET's name:
Their wonted paffport through the gates of fame:
It *bribes* the partial reader into praife,
And throws a glory round the fhelter'd lays:
The dazzled judgment fewer faults can fee,
And gives applaufe to *B——e*, or to me.
But you decline the *miftrefs* we purfue;
Others are fond of *Fame*, but *Fame* of you.
    Inftructive Satire, true to virtue's caufe!
Thou fhining *fupplement* of public *laws!*
When *flatter'd crimes* of a licentious age
Reproach our filence, and demand our rage;

When

When *purchas'd follies*, from each diftant land,
Like arts, improve in *Britain*'s fkilful hand;
When the *Law* fhews her teeth, but dares not bite,
And *South-fea* treafures are not brought to light;
When *Churchmen* Scripture for the Claffics quit,
Polite apoftates from God's *Grace* to *Wit*;
When men grow *great* from their *revenue fpent*,
And fly from bailiffs into parliament;
When dying finners, to blot out their fcore,
Bequeath the *church* the leavings of a *whore*;
To chafe our fpleen, when themes like thefe increafe,
Shall *Panegyric* reign, and *Cenfure* ceafe?

Shall *Poefy*, like *Law*, turn wrong to right,
And dedications wafh an *Æthiop* white,
Set up each fenfelefs wretch for nature's boaft,
On whom praife fhines, as *trophies* on a *poft*?
Shall fun'ral eloquence her colours fpread,
And fcatter rofes on the wealthy dead?
Shall authors fmile on fuch illuftrious days,
And *fatirife* with nothing—but their *praife*?

Why flumbers POPE, who leads the tuneful train,
Nor hears that virtue, which he loves, complain?
DONNE, DORSET, DRYDEN, ROCHESTER, are dead,
And guilt's chief foe, in ADDISON, is fled;
CONGREVE, who, crown'd with laurels, fairly won,
Sits fmiling at the goal, while others run,
He will not write; and (more provoking ftill!)
Ye gods! he will not write, and MÆVIUS will.

Doubly diftreft, what author fhall we find
Difcreetly daring, and feverely kind,
The courtly * *Roman*'s fhining path to tread,
And fharply *fmile* prevailing folly dead?

* HORACE.

Will

Will no fuperior genius fnatch the quill,
And fave me, on the brink, from writing ill?
'Tho' vain the ftrife, I'll ftrive my voice to raife,
What will not men attempt for *facred praife?*

   The *Love of Praife*, howe'er conceal'd by art,
Reigns, more or lefs, and glows, in ev'ry heart:
The *proud*, to gain it, toils on toils endure;
The *modeft* fhun it, but to make it fure.
O'er globes, and fceptres, now on thrones it fwells;
Now, trims the midnight lamp in college cells:
'Tis Tory, Whig; it plots, prays, preaches, pleads,
Harangues in Senates, fqueaks in Mafquerades.
Here, to S——e's *humour* makes a bold pretence;
There, bolder, aims at P——y's *eloquence.*
It aids the *dancer's* heel, the *writer's* head,
And heaps the plain with mountains of the dead;
Nor ends with *life*; but nods in fable *plumes,*
Adorns our *hearfe,* and flatters on our *tombs.*

   What is not *proud?*   The *pimp* is proud to fee
So many like himfelf in high degree:
The *whore* is proud her beauties are the dread
Of peevifh virtue, and the marriage-bed;
And the brib'd *cuckold,* like crown'd victims born
To flaughter, glories in his gilded horn.

   Some go to church, *proud* humbly to repent,
And come back much more guilty than they went:
One way they *look*, another way they *fteer,*
Pray to the gods, but would have mortals hear;
And when their fins they fet fincerely down,
They'll find that their religion has been one.

   Others with wifhful eyes on *glory* look,
When they have got their *picture* tow'rds a book;
Or *pompous* title, like a gaudy fign,
Meant to betray dull fots to wretched wine.

If at his title *T*—— had dropt his quill,
T—— might have pafs'd for a great genius ftill.
But *T*—— alas! (excufe him, if you can)
Is now a *fcribbler*, who was once a *man*.
Imperious fome a claffic *fame* demand,
For heaping up, with a laborious hand,
A waggon-load of meanings for *one* word,
While *A's depos'd*, and B with pomp *reftor'd*.

Some, for *renown*, on fcraps of learning doat,
And think they grow immortal as they *quote*.
To patch-work learn'd quotations are ally'd;
Both ftrive to make our *poverty* our *pride*.
On *glafs* how witty is a noble peer!
Did ever diamond coft a man fo *dear?*

Polite difeafes make fome idiots *vain*
Which, if unfortunately well, they feign.

Of folly, vice, difeafe, men proud we fee;
And (ftranger ftill!) of blockheads' flattery;
Whofe praife defames; as if a fool fhould mean,
By fpitting on your face, to make it clean.

Nor is't enough all hearts are fwoln with *pride*,
Her *power* is mighty, as her *realm* is wide.
What can fhe not perform?   The Love of Fame
Made bold ALPHONSUS his Creator blame:
EMPEDOCLES hurl'd down the-burning fteep:
And (ftronger ftill!)·made ALEXANDER weep.
Nay, it holds DELIA from a fecond bed,
Tho' her lov'd lord has four half months been dead.

This paffion with a *pimple* have I feen
Retard a caufe, and give a judge the fpleen.
By *this* infpir'd (O ne'er to be forgot!)
Some lords have learn'd to *fpell*, and fome to *knot*.
It makes GLOBOSE a fpeaker in the houfe;
He hems, and is deliver'd of his moufe.

It

It makes *dear self* on well-bred tongues prevail,
And *I* the *little hero* of each tale.

   Sick with the *Love of Fame*, what throngs pour in,
Unpeople *court*, and leave the *senate* thin !
My growing subject seems but just begun,
And, chariot-like, I kindle as I run.

   Aid me, great HOMER ! with thy *epic rules*,
To take a catalogue of *British* fools.
Satire ! had I thy DORSET's force divine,
A knave or fool should perish in each line ;
Tho' for the first all *Westminster* should plead,
And for the last, all *Gresham* intercede.

   BEGIN.   Who first the *catalogue* shall grace ?
To *quality* belongs the highest place.
My lord comes forward ; forward let him come !
Ye vulgar ! at your peril, give him room :
He stands for *fame* on his forefathers' feet,
By heraldry prov'd *valiant* or *discreet.*
With what a decent pride he throws his eyes
Above the man by *three descents* less wife !
If virtues at his noble hands you crave,
You bid him raise his fathers from the grave.
Men should press forward in fame's glorious chace ;
Nobles look *backward*, and so lose the race.

   Let high birth triumph ! What can be more great ?
Nothing—but merit in a low estate.
To virtue's humblest son let none prefer
Vice, though descended from the Conqueror.
Shall men, like *figures*, pass for high, or base,
Slight, or important, only by their place ?
Titles are marks of *honest* men, and *wise* ;
The fool, or knave, that wears a title, *lyes.*

   They that on glorious ancestors enlarge,
Produce their *debt*, instead of their *discharge.*

DORSET,

Dorset, let those who proudly boast their line,
Like thee, in worth hereditary, shine.

Vain as false greatness is, the muse must own
We want not fools to buy that *Bristol* stone;
Mean sons of earth, who, on a *South-sea* tide
Of full success, swarm into *wealth* and *pride*;
Knock with a purse of gold at Anstis' gate,
And beg to be descended from the great.

When men of infamy to grandeur soar,
They light a torch to shew their shame the more.
Those governments which *curb* not evils, *cause*!
And a rich knave's a *libel* on our *laws*.

Belus with solid *glory* will be crown'd;
He buys no phantom, no vain empty sound;
But *builds* himself a name; and, to be great,
Sinks in a quarry an immense estate!
In cost and grandeur, C——*dos* he'll out-do;
And, B—*l*—*ton*, thy taste is not so true.
The pile is finish'd; ev'ry toil is past;
And full perfection is arriv'd at last;
When, lo! my lord to some small corner runs,
And leaves state-rooms to *strangers* and to *duns*.

The man who builds, and wants wherewith to pay,
Provides a home from which to run away.
In *Britain*, what is many a lordly seat,
But a discharge in full for an estate?

In smaller compass lies Pygmalion's fame;
Not domes, but antique statues, are his flame:
Not F——*t*——*n*'s self more *Parian* charms has known;
Nor is good P—*b*—*ke* more in love with stone.
The bailiffs come (rude men prophanely bold!)
And bid him turn his Venus into gold.
" No, firs," he cries; " I'll sooner rot in jail;
" Shall *Grecian* arts be truck'd for *English* bail?"

Such

Such *heads* might make their very *busto's* laugh :
His daughter ftarves ; but * CLEOPATRA's fafe.
  Men, overloaded with a large eftate,
May fpill their treafure in a nice conceit :
The *rich* may be polite ; but, oh ! 'tis fad
To fay you're *curious*, when we fwear you're *mad.*
By your revenue meafure your expence ;
And to your *funds* and *acres* join your *fenfe.*
No man is blefs'd by *accident* or *guefs* ;
True *wifdom* is the price of *happinefs :*
Yet few without long difcipline are fage ;
And our *youth* only lays up fighs for *age.*
But how, my mufe, canft thou refift fo long
The bright temptation of the Courtly throng,
Thy moft inviting theme ? The *court* affords
Much food for fatire ;—it abounds in lords.
" What lords are thofe faluting with a grin ?"
One is juft *out*, and one as lately *in.*
" How comes it then to pafs we fee prefide
" On both their brows an equal fhare of *pride ?*"
Pride, that impartial paffion, reigns through all,
Attends our glory, nor deferts our fall.
As in its home it triumphs in *high place*,
And frowns a haughty exile in *difgrace.*
Some lords it bids admire their wands fo white,
Which bloom, like AARON's, to their ravifh'd fight ;
Some lords it bids *refign* ; and turn their wands,
Like MOSES', into ferpents in their hands.
Thefe fink, as divers, for renown ; and boaft,
With pride *inverted*, of their honours loft.
But againft reafon fure 'tis equal fin,
To boaft of merely being *out*, or *in*.

* A famous ftatue.

What

What numbers *here*, through odd ambition strive,
To seem the most transported things alive !
As if by *joy*, *desert* was understood ;
And all the fortunate were *wise* and *good*.
Hence aching bosoms wear a visage gay,
And stifled groans frequent the ball and play.
Completely drest by * MONTEUIL, and grimace,
They take their *birth-day* suit, and *public* face :
Their smiles are only part of what they *wear*,
Put off at night, with lady *B———*'s hair.
What bodily fatigue is half so bad ?
With anxious *care* they labour to be *glad*.

　What numbers, *here*, would into fame advance,
Conscious of merit, in the coxcomb's *dance* ;
The tavern ! park ! assembly ! mask ! and play !
Those dear destroyers of the tedious day !
That wheel of fops ! that saunter of the town !
Call it *diversion*, and the *pill* goes down.
Fools grin on fools, and, *stoic*-like, support,
Without one sigh, tne *pleasures* of a court.
Courts can give nothing, to the *wise* and *good*,
But scorn of pomp, and love of solitude.
High stations *tumult*, but not *bliss*, create :
None think the Great unhappy, but the Great :
Fools gaze, and envy ; envy darts a sting,
Which makes a swain as wretched as a king.

　I envy none their pageantry and show ;
I envy none the *gilding* of their woe.
Give me, indulgent Gods ! with mind serene,
And guiltless heart, to range the sylvan scene ;
No splendid poverty, no smiling care,
No well-bred hate, or servile grandeur, *there* :

.* A famous Taylor.

There

There pleasing objects useful thoughts suggest;
The *sense* is ravish'd, and the *soul* is blest;
On every thorn delightful wisdom grows;
In every rill a sweet instruction flows.
But some, *untaught*, o'erhear the whisp'ring rill,
In spite of sacred leisure, blockheads still;
Nor shoots up folly to a nobler bloom
In her own native soil, the *drawing-room*.

The *Squire* is *proud* to see his coursers strain,
Or well-breath'd beagles sweep along the plain.
Say, dear HIPPOLITUS (whose drink is ale,
Whose erudition is a *Christmas*-tale,
Whose mistress is saluted with a smack,
And friend receiv'd with thumps upon the back)
When thy sleek gelding nimbly leaps the mound,
And RINGWOOD opens on the tainted ground,
Is that *thy* praise? Let RINGWOOD's fame alone;
Just RINGWOOD leaves each animal his own;
Nor envies, when a gypsy *you* commit,
And shake the clumsy *bench* with country wit;
When you the dullest of dull things have said,
And then ask pardon for the *jest* you made.

Here breathe, my muse! and then thy task renew:
Ten thousand fools unsung are still in view.
Fewer lay-atheists made by church debates;
Fewer great beggars fam'd for large estates;
Ladies, whose love is constant as the wind;
Cits, who prefer a guinea to mankind;
Fewer grave lords, to SCR——PE discreetly bend;
And fewer *shocks* a statesman gives his *friend*.

Is there a man of an eternal vein,
Who lulls the town in *winter* with his strain,
At *Bath*, in *summer*, chants the reigning lass,
And sweetly *whistles*, as the *waters* pass?

Is there a tongue, like Delia's o'er her cup,
That runs for ages without winding up?
Is there, whom his *tenth Epic* mounts to fame?
Such, and such only, might exhauft my theme:
Nor would thefe heroes of the tafk be glad;
For who can *write* fo faft as men run *mad*?

SATIRE

S A T I R E   II.

M

Y mufe, proceed, and reach thy deftin'd end;
Though *toils* and *danger* the bold tafk attend.
Heroes and *Gods* make other poems fine;
Plain Satire calls for *fenfe* in every line:
Then, to what fwarms thy faults I dare expofe!
All friends to *vice* and *folly* are thy foes.
When *fuch* the foe, a war eternal wage;
'Tis moft ill-nature to *reprefs* thy rage:
And if thefe ftrains fome nobler mufe excite,
I'll glory in the verfe I did *not* write.
   So weak are human kind by nature made,
Or to fuch weaknefs by their vice betray'd,
Almighty *vanity!* to thee they owe
Their *zeft* of pleafure, and their *balm* of woe.
Thou, like the fun, all *colours* doft contain,
Varying, like rays of light, on drops of rain.
For every foul finds reafons to be proud,
Tho' hifs'd and hooted by the pointing crowd.

Warm in purſuit of foxes, and renown,
* HIPPOLITUS demands the *ſylvan* crown;
But FLORIO's fame, the product of a ſhower,
Grows in his garden, an illuſtrious flower!
Why teems the earth? Why melt the vernal ſkies?
Why ſhines the ſun? To make † *Paul Diack* riſe.
From morn to night has FLORIO gazing ſtood,
And wonder'd how the gods could be ſo good;
What ſhape! What hue! Was ever nymph ſo fair!
He doats! he dies! he too is *rooted* there.
O ſolid bliſs! which nothing can deſtroy,
Except a cat, bird, ſnail, or idle boy.
In fame's full bloom lies FLORIO down at night,
And wakes next day a moſt inglorious wight;
The tulip's dead! See thy fair ſiſter's fate,
O C——! and be kind ere 'tis too late.

   Nor are thoſe enemies I mention'd, all;
Beware, O Floriſt, thy ambition's fall.
A friend of mine indulg'd this noble flame;
A Quaker ſerv'd him, ADAM was his name;
To one lov'd tulip oft the maſter went,
Hung o'er it, and whole days in rapture ſpent;
But came, and miſt it, one ill-fated hour:
He rag'd! he roar'd! " What *dæmon* cropt my flow'r?"
Serene, quoth ADAM, " Lo! 'twas cruſht by me;
" Fall'n is the BAAL to which thou bow'dſt thy knee."

   But all men want *amuſement*; and what crime
In ſuch a paradiſe to fool their time?
None: but why proud of this? To fame they ſoar;
We grant *they're idle*, if they'll aſk no more.

   We ſmile at Floriſts, we deſpiſe their joy,
And think their hearts enamour'd of a toy:

     * This refers to the firſt Satire.
     † The name of a tulip.

                            Bu

But are thofe wifer whom we moft admire,
Survey with envy, and purfue with fire?
What's he who fighs for wealth, or fame, or pow'r?
Another FLORIO doating on a flower;
A fhort-liv'd flower; and which has often fprung
From fordid arts, as FLORIO's out of dung.

With what, O CODRUS! is thy fancy fmit?
The *flow'r* of learning, and the *bloom* of wit.
Thy gaudy fhelves with crimfon bindings glow,
And EPICTETUS is a perfect beau.
How fit for thee! bound up in crimfon too,
Gilt, and, like them, devoted to the view!
Thy books are *furniture.* Methinks 'tis hard
That fcience fhould be purchas'd by the yard;
And T————N, turn'd upholfterer, fend home
The gilded leather to *fit up* thy room.

If not to fome peculiar end defign'd,
Study's the fpecious *trifling* of the mind;
Or is at beft a fecondary aim,
A chace for fport alone, and not for *game.*
If fo, fure they who the *mere volume* prize,
But love the thicket where the *quarry* lies.

On buying books LORENZO long was bent,
But found at length that it reduc'd his rent;
His farms were flown; when, lo! a fale comes on,
A choice collection! what is to be done?
He fells his *laft*; for he the whole will buy;
Sells ev'n his houfe; nay, wants whereon to lie:
So high the gen'rous ardour of the man
For *Romans, Greeks,* and *Orientals* ran.
When terms were drawn, and brought him by the clerk,
LORENZO fign'd the bargain—with his *mark.*
Unlearned men of books affume the care,
As eunuchs are the guardians of the fair.

G 3

Not in his authors' *liveries* alone
Is CODRUS' erudite ambition shown:
Editions various, at high prices bought,
Inform the world what CODRUS would be *thought*;
And to this cost another must succeed
To pay a sage, who *says* that he can read;
Who *titles* knows, and *indexes* has seen;
But leaves to ———— what lies between;
Of pompous books who shuns the proud expence,
And humbly is contented with their *sense*.

O ————, whose accomplishments make good
The *promise* of a long-illustrious blood,
In *arts* and *manners* eminently grac'd,
The strictest *honour !* and the finest *taste !*
Accept this verse; if Satire can agree
With so consummate an *humanity*.

By your example would HILARIO mend,
How would it grace the talents of my friend,
Who, with the charms of his own genius smit,
Conceives all virtues are compriz'd in wit !
But time his fervent petulance may cool;
For though he is a *wit*, he is no *fool*.
In time he'll learn to *use*, not *waste*, his sense;
Nor make a *frailty* of an *excellence*.
He spares nor friend, nor foe; but calls to mind,
Like *doom's-day*, all the faults of all mankind.

What though *wit* tickles ? tickling is unsafe,
If still 'tis *painful* while it makes us *laugh*.
Who, for the poor renown of being *smart*,
Would leave a sting within a brother's heart ?

Parts may be prais'd, *good-nature* is ador'd;
Then draw your *wit* as seldom as your *sword*;
And never on the *weak*; or you'll appear
As *there* no hero, no great genius *here*.

As

As in smooth oil the razor best is whet,
So *wit* is by *politeness* sharpest set :
Their want of edge from their *offence* is seen ;
Both pain us *least* when exquisitely keen.
The *fame* men give is for the *joy* they find;
Dull is the *jester*, when the joke's *unkind*.

Since MARCUS, doubtless, thinks himself a wit,
To pay my compliment, what place so fit ?
His most facetious * letters came to hand,
Which my First Satire sweetly reprimand :
If that a *just* offence to MARCUS gave,
Say, MARCUS, which art thou, a *Fool*, or *Knave?*
For all but such with caution I forbore ;
That thou wast either, I ne'er knew before :
I know thee now, both *what* thou art, and *who* ;
No mask so good, but MARCUS must shine through :
False names are vain, thy lines their author tell;
Thy best concealment had been writing *well :*
But thou a brave neglect of *fame* hast shown,
Of *others'* fame, great genius! and thy *own.*
Write on unheeded; and this maxim know,
The man who *pardons, disappoints* his foe.

In malice to *proud wits,* some proudly lull
Their *peevish* reason ; *vain* of being dull ;
When some home joke has stung their *solemn* souls,
In vengeance they determine to be *fools* ;
Through spleen, that *little* nature gave, make *less,*
Quite zealous in the way of *heaviness* ;
To *lumps* inanimate a fondness take ;
And disinherit sons that are *awake.*
These, when their utmost venom they would spit,
Most barbarously tell you——" *He's a wit.*"

* Letters sent to the author, signed MARCUS.

Poor

Poor *negroes*, thus, to shew their burning spite
To cacodemons, say, they're *dev'lish white*.
  LAMPRIDIUS, from the bottom of his breast,
Sighs o'er one child; but triumphs in the rest.
How just his *grief!* one carries in his head
A less proportion of the father's lead;
And is in danger, without special grace,
To rise above a justice of the peace.
The *dungbill-breed* of men a *diamond* scorn,
And feel a passion for a *grain of corn*;
Some stupid, plodding, money-loving wight,
Who wins their hearts by knowing black from white,
Who with *much* pains, exerting *all* his sense,
Can range aright his shillings, pounds, and pence.
  The booby father craves a booby son;
And by Heav'n's *blessing* thinks himself *undone*.
  Wants of all kinds are made to fame a plea;
One learns to *lisp*; another, *not* to see:
Miss D——, tottering, catches at your hand:
Was ever thing so pretty born to stand?
Whilst these, what nature gave, disown, through pride,
Others affect what nature has deny'd;
What nature has deny'd, fools will pursue,
As *apes* are ever walking upon *two*.
  CRASSUS, a *grateful* sage, our awe and sport!
Supports grave forms; for forms the sage support.
He hems; and cries, with an important air,
" If yonder clouds withdraw it will be fair:"
Then quotes the *Stagyrite*, to prove it true;
And adds, " The learn'd delight in something *new*."
Is't not enough the blockhead scarce can read,
But must he *wisely* look, and *gravely* plead?
As far a *formalist* from *wisdom* sits,
In judging eyes, as *libertines* from *wits*.

Thefe

These subtle wights (so blind are mortal men,
Though Satire *couch* them with her keenest pen)
For ever will hang out a solemn face,
To put off *nonsense* with a better grace :
As pedlars with some hero's head make bold,
Illustrious mark ! where *pins* are to be sold.
What's the bent brow, or neck in thought reclin'd ?
The *body*'s wisdom to conceal the mind.
A man of sense can *artifice* disdain ;
As men of wealth may venture to go *plain* ;
And be this truth eternal ne'er forgot,
Solemnity's a cover for a *sot*.
I find the *fool*, when I behold the *skreen* ;
For 'tis the wise man's interest to be seen.

Hence, ———, that openness of heart,
And just disdain for that poor *mimic* art ;
Hence (manly praise !) that manner nobly free,
Which all admire, and I commend, in thee.

With generous scorn how oft hast thou survey'd
Of *court* and *town* the noontide masquerade ;
Where swarms of *knaves* the vizor quite disgrace,
And hide secure behind a *naked face* ?
Where nature's end of language is declin'd,
And men talk only to *conceal* the mind ;
Where gen'rous hearts the greatest hazard run,
And he who trusts a *brother*, is undone ?

These all their care expend on outward show
For wealth and fame ; for fame alone, the *beau*.
Of late at WHITE's was young FLORELLO seen !
How blank his look ! how discompos'd his mien !
So hard it proves in grief sincere to feign !
Sunk were his spirits ; for his coat was *plain*.

Next day his breast regain'd its wonted peace ;
His health was mended with a *silver lace*.

A curious

A curious artift, long inur'd to toils
Of gentler fort, with combs, and fragrant oils,
Whether by chance, or by fome god infpir'd,
So touch'd his *curls*, his mighty foul was fir'd.
The well-fwoln ties an equal homage claim,
And either fhoulder has its fhare of fame ;
His fumptuous *watch-cafe*, tho' conceal'd it lies,
Like a good *confcience*, folid joy fupplies.
He only thinks himfelf (fo far from vain !)
St——pe in wit, in breeding D—l—e.
Whene'er, by *feeming* chance, he throws his eye
On mirrors that refleâ his *Tyrian* dye,
With how fublime a tranfport leaps his heart !
But fate ordains that deareft friends muft part.
In aâive meafures, brought from *France*, he wheels,
And triumphs, confcious of his learned *heels*.

So have I feen, on fome bright fummer's day,
A calf of genius, debonnair and gay,
Dance on the bank, as if infpir'd by fame,
Fond of the *pretty fellow* in the ftream.

Morose is funk with fhame, whene'er furpris'd
In linen clean, or peruke undifguis'd.
No fublunary chance his veftments fear ;
Valu'd, like leopards, as their *fpots* appear.
A fam'd furtout he wears, which *once* was blue,
And his foot fwims in a capacious fhoe ;
One day his wife (for who can wives reclaim ?)
Levell'd her barb'rous *needle* at his fame :
But open force was vain ; by night fhe went,
And, while he flept, furpris'd the darling *tent :*
Where yawn'd the frieze is now become a doubt ;
And glory, at one entrainçe, quite fhut out *.

* Milton.

He

He scorns FLORELLO, and FLORELLO him;
This hates the *filthy* creature; that, the *prim:*
Thus, in each other, both these fools despise
Their own dear selves, with undiscerning eyes;
Their methods various, but alike their aim;
The *sloven* and the *fopling* are the same.

Ye whigs and tories! thus it fares with you,
When party-rage too warmly you pursue;
Then both club nonsense, and impetuous pride,
And *folly* joins whom *sentiments* divide.
You vent your spleen, as monkeys, when they pass,
Scratch at the mimic monkey in the glass;
While both are *one:* and henceforth be it known,
Fools of both sides shall stand for fools alone.

" But who art Thou ?" methinks FLORELLO cries;
" Of all thy species art Thou only wise ?"
Since smallest things can give our sins a twitch,
As crossing straws retard a passing witch,
FLORELLO, thou my monitor shalt be;
I'll *conjure* thus some profit out of *thee.*
O THOU myself! abroad our counsels roam,
And, like ill husbands, take no care at home:
Thou too art wounded with the common dart,
And Love of Fame lies throbbing at thy heart;
And what wise means to gain it hast thou chose ?
Know, *fame* and *fortune* both are made of prose.
Is thy ambition sweating for a *rhyme,*
Thou unambitious fool, at this late time ?
While I a moment name, a moment's past;
I'm nearer death in *this* verse, than the *last:*
What then is to be done ? Be wise with speed;
A fool at forty is a fool indeed.

And what so foolish as the chance of fame?
How vain the prize! how impotent our aim!

For

For what are men who grasp at praise sublime,
But *bubbles* on the rapid stream of time,
That rise, and fall, that swell; and are no more,
Born, and *forget*, ten thousand in an hour?

SATIRE

S A T I R E   III.

TO THE RIGHT HONOURABLE

Mᴿ. D O D I N G T O N.

L ONG, Dodington, in debt, I long have fought
   To eafe the burthen of my grateful thought;
And now a poet's gratitude you fee;
Grant him *two* favours, and he'll afk for *three :*
For whofe the prefent glory, or the gain?
You give protection, I a worthlefs ftrain.
You love and feel the poet's facred flame,
And know the bafis of a folid fame;
Tho' prone to like, yet cautious to commend,
You read with all the *malice* of a *friend*;
Nor favour my attempts that way alone,
But, more to raife my verfe, *conceal* your own.

 An ill-tim'd modefty! turn ages o'er,
When wanted *Britain* bright examples more?
Her *learning*, and her *genius* too, decays,
And *dark* and *cold* are her declining days;

As

As if men now were of another caſt,
They meanly live *on alms* of ages paſt.
Men ſtill are men ; and they who boldly dare,
Shall triumph o'er the ſons of cold deſpair ;
Or, if they fail, they juſtly ſtill take place
Of ſuch who *run in debt* for their diſgrace ;
Who borrow much, then fairly make it known,
And damn it with *improvements* of their own.
We bring ſome new materials, and what's old
New caſt with care, and in no *borrow'd* mould ;
Late times the verſe may read, if theſe refuſe ;
And from ſour critics vindicate the muſe.

 " Your work is long," the critics cry. 'Tis true,
And lengthens ſtill, to take in fools like you :
Shorten my labour, if its length you blame ;
For, grow but wiſe, you rob me of my game ;
As hunted *hags*, who, while the dogs purſue,
Renounce their four legs, and ſtart up on two.

 Like the bold bird upon the banks of *Nile*,
That picks the teeth of the dire *crocodile*,
Will I enjoy, (dread feaſt !) the critic's rage,
And with the *fell deſtroyer* feed my page.
For what ambitious fools are more to blame,
Than thoſe who thunder in the critic's name ?
Good authors damn'd, have their revenge in *this*,
To ſee what wretches gain the praiſe they miſs.

 BALBUTIUS, muffled in his ſable cloak,
Like an old Druid from his hollow oak,
As ravens ſolemn, and as *boding*, cries,
 " Ten thouſand worlds for the three unities !"
Ye doctors ſage, who thro' *Parnaſſus* teach,
Or quit the tub, or practiſe what you preach.

 One judges *as* the *weather* dictates ; right
The poem is at noon, and wrong at night :

Another

Another judges by a furer gage,
An author's *principles*, or *parentage*;
Since his great anceftors in *Flanders* fell,
The poem doubtlefs muft be written well.
Another judges by the writer's *look*;
Another judges, for he *bought the book*;
'Some judge, their knack of *judging wrong* to keep;
Some judge, becaufe it is too foon to *fleep*.

Thus all will judge, and with one fingle aim,
To gain themfelves, not give the writer, fame.
The very beft *ambitioufly* advife,
Half to ferve you, and half to pafs for wife.

Critics on verfe, as *fquibs* on triumphs wait,
Proclaim the glory, and augment the ftate;
Hot, envious, noify, proud, the fcribbling fry
Burn, hifs, and bounce, wafte paper, ftink, and die.
Rail on, my friends! what more my verfe can crown
Than *Compton*'s fmile, and your obliging frown?

Not all on *books* their *criticifm* wafte:
The genius of a *difh* fome juftly tafte,
And *eat* their way to *fame*; with anxious thought
The *falmon* is refus'd, the *turbot* bought.
Impatient art rebukes the fun's delay,
And bids *December* yield the fruits of *May*;
Their various cares in one great point combine
The bufinefs of their lives, that is—*to dine*.
Half of their precious day they give the *feaft*;
And to a kind *digeftion* fpare the reft.
APICIUS, here, the tafter of the town,
Feeds twice a week, to fettle their renown.

Thefe worthies of the palate guard with care
The facred annals of their *bills of fare*;
In thofe choice books their *panegyrics* read,
And fcorn the creatures that for *hunger* feed.

If

If man by *feeding well* commences *great*,
Much more the worm to whom that man is meat.
  To glory fome advance a lying claim,
Thieves of renown, and *pilferers* of fame :
Their front fupplies what their ambition lacks ;
They know a thoufand lords, *behind their backs.*
Cottil is apt to wink upon a peer,
When turn'd away, with a familiar leer ;
And *H——y's* eyes, unmercifully keen,
Have murder'd fops, by whom fhe ne'er was feen.
NIGER adopts ftray libels ; wifely prone
To covet fhame ftill greater than his own.
BATHYLLUS, in the winter of threefcore,
Belyes his innocence, and keeps a whore.
Abfence of mind BRABANTIO turns to fame,
Learns to *miftake*, nor knows his brother's name ;
Has words and thoughts in nice *diforder* fet,
And takes a memorandum to *forget.*
Thus vain, not knowing what adorns, or blots,
Men *forge the patents*, that create them fots.

  As love of pleafure into pain betrays,
So moft grow infamous thro' love of praife.
But whence for praife can fuch an ardor rife,
When thofe, who bring that incenfe, we defpife ?
For fuch the vanity of great and fmall,
Contempt goes round, and all men laugh at all.

  Nor can ev'n Satire blame them ; for, 'tis true,
They have moft ample caufe for what they do.
O fruitful *Britain !* doubtlefs thou waft meant
A nurfe of *fools*, to ftock the continent.
Tho' PHOEBUS and the Nine for ever mow,
Rank folly underneath the fcythe will grow.
The plenteous harveft calls me forward ftill,
'Till I furpafs in length my lawyer's bill ;

               A WELCH

A Welch defcent, which well-paid heralds damn ;·
Or, longer ftill, a Dutchman's epigram.
When, cloy'd, in fury I throw down my pen,
In comes a coxcomb, and I write again.
　　See Tityrus, with merriment poffeft,
Is burft with laughter, ere he hears the jeft :
What need he ftay ? for when the joke is o'er,
His *teeth* will be no whiter than before.
Is there of *thefe*, ye fair! fo great a dearth,
That you need purchafe *monkeys* for your mirth ?
　　Some, vain of *paintings*, bid the world admire ; ·
Of *houfes* fome ; nay, houfes that they *hire :*
Some (perfect wifdom!) of a beauteous *wife* ;
And boaft, like Cordeliers, a fcourge for life.
　　Sometimes, thro' pride, the fexes change their airs ;
My lord *has vapours,* and my lady *fwears* ;
Then, ftranger ftill! on turning of the wind,
My lord *wears breeches,* and my lady's *kind.*
　　To fhew the ftrength, and infamy of *pride,*
By all 'tis follow'd, and by all deny'd.
What numbers are there, which at once purfue
Praife, and the glory to contemn it, too !
Vincenna knows *felf-praife* betrays to *fhame,*
And therefore lays a ftratagem for fame ;
Makes his approach in modefty's difguife,
To win applaufe ; and takes it by furprize.
" To err," fays he, " in fmall things, is my fate."
You know your anfwer, *he's exact in great.*
" My *ftile,*" fays he, " is rude and full of faults."
But oh! what fenfe! what energy of thoughts!
That he wants algebra, he muft confefs ;
But not a foul to give our arms fuccefs.
" Ah ; That's an hit indeed," *Vincenna* cries ;
" But who in heat of blood was ever wife ?

" I own 'twas wrong, when thoufands call'd me back,

" To make that hopeless, ill-advis'd, attack ;

" All fay, 'twas madness; nor dare I deny ;

" Sure never fool fo well deferv'd to die."

Could *this* deceive in others, to be free,

It ne'er, *Vincenna*, could deceive in *thee*;

Whofe conduct is a comment to thy tongue,

So clear, the dulleft cannot take thee wrong.

Thou on *one fleeve* wilt thy *revenues* wear;

And haunt the court, without a *profpect* there.

Are thefe expedients for renown ?   Confefs

Thy *little felf*, that I may fcorn thee lefs.

   Be wife, *Vincenna*, and the court forfake;

Our fortunes there, nor *thou*, nor *I*, fhall make,

Ev'n *men of merit*, ere their point they gain,

In hardy fervice make a long campaign ;

Moft manfully befiege their patron's gate,

And oft repuls'd, as oft attack the *great*

With painful art, and application warm,

And take, at laft, fome *little place* by ftorm ;

Enough to keep *two fhoes* on *Sunday* clean,

And *ftarve* upon difcreetly, in *Sheer Lane*.

Already *this* thy fortune can afford ;

Then ftarve without the *favour* of my lord.

'Tis true, great fortunes fome great men confer;

But often, ev'n in doing right, they err :

From *caprice*, not from *choice*, their favours come;

They give, but think it *toil* to know to whom :

The man that's neareft, *yawning*, they advance :

'Tis *inhumanity* to *blefs* by chance.

If *merit* fues, and greatnefs is fo loth

To break its downy trance, I pity *both*.

   I grant at court, PHILANDER, at his need,

(Thanks to his lovely wife) finds friends indeed.

                         Of

Of every charm and virtue fhe's poffeft :
Philander ! thou art exquifitely bleft ;
The public envy ! Now then, 'tis allow'd,
The man is found, who may be *juftly* proud :
But, fee ! how fickly is ambition's tafte !
Ambition feeds on trafh, and loaths a feaft ;
For, lo ! *Philander*, of reproach afraid,
In *fecret* loves his wife, but *keeps* her maid.

   Some nymphs fell reputation ; others buy ;
And love a market where the rates run high :
Italian mufic's fweet, becaufe 'tis dear ;
Their *vanity* is tickled, not their *ear :*
Their taftes would leffen, if the prices fell,
And SHAKESPEAR's wretched ftuff do quite as well ;
Away the difinchanted. fair would throng,
And *own*, that *Englifh* is their mother tongue.

   To fhew how much our northern taftes refine,
Imported nymphs our peereffes outfhine ;
While *tradefmen* ftarve, thefe PHILOMELS are gay ;
For generous lords had rather *give* than *pay*.

   Behold the mafquerade's fantaftic fcene !
The *Legiflature* join'd with *Drury-lane !*
When *Britain* calls, th' embroider'd patriots run,
And ferve their *country*—if the *dance* is done.
" Are we not then allow'd to be polite ?"
Yes, doubtlefs ; but firft fet your notions right.
Worth, of *politenefs* is the needful ground ;
Where *that* is wanting, *this* can ne'er be found.
Triflers not e'en in trifles can excel ;
'Tis *folid* bodies only *polifh* well.

   Great, chofen prophet ! For thefe latter days,
To turn a willing world *from* righteous ways !
Well, H——R, doft thou thy *mafter* ferve ;
Well has he feen his *fervant* fhould not ftarve.

Thou

Thou to his name haft fplendid *temples* rais'd ;
In various forms of *worſhip* feen him prais'd,
Gaudy devotion, like a *Roman*, ſhown,
And fung fweet anthems in a tongue *unknown*.
Inferior off'rings to thy god of vice
Are duly paid, in *fiddles, cards,* and *dice* ;
Thy facrifice fupreme, an *hundred maids !*
That folemn rite of midnight mafquerades !
If maids the quite exhaufted town denies,
An hundred heads of *cuckolds* may fuffice.
Thou fmil'ft, well pleas'd with the *converted* land,
To fee the *fifty churches* at a ftand.
And that thy minifter may never fail,
But what thy hand has planted ftill prevail,
Of *minor prophets* a fucceffion fure
The propagation of thy zeal fecure.

　See commons, peers, and minifters of ftate,
In folemn council met, and deep debate !
What Godlike enterprize is taking birth ?
What wonder opens on th' expecting earth ?
'Tis done ! with loud applaufe the council rings !
Fix'd is the fate of *whores* and *fiddle-ſtrings !*

　　Tho' bold thefe truths, thou, Mufe, with truths like thefe,
Wilt none offend, whom 'tis a praife to pleafe :
Let others flatter to be flatter'd, thou,
Like juft *tribunals*, bend an awful brow.
How terrible it were to common fenfe,
To write a *Satire*, which gave none *offence !*
And, fince from *life* I take the draughts you fee,
If men diflike them, do they cenfure *me ?*
The fool, and knave, 'tis glorious to offend,
And Godlike an attempt the world to mend ;
The world, where lucky throws to *blockheads* fall,
Knaves know the game, and *honeſt men* pay all.

                                        How

How hard for real worth to gain its price!
A man ſhall make his fortune in a trice,
If bleſt with pliant, tho' but ſlender, ſenſe,
Feign'd modeſty, and real impudence:
A ſupple knee, ſmooth tongue, an eaſy grace,
A curſe within, a ſmile upon his face;
A beauteous ſiſter, or convenient wife,
Are *prizes* in the lottery of life;
Genius and *virtue* they will ſoon defeat,
And lodge you in the boſom of the *great*.
To *merit*, is but to provide a *pain*
For men's refuſing what you ought to gain.
      May, DODINGTON, this maxim fail in you,
Whom my preſaging thoughts already view
By WALPOLE's conduct fir'd, and friendſhip grac'd,
Still higher in your Prince's favour plac'd;
And lending, *here*, thoſe awful councils aid,
Which you, *abroad*, with ſuch ſucceſs obey'd:
Bear *this* from one, who holds your friendſhip dear;
What moſt we wiſh, with eaſe we fancy near.

S A T I R E . IV.

TO THE RIGHT HONOURABLE

SIR SPENCER COMPTON.

ROUND some fair tree th' ambitious *Woodbine* grows,
    And breathes her sweets on the supporting boughs;
So sweet the *verse*, th' ambitious verse, should be,
(O! pardon mine) that hopes support from thee;
Thee, COMPTON, born o'er senates to preside,
Their *dignity* to raise, their *councils* guide;
Deep to discern, and widely to survey,
And kingdoms fates, without ambition, weigh;
Of distant virtues nice extremes to blend,
The *Crown's* asserter, and the *People's* friend:
Nor dost thou scorn, amid sublimer views,
To listen to the labours of the *muse*;
Thy smiles protect her, while thy talents *fire*,
And 'tis but *half* thy glory to *inspire*.
Vex'd at a public fame, so justly won,
The jealous CHREMES is with spleen undone;

CHREMES,

CHREMES, for airy penfions of *renown*,
Devotes his fervice to the *State* and *Crown*;
All fchemes he knows, and, knowing, all improves,
Tho' *Britain*'s thanklefs, ftill *this patriot* loves:
But patriots differ; fome may fhed their blood,
He *drinks* his *coffee*, for the public good;
Confults the facred fteam, and there forefees
What ftorms, or fun-fhine, Providence decrees;
Knows, for each day, the *weather* of our fate;
A *quid nunc* is an *almanack* of State.

You fmile, and think *this* ftatefman void of ufe:
Why may not time his fecret worth produce?
Since *apes* can roaft the choice *Caftanian Nut*,
Since *fteeds* of genius are expert at *Put*;
Since half the Senate *Not content* can fay,
Geefe nations fave, and *puppies* plots betray.
What makes *him* model realms, and counfel kings?
An incapacity for fmaller things:
Poor CHREMES can't conduct his *own eftate*,
And thence has undertaken *Europe*'s fate.

GEHENNO leaves the realm to CHREMES' fkill,
And boldly claims a province higher ftill:
To raife a name, th' ambitious boy has got,
At once, a *Bible*, and a *fhoulder-knot*;
Deep in the fecret, he looks thro' the whole,
And pities the dull rogue that *faves his foul*;
To talk with rev'rence you muft take good heed,
Nor fhock his *tender reafon* with the Creed:
Howe'er well bred, in public he complies,
Obliging friends alone with *blafphemies*.

Peerage is poifon, good eftates are bad
For this difeafe; poor rogues run feldom mad.
Have not *attainders* brought unhop'd relief,
And *falling ftocks* quite cur'd an unbelief?

H 4

While

While the fun fhines, BLUNT talks with wondrous force;
But thunder mars *fmall beer*, and *weak difcourfe*.
Such ufeful *inftruments* the weather fhow,
Juft as their *Mercury* is high or low:
Health chiefly keeps an Atheift in the dark;
A fever argues better than a *Clarke:*
Let but the logick in his *pulfe* decay,
The *Grecian* he'll renounce, and learn to pray;
While C—— mourns, with an unfeigned zeal,
Th' apoftate youth, who reafon'd *once* fo well.

    C——, who makes fo merry with the Creed,
He almoft thinks he difbelieves *indeed*;
But only thinks fo; to give both their due,
Satan, and *he*, believe, and tremble too..
Of fome for *glory* fuch the boundlefs rage,
That they're the blackeft *fcandal* of their age.

    NARCISSUS the *Tartarian club* difclaims;
Nay, a *Free-mafon*, with fome terror, names;
Omits no duty; nor can *envy* fay,
He mifs'd, thefe many years, the *Church*, or *Play:*
He makes no noife in *Parliament*, 'tis true;
But pays his *debts*, and *vifit*, when 'tis due;
His *character* and *gloves* are ever clean,
And then, he can out-bow the *bowing dean*;
A fmile eternal on his lip he wears,
Which equally the wife and worthlefs fhares.
In gay fatigues, this moft undaunted chief,
Patient of *idlenefs* beyond belief,
Moft charitably lends the town his *face*,
For ornament, in ev'ry public place;
As fure as *cards*, he to th' *affembly* comes,
And is the *furniture* of drawing-rooms:
When *Ombre* calls, his hand and heart are free,
And, join'd to two, he fails not—to make three:

                                 NARCISSUS

NARCISSUS is the glory of his race;
For who does *nothing* with a better grace?
　　To deck my lift, by nature were defign'd
Such fhining *expletives* of human kind,
Who want, while thro' blank life they dream along,
Senfe to be right, and *paffion* to be wrong.
　　To counterpoife this hero of the *mode,*
Some for renown are *fingular* and *odd*;
What other men diflike, is fure to pleafe,
Of all mankind, thefe dear *antipodes*;
Thro' pride, not malice, they run counter ftill,
And *birth-days* are their days of dreffing *ill.*
ARB—T is a fool, and F—— a fage, -
S—LY will fright you, E—— engage;
By nature ftreams run backward, flame defcends,
Stones mount, and S——x is the worft of friends;
They take their reft by *day,* and wake by *night,*
And blufh, if you furprize them in the *right*;
If they by chance blurt out, ere well aware,
A fwan is white, or Q——Y is fair.
　　Nothing exceeds in ridicule, no doubt,
A fool *in* fafhion, but a fool that's *out,*
His paffion for abfurdity's fo ftrong,
He cannot bear a *rival* in the wrong;
Tho' wrong the mode, comply; more fenfe is fhewn
In wearing *others'* follies, than your *own.*
If what is out of fafhion moft you prize,
Methinks you fhould endeavour to be wife.
But what in oddnefs can be more fublime
Than S——, the foremoft *toyman* of his time?
His nice ambition lies in curious fancies,
His daughter's portion a rich *fhell* inhances,
And ASHMOLE's baby-houfe, is, in his view,
Britannia's golden mine, a rich *Peru!*

How

How his eyes languiſh ! how his thoughts adore
That painted coat, which JOSEPH *never* wore !
He ſhews, on *holidays*, a ſacred pin,
That touch'd the ruff, that touch'd queen BESS's chin.
    " Since that great *dearth* our chronicles deplore,
" Since that great *plague* that ſwept as many more,
" Was ever year unbleſt as *this* ?" he'll cry,
" It has not brought us one new *butterfly* !"
In times that ſuffer ſuch learn'd men as *theſe,*
Unhappy I——Y ! how came *you* to pleaſe ?
    Not gaudy butterflies are LICO's game ;
But, in effect, his chace is much the ſame ;
Warm in purſuit, he *levées* all the great,
Stanch to the foot of *title* and *eſtate :*
Where-e'er their *lordſhips* go, they never find
Or LICO, or their *ſhadows*, lag behind ;
He *ſets* them ſure, where-e'er their *lordſhips* run,
Cloſe at their elbows, as a *morning-dun* ;
As if their grandeur, by contagion, wrought,
And *fame* was, like a *fever*, to be caught :
But after ſeven years dance, from place to place,
The * *Dane* is more familiar with his Grace.
    Who'd be a *crutch* to prop a rotten peer ;
Or living *pendant* dangling at his ear,
For ever whiſp'ring ſecrets, which were blown
For months before, by trumpets, thro' the town ?
Who'd be a *glaſs*, with flattering grimace,
Still to reflect the temper of his face ;
Or happy *pin* to ſtick upon his ſleeve,
When my lord's gracious, and vouchſafes *it* leave ;
Or *cuſhion*, when his heavineſs ſhall pleaſe
To loll, or *thump* it, for his better eaſe ;

    * A *Daniſh* dog of the duke of *Argyle.*

Or a vile *butt*, for noon, or night, befpoke,
When the peer *rafhly* fwears he'll club his joke ?
Who'd fhake with laughter, tho' he could not find
His lordfhip's jeft; or, if his nofe broke wind,
For bleffings to the gods profoundly bow,
That can cry, *Chimney fweep*, or drive a *plough ?*
With terms like thefe, how mean the tribe that *clofe !*
Scarce meaner they, who terms like thefe, *impofe.*

But what's the tribe moft likely to comply ?
The men of ink, or antient authors lye;
The writing tribe, who fhamelefs *auctions* hold
Of praife, by inch of candle to be fold :
All men they flatter, but themfelves the moft,
With deathlefs fame, their everlafting boaft :
For fame no cully makes fo much her jeft,
As her old conftant fpark, the bard profeft.
" B—l r fhines in council, M——t in the fight,
" P—l—m's magnificent; but I can write,
" And what to my great foul like glory dear ?"
'Till fome god whifpers in his tingling ear,
That *fame's* unwholefome taken without *meat,*
And life is beft fuftain'd by what is *eat :*
Grown *lean,* and *wife,* he curfes what he writ,
And wifhes all his wants were in his *wit.*

Ah ! what avails it, when his *dinner's* loft,
That his triumphant name adorns a *poft ?*
Or that his fhining page (provoking fate !)
Defends Sirloins, which fons of dulnefs *eat ?*

What foe to verfe without compaffion hears,
What cruel *profe-man* can refrain from tears,
When the poor mufe, for lefs than half a crown,
A *proftitute* on every bulk in town,
With other whores undone, tho' *not* in print,
Clubs *credit* for *Geneva* in the *Mint ?*

Ye bards ! why will you fing, tho' uninfpir'd ?
Ye bards ! why will you *ſtarve,* to be *admir'd ?.*
Defunct by PHOEBUS' laws, beyond redreſs,
Why will your *ſpectres* haunt the frighted preſs ?
Bad metre, that *excreſcence* of the head,
Like *hair,* will ſprout, altho' the poet's *dead.*

    All other trades *demand,* verſe-makers *beg ;*
A dedication is a *wooden leg ;*
A barren *Labeo,* the true *mumper's* faſhion,
Expoſes *borrow'd brats* to move *compaſſion.*
Tho' ſuch myſelf, vile bards I diſcommend ;
Nay more, tho' gentle DAMON is my *friend.*
" Is't then a crime to *write ?*"—If talent rare
Proclaim the god, the crime is to *forbear :*
For ſome, tho' few, there are large-minded men,
Who watch unſeen the labours of the pen ;
Who know the muſe's worth, and therefore court,
Their deeds her theme, their bounty her ſupport ;
Who ſerve, *unaſk'd,* the *leaſt pretence* to wit ;
My ſole excuſe, alas ! for having writ.
A——LE true wit is ſtudious to reſtore ;
And D——T ſmiles, if PHOEBUS ſmil'd before ;
P——KE in years the long-lov'd arts admires,
And HENRIETTA like a muſe inſpires.

    But, ah ! not *inſpiration* can obtain
That fame, which poets languiſh for in vain.
How mad their aim, who thirſt for glory, ſtrive
To graſp, what no man can poſſeſs *alive !*
Fame's a *reverſion* in which men take place
(O late reverſion !) at their own deceaſe.
This truth ſagacious LINTOT knows ſo well,
He *ſtarves* his authors, that their works may *ſell.*

    That *fame* is *wealth,* fantaſtic poets cry ;
That *wealth* is *fame,* another clan reply ;

Who

Who know no guilt, no scandal, but in *rags*;
And *swell* in just proportion to their *bags*.
Nor only the low-born, deform'd, and old,
Think glory nothing but the *beams of gold*;
The first young lord, which in the *Mall* you meet,
Shall match the veriest huncks in *Lombard-street*,
From rescu'd candles' ends, who rais'd a *sum*,
And starves to join a *penny* to a *plumb*.
A *beardless* miser! 'Tis a guilt unknown
To former times, a scandal *all* our own.

  Of ardent lovers, the true modern band
Will mortgage CELIA to redeem their *land*.
For love, young, noble, rich, CASTALIO dies:
Name but the fair, love swells into his eyes.
Divine MONIMIA, thy fond fears lay down;
No rival can prevail,—but *half a crown*.

  He glories to late times to be convey'd,
Not for the poor he has *reliev'd*, but *made*:
Not such ambition his great fathers fir'd,
When HARRY conquer'd, and half *France* expir'd:
He'd be a slave, a pimp, a dog, for gain:
Nay, a *dull sheriff*, for his *golden chain*.

  " Who'd be a slave?" the gallant Colonel cries,
While love of glory sparkles from his eyes:
To deathless fame he loudly pleads his right,—
Just is his title,—for he will not *fight*:
All soldiers *valour*, all divines have *grace*,
As maids of honour *beauty*,—by their *place*:
But, when indulging on the last campaign,
His lofty terms climb o'er the hills of slain;
He gives the foes he slew, at each vain word,
A sweet *revenge*, and *half absolves* his sword.

  Of *boasting* more than of a *bomb* afraid,
A *soldier* should be modest as a *maid*:

Fame

Fame is a bubble the referv'd enjoy;
Who ftrive to grafp it, as they *touch, deftroy:*
'Tis the world's debt to deeds of high degree;
But if you pay yourfelf, the world is free.

    Wete there no tongue to fpeak them but his own,
Augustus' deeds in arms had ne'er been known.
Augustus' deeds ! if that ambiguous name
Confounds my reader, and mifguides his aim,
Such is the Prince's worth, of whom I fpeak,
The Roman would not blufh at the miftake.

S A T I R E   V.

O N

W   O   M   E   N.

O faireſt of creation ! laſt and beſt
Of all God's works ! Creature in whom excell'd
Whatever can to ſight, or thought, be form'd
Holy, divine, good, amiable, or ſweet !
How art thou loſt ! ————   Milton.

✦✦✦✦✦✦✦✦✦✦✦✦

NOR reigns *ambition* in bold *man* alone ;
　Soft *female* hearts the rude invader own :
But *there*, indeed, it deals in nicer things,
Than routing *armies*, and dethroning *kings* :
Attend, and you diſcern it in the fair
Conduct a *finger*, or reclaim a *hair* ;
Or roll the lucid orbit of an *eye* ;
Or, in full joy, elaborate a *ſigh*.
　The ſex we honour, tho' their faults we blame ;
Nay, thank their faults for ſuch a *fruitful* theme :

A theme,

A theme, fair ——— ! doubly kind to me,
Since satyrizing *those* is praising *thee* ;
Who would'st not bear, too modestly refin'd,
A panegyric of a grosser kind.
  BRITANNIA's daughters, much more *fair* than *nice*,
Too fond of admiration, lose their price ;
Worn in the public eye, give cheap delight
To throngs, and tarnish to the sated sight :
As unreserv'd, and beauteous, as the Sun,
Through every *sign* of vanity they run ;
Assemblies, Parks, coarse feasts in *City-halls,*
Lectures, and *Trials, Plays, Committees, Balls,*
Wells, Bedlams, Executions, Smithfield scenes,
And *Fortune-tellers* Caves, and *Lions* Dens,
Taverns, Exchanges, Bridewells, Drawing-rooms,
Installments, Pillories, Coronations, Tombs,
Tumblers, and *Funerals, Puppet-shows, Reviews,*
Sales, Races, Rabbets,. (and still stranger !) *Pews.*
  CLARINDA's bosom burns, but burns for *Fame* ;
And Love lies vanquish'd in a *nobler* flame ;
Warm gleams of hope she, *now,* dispenses ; *then,*
Like *April* suns, dives into clouds again :
With all her lustre, *now,* her lover warms ;
Then, out of *ostentation,* hides her charms :
'Tis, next, her pleasure sweetly to complain,
And to be taken with a sudden pain ;
Then, she starts up, all ecstasy and bliss,
And is, sweet soul ! just as sincere in this :
O how she rolls her charming eyes in *spite !*
And looks delightfully with all her might !
But, like *our* heroes, much more brave than wise,
She conquers for the *triumph,* not the *prize.*
  ZARA resembles *Ætna* crown'd with snows ;
Without she freezes, and within she glows :

                                              Twice

Twice ere the fun defcends, with zeal infpir'd,
From the vain converfe of the world retir'd,
She reads the *pfalms* and *chapters* for the day,
In —— CLEOPATRA, or the laft new play.
Thus gloomy ZARA, with a folemn grace,
Deceives mankind, and *hides* behind her *face.*

Nor far beneath her in *renown,* is fhe,
Who, through good-breeding, is ill company ;
Whofe *manners* will not let her larum ceafe,
Who thinks you are *unhappy,* when *at peace* ;
To find you *news,* who racks her fubtle head,
And vows—*that her great-grandfather is dead.*

A dearth of words a *woman* need not fear;
But 'tis a tafk indeed to learn—*to bear :*
In that the fkill of converfation lies ;
That *fhews,* or *makes,* you both polite and wife.
XANTIPPE cries, " Let nymphs, who nought can fay,
" Be loft in filence, and refign the day ;
" And let the guilty wife her guilt confefs,
" By tame behaviour, and a foft addrefs ;"
Through *virtue, fhe* refufes to comply
With all the dictates of *humanity* ;
Through wifdom, *fhe* refufes to fubmit
To wifdom's rules, and *raves* to prove her *wit* ;
Then, her unblemifh'd honour to maintain,
Rejects her hufband's kindnefs with difdain :
But if, by chance, an ill-adapted word
Drops from the lip of her unwary lord,
Her darling china, in a whirlwind fent,
Juft *intimates* the lady's difcontent.

Wine may indeed excite the meekeft dame ;
But keen XANTIPPE, fcorning *borrow'd* flame,
Can vent her thunders, and her lightnings play,
O'er cooling *gruel,* and compofing *tea :*

Nor rests by night, but, more sincere than nice,
She shakes the curtains with her kind advice :
Doubly, like echo, sound is her delight,
And the last word is her eternal right.
Is't not enough plagues, wars, and famines, rise
To lash our crimes, but must our wives be wise ?

    Famine, plague, war, and an unnumber'd throng
Of guilt-avenging ills, to man belong :
What black, what ceaseless cares besiege our state !
What strokes we feel from fancy, and from fate !
If fate forbears us, fancy strikes the blow ;
We make misfortune ; suicides in woe.
Superfluous aid ! unnecessary skill !
Is nature backward to torment, or kill ?
How oft the noon, how oft the midnight, bell,
(That iron tongue of death !) with solemn knell,
On folly's errands, as we vainly roam,
Knocks at our hearts, and finds our thoughts from home !
Men drop so fast, ere life's mid stage we tread,
Few know so many friends alive, as dead.
Yet, as immortal, in our up-hill chace
We press coy fortune with unslacken'd pace ;
Our ardent labours for the toys we seek,
Join night to day, and Sunday to the week :
Our very joys are anxious, and expire
Between satiety and fierce desire.
Now what reward for all this grief and toil ?
But one ; a female friend's endearing smile ;
A tender smile, our sorrows' only balm,
And, in life's tempest, the sad sailor's calm.

    How have I seen a gentle nymph draw nigh,
Peace in her air, persuasion in her eye ;
Victorious tenderness ! it all o'ercame,
Husbands look'd mild, and savages grew tame.

The

The *Sylvan* race our active nymphs purſue;
Man is not all the game they have in view:
In woods and fields their glory they complete;
There *Maſter* BETTY leaps a five-barr'd gate;
While fair *Miſs* CHARLES to toilets is confin'd,
Nor raſhly tempts the barb'rous ſun and wind.
Some nymphs affect a more heroic breed,
And volt from *hunters* to the *manag'd ſteed*;
Command his prancings with a martial air,
And FOBERT has the forming of the *Fair*.

    More than *one* ſteed muſt DELIA's empire feel,
Who ſits triumphant o'er the flying *wheel*;
And as ſhe guides it thro' th' admiring throng,
With what an air ſhe ſmacks the *ſilken* thong!
Graceful as JOHN, ſhe moderates the reins,
And whiſtles ſweet her *diuretic* ſtrains:
SESOSTRIS like, ſuch charioteers as *theſe*
May drive ſix harneſs'd *monarchs*, if they pleaſe:
They *drive, row, run*, with love of glory ſmit,
Leap, ſwim, ſhoot flying, and pronounce on *wit*.

    O'er the *Belle-lettre* lovely DAPHNE reigns;
Again the god APOLLO wears her chains:
With legs toſs'd high, on her ſophee ſhe ſits,
Vouchſafing audience to contending wits:
Of each performance ſhe's the final teſt;
One act read o'er, ſhe propheſies the reſt;
And then, pronouncing with deciſive air,
Fully convinces all the town—*ſhe*'s *fair*.
Had lovely DAPHNE HECATESSA's face,
How would her elegance of taſte decreaſe!
Some ladies' *judgment* in their *features* lies,
And all their *genius* ſparkles from their *eyes*.

    " But hold," ſhe cries, " lampooner! have a care;
" Muſt I want common ſenſe, becauſe I'm fair?"

O no: fee STELLA; her *eyes* fhine as bright,
As if her tongue was never in the right;
And yet what real learning, judgment, fire!
She feems infpir'd, and can herfelf infpire:
How then (if malice rul'd not all the fair)
Could DAPHNE publifh, and could fhe forbear?
We grant that beauty is no bar to *fenfe*,
Nor is't a fanction for *impertinence*.

   SEMPRONIA lik'd her man; and well fhe might;
The youth in perfon, and in parts, was bright;
Poffefs'd of ev'ry virtue, grace, and art,
That claims juft empire o'er the female heart:
He met her paffion, all her fighs return'd,
And, in full rage of youthful ardour, burn'd:
Large his poffeffions, and beyond her own;
Their blifs the theme, and envy of the town:
The day was fix'd, when, with one acre more,
In ftepp'd deform'd, debauch'd, difeas'd, *threefcore*.
The fatal fequel I, through fhame, forbear:
Of pride, and *av'rice*, who can cure the fair?

   Man's rich with little, were his judgment true;
Nature is frugal, and her wants are few;
Thofe few wants anfwer'd, bring fincere delights;
But fools create themfelves new appetites:
Fancy, and pride, feek things at vaft expence,
Which relifh not to *reafon*, nor to *fenfe*.
When *furfeit*, or *unthankfulnefs*, deftroys,
In *nature's* narrow fphere, our folid joys,
In *fancy's* airy land of noife and fhow,
Where nought but dreams, no real pleafures, grow;
Like cats in air-pumps, to fubfift we ftrive
On joys too thin to keep the foul alive.
LEMIRA's fick; make hafte; the doctor call:
He comes; but where's his patient? At the ball.

The

The doctor stares; her woman curtsies low,
And cries, " My Lady, Sir, is always so:
" Diversions put her maladies to flight:
" True, she can't *stand*, but she can *dance* all night:
" I've known my Lady (for she loves a tune)
" For *fevers* take an opera in *June:*
" And, tho' perhaps you'll think the practice bold,
" A midnight Park is sov'reign for a *cold:*
" With *ebolics*, breakfasts of green fruit agree;
" With *indigestions*, supper just at three."
A strange alternative, replies Sir *Hans*,.
Must women have a *doctor*, or a *dance?*
Though sick to death, *abroad* they safely roam,
But droop and die, in perfect health, *at home:*
For want—but not of health, are ladies ill;
And *tickets* cure beyond the *doctor's pill*.

  Alas, my heart! how languishingly fair
Yon lady lolls! With what a tender air!
Pale as a young dramatic author, when,
O'er darling lines, fell CIBBER waves his pen.
Is her lord angry, or has * *Veny* chid?
Dead is her father, or the mask forbid?
" Late sitting up has turn'd her roses white."
Why went she not to bed? " Because 'twas *night*."
Did she then dance, or play? " Nor this, nor that."
Well night soon steals away in pleasing chat,
" No, all alone, her *pray'rs* she rather chose;
" Than be that *wretch* to sleep till morning rose."
Then Lady CYNTHIA, mistress of the shade,
Goes, with the *fashionable* owls, to bed:
This her *pride* covets, this her *health* denies;
Her soul is silly, but her body's wise.

* Lap-dog.

I 3

Others, with curious arts, dim charms revive,
And triumph in the bloom of *fifty-five.*
You, in the morning, a *fair* nymph invite;
To keep her word, a *brown* one comes at night:
Next day she shines in glossy *black*; and then
Revolves into her native *red* again:
Like a dove's neck, she shifts her transient charms,
And is her own dear rival in your arms.

But *one* admirer has the painted lass;
Nor finds that one, but in her looking-glass:
Yet LAURA's beautiful to such excess,
That all her *art* scarce makes her please us *less.*
To deck the female cheek, HE only knows,
Who paints less fair the *lily,* and the *rose.*

How gay *they* smile! Such blessings *nature* pours,
O'erstock'd mankind enjoy but half her stores:
In distant wilds, by human eyes unseen,
She rears her flow'rs, and spreads her velvet green:
Pure gurgling rills the lonely desart trace,
And *waste* their music on the savage race.
Is *nature* then a niggard of her bliss?
Repine we *guiltless* in a world like this?
But our lewd tastes her lawful charms refuse,
And painted *art's* deprav'd allurements chuse.
Such FULVIA's passion for the town; fresh air
(An odd effect!) gives vapours to the fair;
Green fields, and shady groves, and chrystal springs,
And larks, and nightingales are odious things;
But smoke, and dust, and noise, and crowds, delight;
And to be press'd to death, transports her quite:
Where silver riv'lets play through flow'ry meads,
And *woodbines* give their sweets, and *limes* their shades,
Black kennels' absent *odours* she regrets,
And stops her nose at beds of violets.

Is

Is stormy life preferr'd to the serene ?
Or is the public to the private scene ?
Retir'd, we tread a smooth and open way ;
Through briars and brambles in the world we stray ;
Stiff opposition, and *perplex'd* debate,
And *thorny* care, and *rank* and *stinging* hate,
Which choak our passage, our career controul,
And wound the firmest temper of our soul.
O sacred solitude ! divine retreat !
Choice of the Prudent ! envy of the Great !
By thy pure stream, or in thy waving shade,
We court fair wisdom, that celestial maid :
The genuine offspring of her lov'd embrace,
(Strangers on earth !) are *innocence* and *peace* :
There, from the ways of men laid safe ashore,
We smile to hear the distant tempest roar ;
There, bless'd with health, with business unperplex'd,
This life we relish, and ensure the *next* ;
There too the *Muses* sport ; these numbers free,
Pierian EASTBURY ! I owe to thee.

There sport the *Muses* ; but not there alone :
Their sacred force AMELIA feels in town.
Nought but a genius can a genius fit ;
A wit herself, AMELIA weds a wit :
Both wits ! though miracles are said to cease,
Three days, three wond'rous days ! they liv'd in peace ;
With the fourth sun a warm dispute arose,
On DURFEY's poesy, and BUNYAN's prose :
The learned war both wage with equal force,
And the fifth morn concluded the divorce.

PHOEBE, though she possesses nothing less,
Is proud of being rich in happiness :
Laboriously pursues delusive toys,
Content with pains, since they're reputed joys.

I 4

With

With what well-acted tranſport will ſhe ſay,
" Well, ſure, we were ſo happy *yeſterday !*
" And then that charming party for *to-morrow !*"
Though, well ſhe knows, 'twill languiſh into ſorrow :
But ſhe dares never boaſt the *preſent* hour ;
So groſs that cheat, it is beyond her power :
For ſuch is or our weakneſs, or our curſe,
Or rather ſuch our crime, which ſtill is worſe,
The preſent moment, like a wife, we ſhun,
And ne'er enjoy, becauſe it is *our own.*

    Pleaſures are few, and fewer we enjoy ;
Pleaſure, like *quickſilver*, is *bright*, and *coy* ;
We ſtrive to graſp it with our utmoſt ſkill,
Still it eludes us, and it glitters ſtill :
If ſeiz'd at laſt, compute your mighty gains ;
What is it, but rank poiſon in your veins ?

    As ELAVIA in her glaſs an angel ſpies,
Pride whiſpers in her ear pernicious lyes ;
Tells her, while ſhe ſurveys a face ſo fine,
There's no ſatiety of charms divine :
Hence, if her lover yawns, all chang'd appears
Her temper, and ſhe melts (ſweet ſoul !) in tears:
She, fond and young, laſt week, her wiſh enjoy'd,
In ſoft amuſement all the night employ'd ;
The morning came, when STREPHON, waking, found
(Surpriſing ſight !) his bride in ſorrow drown'd.
" What miracle," ſays STREPHON, " makes thee weep ?"
" Ah, barb'rous man !" ſhe cries, " how could you——
    " *ſleep ?*"

    Men love a *miſtreſs*, as they love a *feaſt* ;
How grateful one to *touch*, and one to *taſte ?*
Yet ſure there is a certain time of day,
We wiſh our miſtreſs, and our meat, away :
But ſoon the ſated appetites return,
Again our ſtomachs crave, our boſoms burn :

                                       Eternal

Eternal Love let man, then, never fwear;
Let women never *triumph*, nor *defpair*;
Nor praife, nor blame, too much, the warm, or chill;
Hunger and Love are foreign to the *will*.

   There is indeed a paffion more refin'd,
For thofe few nymphs whofe charms are of the mind:
But not of that unfafhionable fet
Is PHYLLIS; PHYLLIS and her DAMON met.
Eternal Love exactly hits her tafte;
PHYLLIS demands eternal love at *leaft*.
Embracing PHYLLIS with foft-fmiling eyes,
Eternal Love I vow, the fwain replies:
But fay, my *All*, my *Miftrefs*, and my *Friend!*
What day next week th' *Eternity* fhall *end?*

   Some nymphs prefer *aftronomy* to *love:*
Elope from mortal man, and range above.
The fair philofopher to ROWLEY flies,
Where, in a *box*, the whole creation lies:
She fees the planets in their turns advance,
And fcorns, POITIER, thy fublunary dance:
Of DESAGULIER fhe befpeaks frefh air;
And WHISTON has *engagements* with the fair.
What vain experiments SOPHRONIA tries!
'Tis not in air-pumps the gay colonel dies.
But though to-day this rage of fcience reigns,
(O fickle fex!) foon end her learned pains.
Lo! PUG from JUPITER her heart has got,
Turns out the ftars, and NEWTON is a fot.

   To ——— turn; fhe never took the height
Of SATURN, yet is ever in the right.
She ftrikes each point with native force of mind,
While puzzled learning blunders far behind,
Graceful to fight, and elegant to thought,
The *great* are vanquifh'd, and the *wife* are taught.

                           Her

Her breeding finiſh'd, and her temper ſweet,
When ſerious, eaſy; and when gay, diſcreet;
In glitt'ring ſcenes, o'er her own heart, ſincere;
In crouds, collected; and in courts, ſevere;
Sincere, and warm, with zeal well underſtood,
She takes a noble pride in doing good;
Yet not ſuperior to her ſex's cares,
The mode ſhe fixes by the gown ſhe wears;
Of *ſilks* and *china* ſhe's the laſt appeal;
In theſe great points ſhe *leads* the commonweal;
And if diſputes of *empire* riſe between
Mechlin the queen of lace, and *Colberteen*,
'Tis doubt! 'tis darkneſs! till ſuſpended fate
Aſſumes *her* nod, to cloſe the grand debate.
When ſuch her mind, why will the fair expreſs
Their emulation only in their *dreſs?*

But, oh! the nymph that mounts above the *ſkies*,
And, *gratis*, clears religious myſteries,
Reſolv'd the *church*'s welfare to enſure,
And make her family a *ſine-cure:*
The theme divine at *cards* ſhe'll not forget,
But *takes* in texts of Scripture at *picquet*;
In thoſe licentious meetings acts the prude,
And thanks her *Maker* that her *cards* are good.
What angels would thoſe be, who thus excel
In theologics, could they *ſew* as well!
Yet why ſhould not the fair her text purſue?
Can ſhe more decently the doctor woo?
'Tis hard, too, ſhe who makes no uſe but *chat*
Of her religion, ſhould be barr'd in that.

ISAAC, a brother of the canting ſtrain,
When he has knock'd at his own ſkull in vain,
To beauteous MARCIA often will repair
With a dark text, to light it at the *fair.*

O how

O how his pious foul exults to find
Such love for *holy* men in woman-kind!
Charm'd with her learning, with what rapture he
Hangs on her *bloom*, like an induſtrious *bee*;
Hums round about her, and with all his power
Extracts ſweet wiſdom from ſo fair a *flower* !

　The *young* and *gay* declining, APPIA flies
At nobler game, the *mighty* and the *wiſe*:
By nature more an *eagle* than a *dove*,
She impiouſly prefers the *world* to *love*.

　Can wealth give happineſs? look round, and ſee
What gay diſtreſs! what ſplendid miſery!
Whatever fortune laviſhly can poúr,
The mind annihilates, and calls for more.
Wealth is a cheat; believe not what it ſays;
Like any lord it *promiſes*—and *pays*.
How will the miſer ſtartle, to be told
Of ſuch a wonder, as *inſolvent* gold !
What nature *wants* has an intrinſic weight;
All *more*, is but the faſhion of the plate,
Which, for one moment, charms the fickle view;
It charms us *now*; *anon* we caſt anew;
To ſome freſh birth of *fancy* more inclin'd:
Then wed not acres, but a noble mind.

　Miſtaken lovers, who make worth their care,
And think accompliſhments will win the fair:
The *fair*, 'tis true, by *genius* ſhould be won,
As *flow'rs* unfold their beauties to the *ſun*;
And yet in female ſcales a fop out-weighs,
And wit muſt wear the *willow* and the *bays*.
Nought ſhines ſo bright in vain LIBERIA's eye
As riot, impudence, and perfidy;
The youth of fire, that has drunk deep, and play'd,
And kill'd his man, and triumph'd o'er his maid;

For

For him, as yet unhang'd, she spreads her charms,
Snatches the dear destroyer to her arms;
And amply gives (though treated long amiss)
The *man of merit* his revenge in *this*,
If you resent, and wish a *woman* ill,
But turn her o'er one moment to her *will*.

The *languid* lady next appears in state,
Who was not born to carry her own weight;
She lolls, reels, staggers, till some foreign aid
To her own stature lifts the feeble maid.
Then, if ordain'd to so *severe* a doom,
She, by just stages, *journeys* round the room:
But, knowing her own weakness, she despairs
To scale the *Alps*—that is, ascend the *stairs*.
My fan! let others say, who laugh at toil;
Fan! hood! glove! scarf! is her *laconic* stile;
And that is spoke with such a dying fall,
That *Betty* rather *sees*, than *hears* the call:
The motion of her lips, and meaning eye,
Piece out th' idea her faint words deny.
O listen with attention most profound!
Her voice is but the shadow of a sound.
And help! oh help! her spirits are so dead,
One hand scarce lifts the other to her head.
If, there, a stubborn pin it triumphs o'er,
She pants! she sinks away! and is no more.
Let the robust, and the gigantic *carve*,
Life is not worth so much, she'd rather *starve*:
But chew she must herself; ah cruel fate!
That ROSALINDA can't by *proxy* eat.

An *antidote* in female caprice lies
(Kind heav'n!) against the *poison* of their eyes.

THALESTRIS triumphs in a manly mien;
Loud is her accent, and her phrase obscene.

In

In fair and open dealing where's the shame?
What nature dares to *give*, she dares to *name*.
This *honeft fellow* is fincere and plain,
And juftly gives the jealous hufband pain.
(Vain is the talk to petticoats affign'd,
If wanton language shews a *naked* mind.)
And now and then, to grace her eloquence,
An oath fupplies the vacancies of fenfe.
Hark! the fhrill notes tranfpierce the yielding air,
And teach the neighb'ring echoes how to fwear.
By JOVE, is faint, and for the fimple fwain;
She, on the Chriftian Syftem, is prophane.
But though the volley rattles in your ear,
Believe her *drefs*, she's not a grenadier.
If thunder's awful, how much more our dread,
When JOVE deputes a lady in his ftead?
A *lady*! pardon my miftaken pen,
A fhamelefs woman is the worft of *men*.

    Few to good-breeding make a juft pretence;
Good-breeding is the bloffom of good-fenfe;
The laft refult of an accomplifh'd mind,
With outward grace, the *body's virtue*, join'd.
A violated decency now reigns;
And nymphs for *failings* take peculiar pains.
With *Chinefe* painters modern *toafts* agree,
The point they aim at is *deformity*:
They *throw* their perfons with a hoyden air
Acrofs the room, and *tofs* into the chair.
So far their commerce with mankind is gone,
They, for our manners, have exchang'd their own.
The modeft look, the caftigated grace,
The gentle movement, and flow-meafur'd pace,
For which her lovers *dy'd*, her parents *pray'd*,
Are indecorums with the *modern* maid.

                                                           Stiff

Stiff forms are bad; but let not worfe intrude,
Nor conquer *art* and *nature*, to be rude.
Modern good-breeding carry to its height,
And lady D————'s felf will be polite.

    Ye rifing fair! ye bloom of *Britain's* ifle!
When high-born ANNA, with a foften'd fmile,
Leads on your train, and fparkles at your head,
What feems moft hard, is, not to be well-bred.
Her bright example with fuccefs purfue,
And all, but adoration, is your due.

    But adoration! give me fomething *more*,
Cries LYCE, on the borders of *threefcore*:
Nought treads fo filent as the foot of *time*;
Hence we miftake our autumn for our prime;
'Tis greatly wife to know, before we're told,
The melancholy news, that we *grow old*.
Autumnal LYCE carries in her face
Memento mori to each public place.
O how your beating breaft a miftrefs warms,
Who looks through fpectacles to fee your charms!
While rival *undertakers* hover round,
And with his fpade the *fexton* marks the ground,
Intent not on her own, but others' doom,
She plans new conquefts, and *defrauds* the tomb.
In vain the cock has fummon'd *fprites* away,
She walks at noon, and blafts the bloom of day.
Gay rainbow filks her mellow charms infold,
And nought of LYCE but *herfelf* is old.
Her grizzled locks affume a *fmirking* grace,
And art has *levell'd* her deep-furrow'd face.
Her ftrange demand no mortal can approve,
We'll afk her *bleffing*, but can't afk her *love*.
She grants, indeed, a lady *may* decline
(All ladies *but* herfelf) at *ninety-nine*.

     5

O how

O how unlike her is the facred age
Of prudent PORTIA ! *Her* grey hairs *engage*;
Whofe thoughts are fuited to her life's decline:
Virtue's the paint that can with *wrinkles* fhine.
That, and that *only*, can old age fuftain;
Which yet all wifh, nor know they wifh for *pain*.
Not num'rous are our joys, when life is new;
And yearly fome are falling of the *few*;
But when we conquer life's meridian ftage,
And downward tend into the vale of age,
They drop *apace*; by *nature* fome decay,
And fome the blafts of *fortune* fweep away;
'Till naked quite of happinefs, aloud
We call for death, and *fhelter* in a fhroud.

   Where's PORTIA now ?—But PORTIA left behind
Two lovely copies of her form and mind.
What heart untouch'd their *early* grief can view,
Like blufhing rofe-buds dipp'd in *morning* dew ?
Who into fhelter takes their tender bloom,
And forms their minds to flee from ills to come ?
The mind, when turn'd adrift, no rules to guide,
Drives at the mercy of the wind and tide;
Fancy and *paffion* tofs it to and fro;
Awhile torment, and then quite *fink* in woe.
Ye beauteous orphans, fince in filent duft
Your beft *example* lies, my *precepts* truft.
Life fwarms with ills; the *boldeft* are afraid;
Where then is fafety for a *tender maid ?*
Unfit for conflict, round befet with woes,
And *man*, whom leaft fhe fears, her worft of foes !
When kind, moft cruel; when oblig'd the moft,
The leaft obliging; and by favours loft.
Cruel by nature, they for kindnefs hate;
And fcorn you for thofe ills *themfelves* create.

                                                            If

If on your fame *our* sex a blot has thrown,
'Twill ever stick, through malice of your *own.*
Most hard! in pleasing your chief *glory* lies;
And yet from pleasing your chief *dangers* rise:
Then please the *Best*; and know, for men of sense,
Your strongest charms are native innocence.
Art on the mind, like *paint* upon the face,
Fright him, that's worth your love, from your embrace.
In *simple* manners all the secret lies;
Be kind and virtuous, you'll be blest and wise.
Vain *shew* and *noise* intoxicate the brain,
Begin with *giddiness,* and end in *pain.*
Affect not *empty* fame, and *idle* praise,
Which, all those wretches I describe, betrays.
Your sex's glory 'tis, to shine *unknown*;
Of all applause, be fondest of *your own.*
Beware the fever of the *mind!* that thirst
With which the age is eminently curst:
To drink of *pleasure,* but inflames desire;
And abstinence alone can quench the fire;
Take *pain* from life, and *terror* from the tomb;
Give peace *in hand*; and promise bliss *to come.*

SATIRE

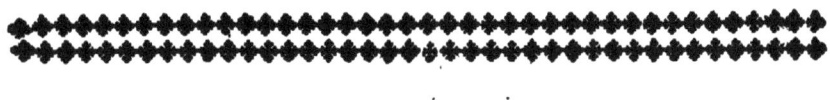

SATIRE VI.

ON

WOMEN.

Infcribed to the RIGHT HONOURABLE the

Lady ELIZABETH GERMAIN.

Interdum tamen & tollit comœdia vocem. HOR.

I SOUGHT a patronefs, but fought in vain.
  APOLLO whifper'd in my ear—" GERMAIN."—
I know her not.—" Your reafon's fomewhat odd;
" Who knows his patron, now ?" reply'd the god.
" Men write, to *me*, and to the *world*, unknown;
" Then fteal great names, to fhield them from the town.
" Detected *worth*, like *beauty* difarray'd,
" To covert flies, of *praife* itfelf afraid:
" Should *fhe* refufe to patronize your lays,
" In vengeance write a volume in *her praife*.

VOL. I.   K   " Nor

" Nor think it hard fo great a length to run ;
" When fuch the theme, 'twill eafily be done."
· Ye fair ! to draw your excellence at length,
Exceeds the narrow bounds of human ftrength ;
You, *here*, in miniature your picture fee ;
Nor hope from ZINCKS more juftice than from me.
My portraits grace your *mind*, as his your *fide* ;
His portraits will *inflame*, mine *quench*, your pride :
He's *dear*, you *frugal* ; choofe my *cheaper* lay ;
And be your *reformation* all my *pay*.

 LAVINIA is *polite*, but not *profane* ;
To *Church* as conftant as to *Drury-lane*.
She decently, *in form*, pays heav'n its due ;
And makes a civil vifit to her pew.
Her lifted fan, to give a folemn air,
Conceals her face, which *paffes* for a *prayer :*
Curtfies to curtfies, then, with grace, fucceed ;
Not one the fair omits, but at the *Creed*.
Or if fhe joins the Service, 'tis to *fpeak* ;
Thro' dreadful *filence* the pent heart might break ;
Untaught to bear it, women *talk away*
To God himfelf, and fondly think they *pray*.
But *fweet* their accent, and their air *refin'd* ;
For they're before their Maker—and *mankind :*
When ladies once are proud of praying well,
SATAN himfelf will toll the parifh bell.

 Acquainted with the world, and quite well-bred,
DRUSA receives her vifitants in bed ;
But, chafte as ice, this *Vefta*, to defy
The very blackeft tongue of calumny,
When from the fheets her lovely form fhe lifts,
She begs you *juft* wou'd *turn you*, while fhe *fhifts*.

 Thofe charms are greateft which decline the fight,
That makes the banquet poignant and polite.

There

There is no *woman*, *where* there's no *reserve* ;
And 'tis on *plenty* your poor lovers *starve*.
But with a modern fair, meridian merit
Is a fierce thing, they call a *nymph of spirit*.
Mark well the rollings of her flaming eye;
And tread on tiptoe, if you dare draw nigh.
" Or if you take a lion by the beard *,
" Or dare defy the fell *Hyrcanian* pard,
" Or arm'd rhinoceros, or rough *Russian* bear,"
First *make your will*, and then *converse* with her.
This lady glories in profuse expence ;
And thinks *distraction* is *magnificence*.
To beggar her gallant, is *some* delight ;
To be more fatal still, is *exquisite* ;
Had ever nymph such reason to be glad ?
In *duel* fell two lovers ; one run *mad*.
Her *foes* their honest execrations pour ;
Her *lovers* only should *detest* her more.

FLAVIA is constant to her old gallant,
And generously supports him in his want ;
But marriage is a fetter, is a snare,
A hell, no lady so polite can bear.
She's faithful, she's observant, and with pains
Her angel-brood of *bastards* she maintains.
Nor least advantage has the fair to plead,
But that of *guilt*, above the *marriage-bed*.

AMASIA hates a prude, and scorns restraint ;
Whate'er she *is*, she'll not *appear* a saint :
Her soul superior flies formality ;
So gay her air, her conduct is so free,
Some might suspect the nymph not *over-good*——
Nor would they be mistaken, if they should.

* SHAKESPEARE.

Unmarried

Unmarried ABRA puts on formal airs;
Her cushion's thread-bare with her constant prayers.
Her only grief is, that she cannot be
At once engag'd in *prayer* and *charity*.
And *this*, to do her justice, must be said,
" *Who would not think that* ABRA *was a maid?*"

     Some ladies are too beauteous to be wed;
For where's the man that's worthy of their bed?
If no disease reduce her pride before,
LAVINIA will be ravish'd at threescore.
Then she submits to venture in the dark;
And nothing now is wanting—but her spark.

     LUCIA thinks happiness consists in state;
She weds an *ideot*, but she eats in *plate*.
The goods of fortune, which her soul possess,
Are but the *ground* of *unmade* happiness;
The rude *material: wisdom* add to *this*,
Wisdom, the sole *artificer* of bliss;
She from herself, if so compell'd by need,
Of *thin content* can draw the subtle thread;
But (no detraction to her sacred skill)
If she can work in *gold*, 'tis better still.

     If TULLIA had been blest with *half* her sense,
None could too much admire her excellence:
But since she can make *error* shine so bright,
She thinks it *vulgar* to defend the *right*.
With understanding she is quite o'er-run;
And by too great accomplishments undone:
With skill she vibrates her eternal tongue,
For ever most *divinely* in the *wrong*.

     Naked in nothing should a woman be;
But veil her very *wit* with *modesty*:
Let man *discover*, let not her *display*,
But yield her *charms of mind* with sweet delay.

                     For

For pleafure form'd, perverfely fome believe,
To make themfelves *important*, men muft *grieve*.
LESBIA the fair, to fire her jealous lord,
Pretends, the fop fhe laughs at, is adored,
In vain fhe's *proud* of fecret innocence;
The fact fhe feigns were fcarce a worfe offence,

MIRA, endow'd with every charm to blefs,
Has no defign, but on her hufband's *peace:*
He lov'd her much; and greatly was he mov'd
At fmall inquietudes in her he lov'd.
" *How charming this!"*—The pleafure lafted long;
Now every day the fits come thick and ftrong:
At laft he found the charmer only *feign'd*;
And was diverted when he *fhould* be pain'd.
What greater vengeance have the gods in ftore?
How tedious life, now fhe can *plague* no more!
She tries a thoufand arts; but none fucceed:
She's forc'd a fever to procure *indeed:*
Thus ftrictly prov'd this virtuous, loving *wife,*
Her hufband's *pain* was dearer than her *life.*

Anxious MELANIA rifes to my view,
Who never thinks her lover pays his due:
Vifit, prefent, treat, flatter, and adore;
Her majefty, to-morrow, calls for *more.*
His wounded ears complaints eternal fill,
As unoil'd hinges, queruloufly fhrill.
" You went laft night with CELIA to the ball."
You prove it falfe. " Not go! that's worft of all."
Nothing can pleafe her, nothing not inflame;
And arrant *contradictions* are the *fame.*
Her lover muft be *fad,* to pleafe her fpleen;
His *mirth* is an inexpiable fin:
For of all *rivals* that can pain her breaft,
There's *one,* that wounds far deeper than the reft;

K 3   To

To wreck her quiet, the moſt dreadful ſhelf
Is if her lover dares enjoy himſelf.

And this, becauſe ſhe's exquiſitely fair:
Should I diſpute her beauty, how ſhe'd ſtare!
How would MELANIA be ſurpriz'd to hear
She's quite deform'd! And yet the caſe is clear;
What's female beauty, but an air divine,
Thro' which the mind's all-gentle graces ſhine?
They, like the ſun, irradiate all between;
The body *charms* becauſe the ſoul is *ſeen*.
Hence, men are often captives of a face,
They know not why, of no peculiar grace:
Some forms, tho' bright, no mortal man can *bear*;
Some, none *reſiſt*, tho' not exceeding fair.

ASPASIA's highly born, and nicely bred,
Of taſte refin'd, in life and manners read;
Yet reaps no fruit from her ſuperior ſenſe,
But to be *teax'd* by her own excellence.
" Folks are ſo aukward! Things ſo unpolite!"
She's *elegantly* pain'd from morn till night.
Her delicacy's ſhock'd where-e'er ſhe goes;
Each *creature's imperfections* are her *woes*.
Heav'n by its favour has the fair diſtreſt,
And pour'd ſuch bleſſings—that ſhe *can't* be bleſt.

Ah! why ſo vain, though blooming in thy ſpring,
Thou *ſhining, frail, ador'd,* and *wretched* thing?
Old-age *will* come; diſeaſe *may* come before;
Fifteen is full as mortal as *threeſcore*.
Thy fortune, and thy charms, may ſoon decay:
But grant theſe *fugitives* prolong their ſtay,
Their baſis totters, their foundation ſhakes;
Life, that ſupports them, in a moment breaks;
Then *wrought* into the ſoul let virtues ſhine;
The *ground* eternal, as the *work* divine.

JULIA's

JULIA's a manager; she's born for rule;
And knows her *wiser* husband is a *fool*;
Assemblies holds, and spins the *subtle thread*
That guides the lover to his fair one's bed:
For difficult amours can smooth the way,
And tender letters *dictate*, or *convey*.
But if depriv'd of such important cares,
Her wisdom condescends to less affairs.
For her *own* breakfast she'll *project a scheme*,
Nor *take* her *tea* without a *stratagem*;
Presides o'er *trifles* with a *serious* face;
Important, by the virtue of *grimace*.

Ladies supreme among amusements reign;
By nature born to *sooth*, and *entertain*.
Their *prudence* in a share of folly lies:
Why will they be so *weak*, as to be *wise*?

SYRENA is for ever in extremes,
And *with a vengeance* she commends, or blames,
Conscious of her discernment, which is good,
She strains too much to make it understood.
Her *judgment* just, her *sentence* is too strong;
Because she's right, she's ever in the wrong.

BRUNETTA's wife in actions great, and rare;
But scorns on *trifles* to bestow her care.
Thus ev'ry hour BRUNETTA is to blame,
Because th' occasion is beneath her aim.
Think nought a *trifle*, though it small appear;
Small sands the mountain, moments make the year,
And trifles life. Your care to trifles give,
Or you may die, before you truly live.

Go breakfast with ALICIA, there you'll see,
Simplex munditiis, to the last degree:
Unlac'd her stays, her night-gown is unty'd,
And what she has of head-dress is aside,

She

She drawls her words, and waddles in her pace;
Unwaſh'd her hands, and much beſnuff'd her face,
A nail uncut, and head uncomb'd, ſhe loves;
And would draw on jack-boots, as ſoon as gloves.
Gloves by queen BESS's maidens might be miſt;
Her bleſſed eyes ne'er ſaw a female fiſt.
Lovers, beware! to *wound* how can ſhe fail
With ſcarlet finger, and long jetty nail?
For H——r the firſt *wit* ſhe cannot be,
Nor, cruel R——D, the firſt *toaſt*, for thee.
Since full each other ſtation of *renown*,
Who would not be the greateſt *trapes* in town?
Women were made to give our eyes delight;
A *female ſloven* is an odious fight.

Fair ISABELLA is ſo fond of *fame*,
That her *dear ſelf* is her eternal theme;
Through hopes of contradiction, oft ſhe'll ſay,
" Methinks I look ſo wretchedly to-day!"
When moſt the world applauds you, moſt beware;
'Tis often leſs a *bleſſing* than a *ſnare*.
Diſtruſt *mankind*; with your own *heart* confer;
And dread even *there* to find a flatterer.
The breath of *others* raiſes our renown;
Our *own* as ſurely blows the pageant down.
Take up no more than you by worth can claim,
Leſt ſoon you prove a *bankrupt* in your fame.

But own I muſt, in this perverted age,
Who moſt *deſerve*, can't always moſt *engage*.
So far is worth from making glory ſure,
It often hinders what it *ſhould* procure.
Whom praiſe we *moſt?* The virtuous, brave, and *wiſe?*
No; wretches, whom, in ſecret, we deſpiſe.
And who ſo blind, as not to ſee the cauſe?
No rivals rais'd by ſuch *diſcreet* applauſe;

And

And yet, of credit it lays in a ſtore,
By which our ſpleen may wound *true* worth the more.
　Ladies there are who think *one* crime is *all*:
Can women, then, no way but *backward* fall?
So ſweet is *that one* crime they don't purſue,
To pay its loſs, they think *all* others *few*.
Who hold *that* crime ſo dear, muſt never claim
Of *injur'd modeſty* the ſacred name.
　But CLIO thus: " What! railing without end?
" Mean taſk! how much more gen'rous to commend!"
Yes, to commend as you are wont to do,
My kind *inſtructor*, and *example* too.
" DAPHNIS," ſays CLIO, " has a charming eye:
" What pity 'tis her ſhoulder is awry!
" ASPASIA's ſhape indeed—But then her air—
" The man has parts who finds deſtruction there.
" ALMERIA's wit has ſomething that's divine;
" And wit's enough—how few in all things ſhine!
" SELINA ſerves her friends, relieves the poor—
" Who was it ſaid SELINA's near threeſcore?
" At LUCIA's match I from my ſoul rejoice;
" The world congratulates ſo wiſe a choice;
" His lordſhip's rent-roll is exceeding great—
" But mortgages will ſap the beſt eſtate.
" In SHERLEY's form might cherubims appear;
" But then—ſhe has a *freckle* on her *ear*."
Without a *but*, HORTENSIA ſhe commends,
The firſt of women, and the beſt of friends;
Owns her in perſon, wit, fame, virtue, bright:
But how comes this to paſs?—She dy'd laſt night.
　Thus nymphs commend, who yet at ſatire rail:
Indeed *that*'s needleſs, if *ſuch praiſe* prevail.
And whence ſuch praiſe? Our virulence is thrown
On *others*' fame, thro' fondneſs for our *own*.

Of

Of rank and riches proud, CLEORA frowns;
For are not *coronets* akin to *crowns?*
Her greedy eye, and her fublime addrefs,
The height of *avarice* and *pride* confefs.
You feek perfections worthy of her rank;
Go, feek for her perfections at the Bank.
By wealth unquench'd, by reafon uncontroul'd,
For ever burns her facred thirft of gold.
As fond of five-pence, as the verieft *cit*;
And quite as much detefted as a *quit.*

　Can gold calm *paffion,* or make *reafon* fhine?
Can we dig *peace,* or *wifdom,* from the mine?
Wifdom to gold prefer; for 'tis much lefs
To make our *fortune,* than our *happinefs.*
That happinefs which great ones often fee,
With rage and wonder, in a low degree;
Themfelves unbleft.　The poor are *only* poor;
But what are they who *droop* amid their ftore?
Nothing is meaner than a wretch *of ftate*;
The *happy* only are the truly *great.*
Peafants enjoy like appetites with kings;
And thofe beft fatisfied with cheapeft things.
Could *both* our *Indies* buy but *one* new *fenfe,*
Our envy would be due to large expence.
Since not, thofe pomps which to the great belong,
Are but poor arts to mark them from the throng.
See how they beg an alms of flattery!
They languifh! oh fupport them with a *lye!*
A *decent competence* we fully tafte;
It ftrikes our *fenfe,* and gives a conftant feaft:
More, we perceive by dint of thought alone;
The rich muft *labour* to poffefs *their own,*
To feel their great abundance; and requeft
Their humble friends to *help* them to be bleft;

　　　　　　　　　　　　　　　　To

To *see* their treasures, *hear* their glory told,
And *aid* the wretched impotence of gold. ,
    But some, great souls ! and touch'd with warmth divine,
Give *gold* a *price*, and teach its *beams* to *shine*.
All *hoarded* treasures they repute a load ;
Nor think their wealth *their own*, till well bestow'd.
Grand *reservoirs* of public happiness,
Through *secret* streams diffusively they bless ;
And, while their bounties glide conceal'd from view,
Relieve our *wants*, and *spare* our *blushes* too.
But Satire is my task ; and *these* destroy
Her gloomy province, and malignant joy.
Help me, ye misers ! help me to complain,
And blast our common enemy, G———n :
But our *invectives* must despair success ;
For next to *praise*, she values nothing less.
    What picture's yonder, loosen'd from its frame ?
Or is't Asturia ? that affected dame.
The brightest forms, through *affectation*, fade
To strange *new* things, which *nature* never made.
Frown not, ye fair ! so much your sex we prize,
We hate those *arts* that take you from our eyes.
In Albucinda's native grace is seen
What you, who *labour* at perfection, mean.
Short is the rule, and to be learnt with ease,
Retain your gentle selves, and you *must* please.
Here might I sing of Memmia's mincing'mien,
And all the movements of the soft machine :
How two red lips affected *Zephyrs* blow,
To cool the *Bohea*, and inflame the *Beau* :
While one white *finger*, and a *thumb*, conspire
To lift the *cup*, and make the world admire.
    Tea ! how I tremble at thy fatal stream !
As Lethe, dreadful to the *Love of Fame*.

What

What devaftations on thy banks are feen!
What *ſhades* of mighty names which *once* have been!
An *becatomb* of characters fupplies
Thy painted altars daily facrifice.
H——, P——, B——, afpers'd by thee, decay,
As grains of fineft fugars melt away,
And recommend thee more to mortal tafte:
Scandal's the fweet'ner of a *female* feaft.

But this inhuman triumph fhall decline,
And thy revolting *Naiads* call for *wine*;
Spirits no longer fhall ferve *under* thee;
But reign in thy own cup, *exploded tea!*
CITRONIA's nofe declares thy ruin nigh,
And who dares give CITRONIA's nofe the lie? *

The ladies long at men of drink exclaim'd,
And what impair'd both health and virtue, blam'd;
At length, to refcue man, the generous lafs
Stole from her confort the pernicious glafs;
As glorious as the *Britiſh* queen renown'd,
Who fuck'd the poifon from her hufband's wound.

Nor to the *glaſs* alone are nymphs inclin'd,
But every bolder vice of bold mankind.

O JUVENAL! for thy feverer rage!
To laſh the ranker follies of our age.

Are there, among the females of our ifle,
Such faults, at which it is a fault to *ſmile?*
There are. Vice, once by *modeſt nature* chain'd
And *legal ties*, expatiates unreftrain'd;
Without thin *decency* held up to view,
Naked fhe ftalks o'er *Law* and *Goſpel* too.
Our matrons lead fuch exemplary lives,
Men figh in vain for *none*, but for their *wives*;

* —— *Solem quis dicere falfum*
  Audeat?   VIRG.

Wh°

Who *marry* to be *free*, to range the more,
And wed one man, to wanton with a fcore.
Abroad too kind, at home 'tis ftedfaft hate,
And one eternal tempeft of debate.
What foul eruptions, from a look moft meek!
What thunders burfting, from a dimpled cheek!
Their *paffions* bear it with a lofty hand!
But then, their *reafon* is at due command.
Is there whom you deteft, and feek his life?
Truft no foul with the fecret—but his wife.
Wives wonder that their conduct I condemn,
And afk, what kindred is a *fpoufe* to them?

    What fwarms of am'rous *grandmothers* I fee!
And miffes, *antient* in iniquity!
What blafting whifpers, and what loud declaiming!
What lying, drinking, bawding, fwearing, gaming!
Friendfhip fo cold, fuch warm incontinence;
Such griping av'rice, fuch profufe expence;
Such dead devotion, fuch a zeal for crimes;
Such licens'd ill, fuch mafquerading times;
Such venal faith, fuch mifapply'd applaufe;
Such flatter'd guilt, and fuch inverted laws;
Such diffolution through the whole I find,
'Tis not a world, but chaos of mankind.

    Since *Sundays* have no balls, the well-drefs'd *belle*
Shines in the pew, but fmiles to hear of *hell*;
And cafts an eye of fweet difdain on all,
Who liftens lefs to C——ns, than St. *Paul*.
Atheifts have been but rare; fince nature's birth,
Till now, She-atheifts ne'er appear'd on earth.
Ye men of deep refearches, fay, whence fprings
This daring character, in timorous things?
Who ftart at *feathers*, from an *infect* fly,
A match for nothing—but the *Deity*.

                                                    But,

But, not to wrong the fair, the muse must own
In this pursuit they court not fame alone ;
But join to that a more substantial view,
" From thinking free, to be free agents too."
They strive with their own hearts, and keep them down,
In complaisance to all the fools in town.
O how they tremble at the name of *prude* !
And die with shame at thought of being *good* !
For what will ARTIMIS, the rich and gay,
What will the wits, that is, the coxcombs say ?
They heav'n defy, to earth's vile dregs a slave ;
Thro' cowardice, most execrably brave.
With our own judgments durst we to comply,
In virtue should we live, in glory die.
Rise then, my muse, in honest fury rise ;
They dread a Satire, who defy the Skies.
    Atheists are few : most nymphs a Godhead own ;
And nothing but his *attributes* dethrone.
From atheists far, they stedfastly believe
God is, and is Almighty——to *forgive*.
His other excellence they'll not dispute ;
But *mercy*, sure, is his chief attribute.
Shall pleasures of a short duration chain
A *lady*'s soul in everlasting pain ?
Will the great Author us poor worms destroy,
For now and then a *sip* of transient joy ?
No, he's for ever in a smiling mood ;
He's like themselves ; or how could he be good ?
And they blaspheme, who blacker schemes suppose.——
Devoutly, thus, JEHOVAH they depose,
The *pure* ! the *just* ! and set up, in his stead,
A deity, that's perfectly *well-bred*.
    " Dear T—L—N ! besure the best of men ;
" Nor thought he more, than thought great ORIGEN.
                              " Though

" Though once upon a time he milbehav'd;

" Poor SATAN ! doubtlefs, he'll at length be fav'd.

" Let priefts do fomething for their One in Ten;

" It is their *trade*; fo far they're honeft men.

" Let them cant on, fince they have got the knack,

" And drefs their notions, like themfelves, in *black*;

" Fright us with terrors of a world *unknown*,

" From joys of this, to keep them all their *own*.

" Of earth's fair fruits, indeed, they claim a fee;

" But then they leave our *untyth'd virtue* free.

" *Virtue's a pretty thing to make a fhow*:

" Did ever mortal write like ROCHEFOCAUT ?"

Thus pleads the devil's fair apologift,

And, pleading, fafely enters on his lift.

Let angel-forms angelic truths maintain;

Nature disjoins the *beauteous* and *profane*.

For what's true beauty, but fair virtue's *face*?

Virtue made *vifible* in outward grace?

She, then, that's haunted with an impious mind,

The more fhe *charms*, the more fhe *fhocks* mankind.

But charms decline: the Fair long vigils keep:

They fleep no more ! * *Quadrille* has murder'd fleep.

" Poor K—p ! cries LIVIA; I have not been there

" Thefe two nights; the poor creature will defpair.

" I hate a crowd—but to do good, you know—

" And people of condition fhould beftow."

Convinc'd, o'ercome, to K—p's grave matrons run;

Now *fet* a daughter, and now *ftake* a fon;

Let health, fame, temper, beauty, fortune, fly;

And beggar half their race—thro' *charity*.

Immortal were we, or elfe mortal *quite*,

I lefs fhould blame this criminal delight :

* SHAKESPEARE.

But

But since the gay assembly's gayest room
Is but an upper story to some tomb,
Methinks, we need not our *short* beings shun,
And, *thought* to fly, *contend* to be undone.
We need not buy our *ruin* with our *crime*,
And give *eternity* to murder *time*.

    The love of gaming is the worst of ills ;
With ceaseless storms the blacken'd soul it fills ;
Inveighs at heav'n, neglects the ties of blood ;
Destroys the pow'r and will of doing good ;
Kills health, pawns honour, plunges in disgrace,
And, what is still more dreadful—spoils your face.

    See yonder set of thieves that live on spoil,
The *scandal*, and the *ruin* of our isle !
And see, (strange sight !) amid that ruffian band,
A form divine high wave her snowy hand ;
That rattles loud a small enchanted box,
Which, loud as thunder, on the board she knocks.
And as fierce storms, which earth's foundation shook,
From Æolus's cave impetuous broke,
From this small cavern a mix'd tempest flies,
Fear, rage, convulsion, tears, oaths, blasphemies !
For men, I mean,—the fair discharges none ;
She (guiltless creature !) swears to heav'n alone.

    See her eyes start ! cheeks glow ! and muscles swell !
Like the mad maid in the *Cumean* cell.
Thus that divine one her *soft* nights employs !
Thus tunes her soul to tender nuptial joys !
And when the cruel morning calls to bed,
And on her pillow lays her aking head,
With the dear images her dreams are crown'd,
The *die* spins lovely, or the *cards* go round ;
Imaginary ruin charms her still ;
Her happy lord is cuckol'd by *spadil* :

                                   And

And if she's brought to bed, 'tis ten to one,
He marks the forehead of her darling son.
  O scene of horror, and of wild despair,
Why is the rich ATRIDES' splendid heir
Constrain'd to quit his antient lordly seat,
And hide his glories in a mean retreat?
Why that drawn sword? And whence that dismal cry?
Why pale distraction thro' the family?
See my lord threaten, and my lady weep,
And trembling servants from the tempest creep.
Why that gay *son* to distant regions sent?
What fiends that *daughter*'s destin'd match prevent?
Why the whole house in sudden ruin laid?
O nothing, but last night—my lady *play'd*.
  But wanders not my Satire from my theme?
Is *this* too owing to the love of *fame?*
Though now your hearts on *lucre* are bestow'd,
'Twas first a *vain devotion* to the *mode;*
Nor cease we *here,* since 'tis a vice so strong,
The torrent sweeps all womankind along;
This may be said, in honour of our times,
That none now stand *distinguish'd* by their crimes.
  If sin you must, take nature for your guide:
Love has some soft excuse to sooth your pride:
Ye fair apostates from love's antient pow'r!
Can nothing *ravish,* but a *golden show'r?*
Can cards alone your glowing fancy seize;
Must CUPID learn to *punt,* ere he can *please?*
When you're enamour'd of a *lift* or *cast,*
What can the *preacher* more, to make us *chaste?*
Why must strong youths *unmarry'd* pine away?
They find no woman disengag'd——*from play.*
Why pine the *marry'd*—O severer fate!
They find from play no disengag'd—*estate.*

FLAVIA, at lovers falfe, *untouch'd* and *hard*,
Turns pale, and trembles at a *cruel* card.
Nor ARRIA s bible can fecure her age;
Her threefcore years are fhuffling with her page.
While *death* ftands by, but till the game is done,
To fweep *that ftake*, in juftice, long his *own*;
Like old cards ting'd with fulphur, fhe takes fire;
Or, like fnuffs funk in fockets, blazes higher.
Ye gods! with *new* delights infpire the Fair;
Or give us *fons*, and fave us from defpair.

    Sons, brothers, fathers, hufbands, *tradefmen*, clofe
In my complaint, and brand your fins in *profe*:
Yet I believe, as firmly as my Creed,
In fpite of all our wifdom, you'll proceed:
Our pride fo great, our paffion is fo ftrong,
Advice to *right* confirms us in the *wrong*.
I hear you cry, " This fellow's very odd."
When *you* chaftife, who would not kifs the rod?
But I've a charm your anger fhall controul,
And turn your eyes with coldnefs on the *vole*.

    The charm begins! To yonder flood of light,
That burfts o'er gloomy *Britain*, turn your fight.
What guardian pow'r o'erwhelms your fouls with awe?
Her deeds are precepts, her example law;
'Midft empire's charms, how CAROLINA's heart
Glows with the love of *virtue*, and of *art!*
Her favour is diffus'd to that degree,
Excefs of goodnefs! it has dawn'd on me:
When in my page, to balance numerous faults,
Or godlike deeds were fhown, or gen'rous thoughts,
She fmil'd, *induftrious* to be pleas'd, nor knew
From whom my pen the *borrow'd* luftre drew.

    * Thus the majeftic mother of mankind,
To her own charms moft amiably blind,

         * MILTON.

On

On the green margin innocently ftood,
And gaz'd indulgent on the chryftal flood;
Survey'd the ftranger in the painted wave,
And, fmiling, prais'd the beauties which fhe gave,

SATIRE VII.

TO THE RIGHT HONOURABLE

SIR ROBERT WALPOLE.

Carmina tum melius, cum venerit IPSE, *canemus.*   VIRG.

ON this laſt labour, this my cloſing ſtrain,
Smile, WALPOLE! or the *Nine* inſpire in vain:
To *thee*, 'tis due; that verſe how juſtly thine,
Where BRUNSWICK's glory crowns the whole deſign!
That glory, which thy counſels make ſo bright;
That glory, which on thee reflects a light.
Illuſtrious commerce, and but rarely known!
To *give*, and *take*, a luſtre from the throne.
  Nor think that thou art foreign to my theme;
The *fountain* is not foreign to the *ſtream.*
How all mankind will be ſurpriz'd, to ſee
This flood of *Britiſh* folly charg'd on thee!
Say, *Britain!* whence this caprice of thy ſons,
Which thro' their various ranks with fury runs?

The

The cause is plain, a cause which we muſt bleſs;
For caprice is the daughter of *ſucceſs*,
(A bad effect, but from a pleaſing cauſe!)
And gives our rulers undeſign'd applauſe;
'Tells how their conduct bids our *wealth* increaſe,
And lulls us in the downy lap of *peace*.

While I ſurvey the bleſſings of our iſle,
Her *arts* triumphant in the royal ſmile,
Her public *wounds* bound up, her *credit* high,
Her *commerce* ſpreading ſails in every ſky,
The pleaſing ſcene recalls my theme again;
And ſhews the madneſs of ambitious men,
Who, fond of bloodſhed, draw the murd'ring ſword,
And burn to give mankind a ſingle lord.

The follies paſt are of a private kind;
Their ſphere is ſmall; their miſchief is confin'd:
But daring men there are (Awake, my muſe,
And raiſe thy verſe!) who bolder frenzy chuſe;
Who ſtung by glory, rave, and bound away;
The *world* their field, and *humankind* their prey.

The *Grecian* chief, th' enthuſiaſt of his *pride*,
With rage and terror ſtalking by his ſide,
Raves round the globe; he ſoars into a god!
Stand faſt, *Olympus!* and ſuſtain his nod.
The peſt divine in horrid grandeur reigns,
And thrives on mankind's miſeries and pains.
What ſlaughter'd *hoſts!* what *cities* in a blaze!
What waſted *countries!* and what crimſon *ſeas!*
With orphans tears his impious bowl o'erflows,
And cries of kingdoms lull him to repoſe.

And cannot thrice ten hundred years unpraiſe
The boiſt'rous boy, and blaſt his guilty bays?
Why want we then encomiums on the *ſtorm*,
Or *famine*, or *volcano?* They perform

Their

Their mighty deeds: they, hero-like, can slay,
And spread their ample defarts in a day.
O great alliance! O divine renown!
With *dearth*, and *peftilence*, to share the crown:
When men extol a wild deftroyer's name,
Earth's Builder and Preferver they blafpheme:

 One to deftroy, is murder by the law;
And gibbets keep the lifted hand in awe;
To murder *thoufands*, takes a fpecious name,
War's glorious art, and gives immortal *fame*.

 When, after battle, I the field have feen
Spread o'er with ghaftly fhapes, which once were men;
A *nation* crufh'd, a nation of the *brave*!
A realm of death! and on this fide the grave!
Are there, faid I, who from this fad furvey,
This *human chaos*, carry fmiles away?
How did my heart with indignation rife!
How honeft nature fwell'd into my eyes!
How was I fhock'd to think the hero's trade
Of fuch materials, *fame* and *triumph* made!

 How guilty thefe! Yet not lefs guilty they,
Who reach falfe glory by a fmoother way:
Who wrap deftruction up in gentle words,
And bows, and fmiles, more fatal than their fwords;
Who ftifle *nature*, and fubfift on *art*;
Who coin the *face*, and petrify the *heart*;
All real kindnefs for the fhew difcard,
As marble polifh'd, and as marble hard;
Who do for gold what Chriftians do thro' Grace,
" With open arms their enemies embrace:"
Who give a nod when broken hearts repine;
" The thinneft food on which a wretch can dine:"
Or, if they ferve you, ferve you difinclin'd,
And, in their height of kindnefs, are unkind.

5   Such

Such *courtiers* were, and such again may be,
WALPOLE! when men forget to copy thee.

    Here ceafe, my Mufe! the *catalogue* is writ;
Nor one more candidate for *fame* admit,
Tho' difappointed thoufands juftly blame
Thy partial pen, and boaft an equal claim:
Be this their comfort, fools, omitted here,
May furnifh laughter for another year.
Then let CRISPINO, who was ne'er refus'd
The *juftice* yet of being well abus'd,
With patience wait; and he content to reign
The pink of puppies in fome future ftrain.

    Some future ftrain, in which the Mufe fhall tell
How *fcience* dwindles, and how *volumes* fwell.

    How commentators each *dark* paffage fhun,
And hold their farthing candle to the *fun*.

    How tortur'd texts to fpeak our fenfe are made,
And every vice is to the Scripture laid.

    How mifers fqueeze a young voluptuous peer;
His fins to LUCIFER not half fo dear.

    How VERRES is lefs qualify'd to fteal
With fword and piftol, than with wax and feal.

    How lawyers' fees to fuch excefs are run,
That clients are redrefs'd till they're undone.

    How one man's anguifh is another's fport;
And ev'n denials coft us dear at court.

    How man eternally falfe judgments makes,
And all his joys and forrows are *miftakes*.

    This fwarm of themes that fettles on my pen,
Which I, like fummer flies, fhake off again,
Let others fing; to whom my weak effay
But founds a prelude, and points out their prey:
That duty done, I haften to complete
My own defign; for TONSON's at the gate.

            The

The love of Fame in its *effect* survey'd,
The Muse has sung; be now the *cause* display'd:
Since so diffusive, and so wide its sway,
What is this power, whom all mankind obey?

Shot from above, by heav'n's indulgence, came
This generous ardor, this unconquer'd flame,
To warm, to raise, to deify, mankind,
Still burning brightest in the noblest mind.
By large-soul'd men, for thirst of fame renown'd,
Wise *laws* were fram'd, and sacred *arts* were found;
Desire of praise first broke the *patriot*'s rest;
And made a bulwark of the *warrior*'s breast;
It bids ARGYLL in fields and senates shine.
What more can prove its origin divine?

But, oh! this passion planted in the soul,
On eagle's wings to mount her to the pole,
The flaming minister of *virtue* meant,
Set up false gods, and wrong'd her high descent.

AMBITION, hence, exerts a doubtful force,
Of blots, and beauties, an alternate source;
Hence GILDON rails, that raven of the pit,
Who thrives upon the carcases of wit;
And in art-loving SCARBOROUGH is seen
How kind a pattern POLLIO *might* have been.
Pursuit of fame with pedants fills our schools,
And into *coxcombs* burnishes our *fools*;
Pursuit of fame makes solid learning bright,
And NEWTON lifts above a mortal height;
That key of nature, by whose wit she clears
Her long, long secrets of five thousand years.

Would you then fully comprehend the whole,
Why, and in what *degrees*, pride sways the soul?
(For though in all, not equally, she reigns)
Awake to knowledge, and attend my strains.

Ye

Ye doctors! hear the doctrine I disclose,
As true, as if 'twere writ in dullest prose;
As if a letter'd dunce had said, " 'Tis right,"
And *imprimatur* usher'd it to light.
   AMBITION, in the *truly noble mind,*
With Sister-virtue is for ever join'd;
As in fam'd LUCRECE, who, with equal dread,
From *guilt,* and *shame,* by her last conduct, fled:
Her *virtue* long rebell'd in firm disdain,
And the sword pointed at her heart in vain;
But, when the slave was threaten'd to be laid
Dead by her side, her *Love of Fame* obey'd.
   In *meaner minds* ambition works alone;
But with such art puts virtue's aspect on,
That not more like in feature and in mien,
* The God and mortal in the comic scene.
False JULIUS, ambush'd in this fair disguise,
Soon made the *Roman* liberties his prize.
   No mask in *basest minds* ambition wears,
But in full light pricks up her ass's ears:
All I have sung are instances of *this,*
And prove my theme unfolded not amiss.
   Ye *vain!* desist from your erroneous strife;
Be wise, and quit the *false* sublime of life,
The *true* ambition there alone resides,
Where *justice* vindicates, and *wisdom* guides;
Where *inward* dignity joins *outward* state;
Our *purpose* good, as our *atchievement* great;
Where public *blessings* public *praise* attend;
Where glory is our *motive,* not our *end.*
Would'st thou be *fam'd?* Have those high deeds in view
Brave men would act, though *scandal* should ensue.

* AMPHITRYON.

Behold

Behold a Prince ! whom no fwoln thoughts inflame ;
No pride of thrones, no fever after *Fame !*
But when the welfare of mankind infpires,
And death in view to dear-bought glory fires,
Proud conquefts then, then regal pomps delight;
Then crowns, then triumphs, fparkle in his fight ;
Tumult and *noife* are dear, which with them bring
His people's bleffings to their ardent king :
But, when thofe great heroic motives ceafe,
His fwelling foul fubfides to native peace ;
From tedious grandeur's faded charms withdraws,
A *fudden* foe to fplendor and applaufe ;
Greatly deferring his arrears of fame,
Till men and angels jointly fhout his name.
O pride celeftial ! which can pride difdain ;
O bleft ambition ! which can ne'er be *vain.*

From one fam'd *Alpine* hill, which props the fky,
In whofe deep womb unfathom'd waters lie,
Here burft the *Rhone*, and founding *Po* ; there fhine,
In infant rills, the *Danube* and the *Rhine* ;
From the rich ftore one fruitful urn fupplies,
Whole kingdoms fmile, a thoufand harvefts rife.

In BRUNSWICK fuch a fource the Mufe adores,
Which public bleffings thro' half *Europe* pours.
When his heart burns with fuch a godlike aim,
Angels and GEORGE are *rivals* for the fame ;
GEORGE ! who in foes can foft affections raife,
And charm envenom'd Satire into praife.

* Nor *human* rage alone his pow'r perceives,
But the mad *winds,* and the tumultuous *waves.*
Ev'n ftorms (death's fierceft minifters !) forbear,
And, in their own wild empire, learn to fpare.

* The king in danger by fea.

Thus,

Thus, *nature's self*, fupporting *man's* decree,
Stiles *Britain's* fovereign, fovereign of the *fea*.

   While *fea* and *air*, great BRUNSWICK! fhook our State,
And fported with a king's and kingdom's fate,
Depriv'd of what fhe lov'd, and prefs'd by fear,
Of *ever* lofing what fhe held moft dear,
How did BRITANNIA, like * ACHILLES, weep,
And tell her forrows to the *kindred deep!*
Hang o'er the floods, and, in devotion warm,
Strive, for Thee, with the furge, and fight the ftorm!

   What felt thy WALPOLE, pilot of the realm!
Our PALINURUS † flept not at the helm;
His eye ne'er clos'd; long fince enur'd to wake,
And out-watch every ftar for BRUNSWICK'S fake:
By thwarting paffions toft, by cares oppreft,
He found the tempeft pictur'd in his breaft:
But, *now*, what joys that gloom of heart difpel,
No pow'rs of language—but his own, can tell;
His own, which *nature* and the *graces* form,
At will, to raife, or hufh, the *civil* ftorm.

* HOM. Il. lib. I.
† *Ecce Deus remum Lethæo rore madentem*, &c.   VIRG. lib. V.

O D E,

O D E,

OCCASIONED BY

H I S   M A J E S T Y's

ROYAL ENCOURAGEMENT OF THE

S E A   S E R V I C E.

I THINK

I THINK Myſelf obliged to recommend to you a Conſideration of the greateſt Importance; and I ſhould look upon it as a great Happineſs, if, at the Beginning of My Reign, I could ſee the Foundation laid of ſo great and neceſſary a Work, as the Increaſe and Encouragement of our Seamen in general; that they may be invited, rather than compelled by Force and Violence, to enter into the Service of their Country, as oft as Occaſion ſhall require it: A Conſideration worthy the Repreſentatives of a People great and flouriſhing in Trade and Navigation. This leads Me to mention to you the caſe of *Greenwich Hoſpital,* that Care may be taken, by ſome Addition to that Fund, to render comfortable and effectual that charitable Proviſion, for the Support and Maintenance of Our Seamen, worn out, and become decrepit by Age and Infirmities, in the Service of their Country.

[SPEECH, *Jan.* 27, 1727-8.]

T O

⁎⁎⁎⁎⁎⁎⁎⁎⁎⁎⁎⁎⁎⁎⁎⁎⁎⁎⁎⁎⁎⁎⁎⁎⁎⁎⁎⁎⁎⁎⁎⁎⁎⁎⁎⁎⁎⁎
⁎⁎⁎⁎⁎⁎⁎⁎⁎⁎⁎⁎⁎⁎⁎⁎⁎⁎⁎⁎⁎⁎⁎⁎⁎⁎⁎⁎⁎⁎⁎⁎⁎⁎⁎⁎⁎⁎

TO THE

K I N G.

M.DCC.XXVIII.

⁎⁎⁎⁎⁎⁎⁎⁎⁎⁎⁎⁎

I.

OLD OCEAN's praise
Demands my lays;
A truly *British* theme I sing;
A theme so great,
I dare complete,
And join with OCEAN, *Ocean*'s King.

II.

The *Roman* Ode
Majestic flow'd:
Its *stream* divinely clear, and strong;
In sense, and sound,
Thebes roll'd profound;
The *torrent* roar'd, and foam'd along.

III. Let

III.

Let *Thebes*, nor *Rome*,
So fam'd, prefume
To triumph o'er a northern ifle;
Late time fhall know
The *North* can *glow*,
If dread Augustus deign to fmile.

IV.

The Naval crown
Is all His own!
Our Fleet, if *war*, or *commerce*, call,
His will performs
Through waves and ftorms,
And rides in triumph round the ball.

V.

No former race,
With ftrong embrace,
This theme to ravifh durft afpire;
With virgin charms
My foul it warms,
And melts melodious on my lyre.

VI.

My lays I file
With cautious toil;
Ye graces! turn the glowing lines;
On anvils neat
Your ftrokes repeat;
At every ftroke the work refines!

VII. How

VII.

How mufic charms!
How metre warms!
Parent of actions, good and brave!
How vice it tames!
And worth inflames!
And holds proud empire o'er the grave!

VIII.

Jove mark'd for man
A fcanty fpan,
But lent him wings to fly his doom;
Wit fcorns the grave;
To Wit he gave
The life of gods! immortal bloom!

IX.

Since *years* will fly,
And *pleafures* die,
Day after day, as years advance;
Since, while life lafts,
Joy fuffers blafts
From frowning *Fate*, and fickle *Chance*;

X.

Nor life is long;
But foon we throng,
Like autumn leaves, death's pallid fhore;
We make, at leaft,
Of *bad* the *beft*,
If in life's phantom, *Fame*, we foar.

XI.

Our ſtrains divide
The laurel's pride;
With thoſe we lift to life, to live;
By fame enroll'd
With heroes bold,
And ſhare the bleſſings which we give.

XII.

What hero's praiſe
Can fire my lays,
Like His, with whom my lay begun?
" *Juſtice* ſincere,
" And *courage* clear,
" Riſe the two columns of his throne.

XIII.

" How form'd for ſway!
" Who look, obey;
" They read the monarch in his *port*:
" Their love and awe
" Supply the *law*;
" And his *own* luſtre makes the court:"

XIV.

On yonder height,
What golden light
Triumphant ſhines? And ſhines *alone?*
Unrivall'd blaze!
The nations gaze!
'Tis not the Sun; 'tis *Britain's* throne.

XV. Our

XV.

Our Monarch, there,
Rear'd high in air,
Should tempefts rife, difdains to bend;
Like *Britifh* oak,
Derides the ftroke;
His blooming honours far extend!

XVI.

Beneath them lies,
With lifted eyes,
Fair *Albion*, like an amorous maid;
While *intereft* wings
Bold foreign kings
To fly, like eagles, to his fhade.

XVII.

At his proud foot
The *fea*, pour'd out,
Immortal nourifhment fupplies;
Thence *wealth* and *ftate*,
And *power* and *fate*,
Which *Europe* reads in GEORGE's eyes.

XVIII.

From what we view,
We take the clue,
Which leads from great to greater things:
Men doubt no more,
But gods adore,
When fuch refemblance fhines in kings.

EPISTLES

EPISTLES

TO

MR. POPE,

CONCERNING THE

AUTHORS OF THE AGE.

M.DCC.XXX.

EPISTLE I.

to

MR. POPE.

WHILST you at *Twick'nham* plan the future wood,
Or turn the volumes of the wife and good,
Our fenate meets; at parties, parties bawl.
And pamphlets ftun the ftreets, and load the ftall;
So rufhing tides bring things obfcene to light,
Foul wrecks emerge, and dead dogs fwim in fight;
The civil torrent foams, the tumult reigns,
And CODRUS' profe works up, and LICO's ftrains.
Lo! what from *cellars* rife, what rufh from high,
Where fpeculation roofted near the fky;
Letters, Effays, Sock, Bufkin, Satire, Song,
And all the *Garret* thunders on the throng!
　O POPE! I burft; nor can, nor will, refrain;
I'll write; let others, in their turn, complain:

M 4

Truce,

Truce, truce, ye *Vandals!* my tormented ear
Lefs dreads a pillory than a pamphleteer;
I've *heard* myfelf to death; and, plagu'd each hour,
Shan't I return the vengeance in my pow'r?
For who can write the true abfurd like me? ——
Thy pardon, CODRUS! who, I mean, but thee?

    POPE! if like mine, or CODRUS', were thy ftyle,
The blood of vipers had not ftain'd thy file;
Merit lefs folid, lefs defpite had bred;
They had not *bit,* and then they had not *bled.*
Fame is a public miftrefs, none enjoys,
But, more or lefs, his rival's peace deftroys;
With *fame,* in juft proportion, *envy* grows;
The man that makes a charaƐter, makes foes:
Slight, peevifh infeƐts round a genius rife,
As a bright day awakes the world of flies;
With hearty malice, but with feeble wing,
(To fhew they live) they flutter, and they fting:
But as by depredations wafps proclaim
The faireft fruit, fo thefe the faireft fame.

    Shall we not cenfure all the motley train,
Whether with ale irriguous, or champaign?
Whether they tread the vale of profe, or climb,
And whet their appetites on cliffs of rhyme;
The college floven, or embroider'd fpark;
The purple prelate, or the parifh clerk;
The quiet *quidnunc,* or demanding prig;
The plaintiff tory, or defendant whig;
Rich, poor, male, female, young, old, gay, or fad;
Whether extremely witty, or quite mad;
Profoundly dull, or fhallowly polite;
Men that read well, or men that only write;
Whether peers, porters, taylors, tune the reeds,
And meafuring words to meafuring fhapes fucceeds;

                             For

For bankrupts write, when ruin'd shops are shut,
As maggots crawl from out a perish'd nut.
His hammer this, and that his trowel quits,
And, wanting sense for tradesmen, serve for wits.
By thriving men subsists each other trade;
Of every *broken* craft a *Writer's* made:
Thus his material, Paper, takes its birth
From tatter'd rags of all the stuff on earth.

   Hail, fruitful *isle!* to thee alone belong
Millions of wits, and brokers in old song:
Thee well a land of liberty we name,
Where all are free to scandal and to shame;
Thy sons, by print, may set their hearts at ease,
And be mankind's contempt, whene'er they please;
Like trodden filth, their vile and abject sense
Is unperceiv'd, but when it gives offence:
This heavy prose our injur'd reason tires;
Their verse immoral kindles loose desires:
Our age they puzzle, and corrupt our prime,
Our sport and pity, punishment and crime.

   What glorious motives urge our Authors on,
Thus to undo, and thus to be undone?
One loses his estate, and down he sits,
To shew (in vain!) he still retains his wits:
Another marries, and his dear proves keen;
He writes as an *Hypnotic* for the spleen:
Some write, confin'd by physic; some, by debt;
Some, for 'tis *Sunday*; some, because 'tis wet;
Through private pique some do the public right,
And love their king and country out of spite:
Another writes because his father writ,
And proves himself a bastard by his wit.

   Has Lico learning, humour, thought profound?
Neither: Why write then? He wants twenty pound:

His

His belly, not his brains, this impulse give;
He'll grow immortal; for he cannot live:
He rubs his awful front, and takes his ream,
With no provision made, but of his theme;
Perhaps a *title* has his fancy smit,
Or a quaint *motto*, which he thinks has wit:
He writes, in infpiration puts his truft,
Tho' wrong his thoughts, the *gods* will make them juft;
Genius directly from the *gods* defcends,
And who by labour would diftruft his *friends?*
Thus having reafon'd with confummate fkill,
In immortality he dips his quill:
And, fince blank paper is deny'd the prefs,
He mingles the whole alphabet by guefs:
In various fets, which various words compofe,
Of which, he hopes, mankind the meaning knows.

So founds fpontaneous from the *Sibyl* broke,
Dark to herfelf the wonders which fhe fpoke;
The priefts found out the meaning, if they cou'd;
And nations ftar'd at what none underftood.

CLODIO drefs'd, danc'd, drank, vifited, (the whole
And great concern of an immortal foul!)
Oft have I faid, " Awake! exift! and ftrive
" For birth! nor think to loiter is to live!"
As oft I overheard the *demon* fay,
Who daily met the loit'rer in his way,
" *I'll meet thee, youth, at* WHITE's:" The youth replies,
" *I'll meet thee there,*" and falls his facrifice;
His fortune fquander'd, leaves his virtue bare
To ev'ry bribe, and blind to ev'ry fnare:
CLODIO for bread his indolence muft quit,
Or turn a foldier, or commence a wit.
Such heroes have we! all, but life, they ftake;
How muft *Spain* tremble, and the *German* fhake!

                                                  Such

Such writers have we all, but sense, they print;
Ev'n GEORGE's praise is dated from the *Mint.*
In arms contemptible, in arts profane,
Such swords, such pens, disgrace a monarch's reign.
Reform your lives before you thus aspire,
And steal (for you *can steal*) celestial fire.

O! the just contrast! O the beauteous strife!
'Twixt their cool writings, and *pindaric* life:
They write with phlegm, but then they live with fire;
They cheat the leader, and their *works* the buyer.

I reverence misfortune, not deride;
I pity poverty, but laugh at pride:
For who so sad, but must some mirth confess
At gay CASTRUCHIO's miscellaneous dress?
Though there's but one of the dull works he wrote,
There's ten editions of his old lac'd coat.

These, nature's commoners, who want a home,
Claim the wide world for their majestic dome;
They make a private study of the street;
And looking full on every man they meet,
Run souse against his chaps; who stands amaz'd
To find they did not see, but only gaz'd.
How must these bards be rapt into the skies!
You need not *read,* you *feel* their ecstasies.

Will they persist? 'Tis madness; *Lintot,* run,
See them confin'd—— "O that's already done."
Most, as by leases, by the works they print,
Have took, for life, possession of the *Mint.*
If you mistake, and pity these poor men,
Est Ulubris, they cry, and write again.

Such wits their nuisance manfully expose,
And then pronounce just judges learning's foes;
O frail conclusion; the reverse is true;
If foes to learning, they'd be friends to you:

Treat

Treat them, ye judges! with an honeſt ſcorn,
And weed the cockle from the generous corn:
There's true good-nature in your diſreſpeƈt;
In juſtice to the good, the bad negleƈt:
For immortality, if hardſhips plead,
It is not theirs who write, but ours who read.

But, O! what wiſdom can convince a fool,
But that 'tis dulneſs to conceive him dull?
'Tis ſad experience takes the cenſor's part,
Conviƈtion, not from reaſon, but from ſmart.

A virgin-author, recent from the preſs,
The ſheets yet wet, applauds his great ſucceſs;
Surveys them, reads them, takes their charms to bed,
Thoſe in his hand, and glory in his head;
'Tis joy too great; a fever of delight!
His heart beats thick, nor cloſe his eyes all night:
But riſing the next morn to claſp his fame,
He finds that without ſleeping he could dream:
So ſparks, they ſay, take goddeſſes to bed,
And find next day the devil in their ſtead.

In vain *advertiſements* the town o'erſpread;
They're epitaphs, and ſay the work is dead.
Who *preſs* for fame, but ſmall recruits will raiſe;
'Tis *volunteers* alone can give the bays.

A famous author viſits a great man,
Of his immortal work diſplays the plan,
And ſays, " Sir, I'm your friend; all fears diſmiſs;
" Your glory, and my own, ſhall live by this;
" Your pow'r is fixt, your fame thro' time convey'd,
" And *Britain Europe*'s Queen—if I am paid."
A Stateſman has his anſwer in a trice;
" Sir, ſuch a genius is beyond all price;
" What man can pay for this?"—Away he turns;
His work is folded, and his boſom burns:

His

His patron he will patronize no more;
But rushes like a tempest out of door.
Lost is the patriot, and extinct his name!
Out comes the piece, another, and the same;
For *A*, his magic pen evokes an *O*,
And turns the tide of *Europe* on the foe:
He rams his quill with scandal, and with scoff;
But 'tis so very foul, it won't go off:
Dreadful his thunders, while unprinted, roar;
But when once publish'd, they are heard no more.
Thus distant bugbears fright, but, nearer draw,
The block's a block, and turns to mirth your awe.

 Can those oblige, whose heads and hearts are such?
No; every party's tainted by their touch.
Infected persons fly each public place;
And hone, or enemies alone, embrace:
To the foul fiend their every passion's sold:
They love, and hate, *extempore*, for gold:
What image of their fury can we form?
Dulness and rage, a puddle in a storm.
Rest they in peace? If you are pleas'd to *buy*,
To swell your sails, like *Lapland* winds, they fly:
Write they with rage? The tempest quickly flags;
. A *State-Ulysses* tames 'em with his bags;
Let him be what he will, *Turk*, *Pagan*, *Jew*:
For *Christian* ministers of state are few.

 Behind the curtain lurks the fountain head,
That pours his politics through pipes of lead,
Which far and near ejaculate, and spout
O'er tea and coffee, poison to the rout:
But when they have bespatter'd all they may,
The statesman throws his filthy squirts away!

 With *golden* forceps, these, another takes,
And state elixirs of the vipers makes.

The

The *richest* statesman wants wherewith to pay
A servile sycophant, if well they weigh
How much it costs the wretch to be so base;
Nor can the *greatest* pow'rs enough *disgrace,*
Enough *chastise,* such prostitute applause;
If well they weigh how much it stains their cause.

But are our writers ever in the wrong?
Does virtue ne'er seduce the venal tongue?
Yes; if well-brib'd, for virtue self they fight;
Still in the wrong, tho' champions for the right:
Whoe'er their crimes for interest only quit,
Sin on in virtue, and good deeds *commit.*

Nought but inconstancy *Britannia* meets,
And broken faith in their abandon'd sheets;
From the same hand how various is the page!
What civil war their brother pamphlets wage!
Tracts battle tracts, self-contradictions glare;
Say, is this lunacy?—I wish it were.
If such our writers, startled at the sight,
Felons may bless their stars they cannot write!

How justly PROTEUS' transmigrations fit
The monstrous changes of a modern wit?
Now, such a gentle *stream* of eloquence
As seldom rises to the verge of sense;
Now, by mad rage, transform'd into a *flame,*
Which yet fit engines, well apply'd, can tame;
Now, on immodest trash, the *swine obscene,*
Invites the town to sup at *Drury-lane;*
A dreadful *lion,* now he roars at pow'r,
Which sends him to his brothers at the *Tow'r;*
He's now a *serpent,* and his double tongue
Salutes, nay licks, the feet of those he stung;
What knot can bind him, his evasion such?
One knot he well deserves, which might do much.

The

'The flood, flame, fwine, the lion, and the fnake,
Thofe fivefold monfters, modern authors make:
The *Snake* reigns moft; Snakes, PLINY fays, are bred,
When the *brain*'s perifh'd in a human head.
Ye grov'ling, trodden, whipt, ftript, turncoat things,
Made up of venom, volumes, ftains, and ftings!
Thrown from the *Tree of Knowledge*, like you, curft
To fcribble in the duft, was Snake the firft.

What if the *figure* fhould in *fact* prove true!
It did in ELKENAH, why not in you?
Poor ELKENAH, all other changes paft,
For bread in *Smithfield dragons* hift at laft,
Spit ftreams of fire to make the butchers gape,
And found his manners fuited to his fhape:
Such is the fate of talents mifapply'd;
So liv'd your *Prototype*; and fo he dy'd.

Th' abandon'd manners of our writing train
May tempt mankind to think religion vain;
But in their fate, their habit, and their mien,
That gods there are is eminently feen:
Heav'n ftands abfolv'd by vengeance on their pen,
And marks the murderers of fame from men:
Through meagre jaws they draw their venal breath,
As ghaftly as their brothers in *Macbeth*:
Their feet through faithlefs leather meet the dirt,
And oftner chang'd their principles than fhirt.
The tranfient veftments of thefe frugal men,
Haftens to paper for our mirth again:
Too foon (O merry-melancholy fate!)
They beg in rhyme, and warble through a grate:
The man lampoon'd forgets it at the fight;
The friend through pity gives, the foe through fpite;
And though full confcious of his injur'd purfe,
LINTOT relents, nor CURLL can wifh them worfe.

5

So fare. the men, who writers dare commence
Without their *patent*, probity, and fenfe.
   From *thefe*, their politics our *quidnuncs* feek,
And *Saturday*'s the learning of the week :
Thefe labouring wits, like paviours, mend our ways, .
With heavy, huge, repeated, flat, effays;
Ram their coarfe nonfenfe down, though ne'er fo dull;
And hem at every thump upon your fkull :
Thefe ftaunch-bred writing hounds begin the cry,
And honeft folly echoes to the lye.
O how I laugh, when I a blockhead fee,
Thanking a villain for his *probity* ;
Who ftretches out a moft refpectful ear,
With fnares for woodcocks in his holy leer ;
It tickles thro' my foul to hear the *cock*'s
Sincere encomium on his friend the *fox*,
Sole *patron* of his *liberties* and *rights* !
While gracelefs *Reynard* liftens—till he bites.
   As when the trumpet founds, th' o'erloaded ftate
Difcharges all her *poor* and *profligate* ;
Crimes of all kinds difhonour'd weapons wield,
And *prifons* pour their filth into the field ;
Thus nature's refufe, and the dregs of men,
Compofe the *black militia* of the *pen.*

E P I S T L E II.

F R O M

O X F O R D.

ALL write at *London*; fhall the rage abate
Here, where it moft fhould fhine, the *Mufes feat?*
Where, mortal or immortal, as they pleafe,
The learn'd may chufe eternity, or eafe?
Has not a * ROYAL PATRON wifely ftrove
To woo the mufe in her *Athenian* grove?
Added new ftrings to her harmonious fhell,
And giv'n new tongues to thofe who fpoke fo well?
Let *thefe* inftruct, with truth's illuftrious ray,
Awake the world, and fcare our owls away.

    Mean while, O friend! indulge me, if I give
Some needful precepts how to *write*, and *live!*

* His late Majefty's benefaction for modern languages.

Serious ſhould be an author's final views;
Who write for pure amuſement, ne'er amuſe.
An *Author* ! 'Tis a venerable-name !
How few deſerve it, and what numbers claim !
Unbleſt with ſenſe above their peers refin'd,
Who ſhall ſtand up, *dictators* to mankind ?
Nay, who dare *ſhine*, if not in *virtue*'s cauſe ?
That ſole proprietor of juſt applauſe.

Ye reſtleſs men, who pant for letter'd praiſe,
With whom would you conſult to gain the bays ?—
With thoſe great authors whoſe fam'd works you read ?
'Tis well : go, then, conſult the laurell'd ſhade.
What anſwer will the laurell'd ſhade return ?
Hear it, and tremble ! he commands you burn
The nobleſt works his envy'd genius writ,
That boaſt of nought more excellent than *wit*.
If this be true, as 'tis a truth moſt dread,
Woe to the page which has not *that* to plead !
Fontaine and *Chaucer*, dying, wiſh'd unwrote,
The ſprightlieſt efforts of their wanton thought :
Sidney and *Waller*, brighteſt ſons of fame,
Condemn the charm of ages to the flame :
And in one point is all true wiſdom caſt,
To think that *early* we muſt think *at laſt*.

Immortal wits, ev'n *dead*, break nature's laws,
Injurious ſtill to virtue's ſacred cauſe ;
And their guilt growing, as their bodies rot,
(Revers'd ambition !) pant to be *forgot*.

Thus ends your courted *fame :* does lucre then,
The ſacred *thirſt* of *gold*, betray your pen ?
In proſe 'tis blameable, in verſe 'tis worſe,
Provokes the muſe, extorts *Apollo*'s curſe :
His ſacred influence never ſhould be ſold ;
'Tis arrant *Simony* to ſing for gold :

'Tis

'Tis immortality fhould fire your mind;
Scorn a lefs paymafter than all mankind.
   If bribes you feek, know this, ye wriing tribe!
Who writes for virtue has the largeft bribe:
All's on the party of the virtuous man;
The good will furely ferve him, if they can;
The bad, when intereft, or ambition guide,
And 'tis at once their *intereft* and their *pride:*
But fhould both fail to take him to their care,
He boafts a *greater* friend, and both may fpare.
   Letters to man uncommon light difpenfe;
And what is virtue, but fuperior fenfe?
In parts and learning you who place your pride,
Your faults are crimes, *your* crimes are double-dy'd.
What is a fcandal of the firft renown,
But letter'd knaves, and *atheifts* in a gown?
   'Tis harder far to pleafe than give offence;
The leaft mifconduct damns the brighteft fenfe;
Each fhallow pate, that cannot read your name,
Can read your life, and will be proud to blame.
Flagitious manners make impreffions deep
On thofe, that o'er a page of *Milton* fleep:
Nor in their dulnefs think to fave your fhame,
True, thefe are fools; but wife men fay the fame.
   Wits are a defpicable race of men,
If they confine their talents to the pen;
When the man fhocks us, while the writer fhines,
Our fcorn in life, our envy in his lines.
Yet, proud of parts, with prudence fome difpenfe,
And play the fool, becaufe they're men of fenfe.
What inftances bleed recent in each thought,
Of men to ruin by their *genius* brought!
Againft their wills what numbers ruin fhun,
Purely through want of wit to be undone!

Nature

Nature has fhewn, by making it fo rare,
That *wit*'s a jewel which we need not wear.
Of plain found *fenfe* life's current coin is made;
With that we drive the moft fubftantial trade.

    Prudence protects and guides us; wit betrays;
A fplendid fource of ill ten thoufand ways;
A certain fnare to miferies immenfe;
A gay prerogative from common fenfe;
Unlefs ftrong judgment that wild thing can tame,
And break to paths of virtue and of fame.

    But grant your judgment equal to the beft,
Senfe fills your head, and genius fires your breaft;
Yet ftill forbear: your wit (confider well)
'Tis great to fhew, but greater to conceal;
As it is great to feize the golden prize
Of place or power; but greater to defpife.

    If ftill you languifh for an author's name,
Think private merit lefs than public fame,
And fancy not to write is not to live;
Deferve, and take, the great prerogative.
But ponder what it is; how dear 'twill coft,
To write one page which you may juftly boaft.

    Senfe may be good, yet not deferve the prefs;
Who write, an awful character profefs;
The world as pupil of their wifdom claim,
And for their ftipend an immortal fame:
Nothing but what is folid or refin'd,
Should dare afk public audience of mankind.

    Severely weigh your learning and your wit:
Keep down your pride by what is nobly writ:
No writer, fam'd in your own way, pafs o'er;
Much truft example, but reflection more:
More had the ancients writ, they more had taught;
Which fhews fome work is left for modern thought.

This

This weigh'd, perfection know; and, known, adore;
Toil, burn for that; but do not aim at more;
Above, beneath it, the juft limits fix;
And zealoufly prefer four lines to fix.
    Write, and re-write, blot out, and write again,
And for its *fwiftnefs* ne'er applaud your pen.
Leave to the jockeys that *Newmarket* praife,
Slow runs the *Pegafus* that wins the bays.
Much time for *immortality* to pay,
Is juft and wife; for *lefs* is thrown away.
Time only can mature the labouring brain;
Time is the father, and the midwife *pain*:
The fame good fenfe that makes a man excel,
Still makes him doubt he ne'er has written well.
Downright impoffibilities they feek;
What man can be immortal in a week?
    Excufe no *fault*; though beautiful, 'twill harm;
One fault fhocks more than twenty beauties charm.
Our age demands correctnefs; *Addifon*
And *you* this commendable hurt have done.
Now writers find, as once *Achilles* found,
The *whole* is mortal, if a *part's* unfound.
    He that *ftrikes out*, and ftrikes not out the *beft*,
Pours luftre in, and dignifies the reft:
Give e'er fo little, if what's right be there,
We praife for what you *burn*, and what you *fpare*:
The part you burn, fmells fweet before the fhrine,
And is as incenfe to the part divine.
    Nor *frequent* write, though you can do it well;
Men may too *oft*, though not too *much*, excel.
A few good works gain fame; more fink their price;
Mankind are fickle, and hate paying twice:
They granted you writ well, what can they more,
Unlefs you let them praife for giving o'er?

Do

Do *boldly* what you do, and let your page
Smile, if it fmiles, and if it rages, rage.
So faintly *Lucius* cenfures and commends,
That *Lucius* has no foes, except his friends.

Let *fatire* lefs engage you than *applaufe* ;
It fhews a gen'rous mind to wink at flaws :
Is genius yours ? be yours a glorious end,
Be your *king's, country's, truth's, religion's* friend ;
The public glory by your own beget ;
Run nations, run pofterity, in debt.
And fince the fam'd alone make others **live**,
Firft *have* that glory you prefume to *give*.

If fatire charms, ftrike faults, but fpare the man :
'Tis dull to be as witty as you can.
Satire recoils whenever charg'd too high ;
Round your own fame the fatal fplinters fly.
As the foft plume gives fwiftnefs to the dart,
Good-breeding fends the fatire to the heart.

Painters and furgeons may the *ftructure* fcan ;
Genius and *morals* be with you the *man* :
Defaults in thofe alone fhould give offence !
Who ftrikes the *perfon*, pleads his innocence.
My narrow-minded fatire can't extend
To *Codrus'* form ; I'm not fo much his friend :
Himfelf fhould publifh that (the world agree)
Before his works, or in the pillory.
Let him be black, fair, tall, fhort, thin, or fat,
Dirty. or clean, I find no theme in that.
Is that call'd *humour ?* It has this pretence,
'Tis neither virtue, breeding, wit, or fenfe,
Unlefs you boaft the genius of a *Swift*,
Beware of *humour*, the dull rogue's *laft fhift*.

Can others write like you ? Your tafk give o'er,
'Tis printing what was publifh'd long before.

3   If

If nought peculiar through your labours run,
They're duplicates, and twenty are but one.
Think frequently, think clofe, read nature, turn
Mens manners o'er, and half your volumes burn;
To nurfe with quick reflection be your ftrife,
Thoughts born from prefent objects, warm from life:
When moft unfought, fuch infpirations rife,
Slighted by fools, and cherifh'd by the wife:
Expect peculiar fame from thefe alone;
Thefe make an author, thefe are all your own.

Life, like their bibles, coolly men turn o'er;
Hence unexperienc'd children of threefcore.
True, all men think of courfe, as all men dream;
And if they flightly think, 'tis much the fame.

Letters admit not of a half-renown;
They give you *nothing*, or they give a *crown*.
No work e'er gain'd *true* fame, or ever can,
But what did honour to the name of man.

Weighty the *fubject*, cogent the *difcourfe*,
Clear be the *ftyle*, the very *found* of force;
Eafy the *conduct*, fimple the *defign*,
Striking the *moral*, and the *foul* divine:
Let nature art, and judgment wit, exceed;
O'er learning reafon reign; o'er that, your *Creed*:
Thus *virtue's feeds*, at once, and *laurel's*, grow;
Do thus, and rife a *Pope*, or a *Defpreau*:
And when your genius exquifitely fhines,
Live up to the full luftre of your lines:
Parts but expofe thofe men who virtue quit;
A fallen angel is a fallen wit;
And they plead *Lucifer's* detefted caufe,
Who for bare talents challenge our applaufe.
Would you reftore juft honours to the pen?
From able writers *rife* to worthy men.

N 4

" Who's this with nonsense, nonsense would restrain ?
" Who's this (they cry) so vainly schools the vain ?
" Who damns our trash, with so much trash replete ?
" As, three ells round, huge *Cheyne* rails at meat ?"
   Shall I with *Bavius* then my voice exalt,
And challenge all mankind to find one fault ?
With huge *Examens* overwhelm my page,
And darken reason with dogmatic rage ?
As if, one tedious volume writ in rhime,
In prose a duller could excuse the crime :
Sure, next to writing, the most idle thing
Is gravely to harangue on what we sing.
   At that tribunal stands the writing tribe,
Which nothing can intimidate or bribe :
Time is the judge ; *Time* has nor friend nor foe ;
False fame *must* wither, and the true *will* grow.
Arm'd with this truth, all critics I defy ;
For if I fall, by my *own* pen I die ;
While snarlers strive with proud but fruitless pain,
To *wound immortals*, or to *slay the slain*.
   Sore prest with danger, and in awful dread
Of twenty pamphlets levell'd at my head,
Thus have I forg'd a buckler in my brain,
Of recent form, to serve me this campaign :
And safely hope to quit the dreadful field
Delug'd with ink, and sleep behind my shield ;
Unless dire *Codrus* rouses to the fray
In all his might, and damns me—for a day.
   As turns a flock of geese, and, on the green,
Poke out their foolish necks in awkward spleen,
(Ridiculous in rage !) to *hiss*, not *bite*,
So war their quills, when *sons* of *dulness* write.

A P A R A.

A

PARAPHRASE

ON PART OF THE

BOOK OF JOB.

A

PARAPHRASE

ON PART OF THE

BOOK OF JOB *.

THRICE happy Job † long liv'd in Regal State,
Nor faw the fumptuous Eaft a prince fo great;
Whofe worldly ftores in fuch abundance flow'd,
Whofe heart with fuch exalted virtue glow'd.

At

---

* It is difputed amongft the critics who was the author of the book of *Job*; fome give it to *Mofes*, fome to others. As I was engaged in this little performance, fome arguments occurred to me which favour the former of thofe opinions; which arguments I have flung into the following notes, where little elfe is to be expected.

† The Almighty's fpeech, chapter xxxviii, &c. which is what I paraphrafe in this little work, is by much the fineft part of the nobleft and moft ancient Poem in the world. Bifhop *Patrick* fays, its grandeur is as much above all other poetry, as thunder is louder than a whifper. In order to fet this diftinguifhed part of the poem in a fuller light, and give the reader a clearer conception of it, I have
abridged

At length misfortunes take their turn to reign,
And ills on ills succeed; a dreadful train!
What now but deaths, and poverty, and wrong,
The sword wide-wasting, the reproachful tongue,
And spotted plagues, that mark'd his limbs all o'er
So thick with pains, they wanted room for more?
A change so sad what mortal heart could bear?
Exhausted woe had left him nought to fear;
But gave him all to grief. Low earth he prest,
Wept in the dust, and sorely smote his breast.
His friends around the deep affliction mourn'd,
Felt all his pangs, and groan for groan return'd;
In anguish of their hearts their mantles rent,
And sev'n long days in solemn silence spent;
A debt of rev'rence to distress so great!
Then Job contain'd no more; but curs'd his fate.

abridged the preceding and subsequent parts of the poem, and joined
them to it; so that this piece is a sort of an epitome of the whole
book of *Job*.

I use the word *paraphrase*, because I want another which might
better answer to the uncommon liberties I have taken. I have
omitted, added, and transposed. The *mountain*, the *comet*, the *sun*, and
other parts, are entirely added: those upon the *peacock*, the *lion*, &c.
are much enlarged; and I have thrown the whole into a method
more suited to our notions of regularity. The judicious, if they com-
pare this piece with the original, will, I flatter myself, find the rea-
sons for the great liberties I have indulged myself in through the
whole.

Longinus has a chapter on interrogations, which shews that they
contribute much to the sublime. This speech of the Almighty is
made up of them. Interrogation seems indeed the proper style of
majesty incensed. It differs from other manner of reproof, as bid-
ding a person execute himself, does from a common execution; for
he that asks the guilty a proper question, makes him, in effect, pass
sentence on himself.

His

His day of birth, its inaufpicious light
He wifhes funk in fhades of endlefs night,
And blotted from the year; nor fears to crave
Death, inftant death; impatient for the grave,
That feat of blifs, that manfion of repofe,
Where reft and mortals are no longer foes;
Where counfellors are hufh'd, and mighty kings
(O happy turn!) no more are wretched things.

   His words were daring, and difpleas'd his friends;
His conduct they reprove, and he defends;
And now they kindled into warm debate,
And fentiments oppos'd with equal heat;
Fix'd in opinion, both refufe to yield,
And fummon all their reafon to the field:
So high at length their arguments were wrought,
They reach'd the laft extent of human thought:
A paufe enfu'd.—When, lo! Heav'n interpos'd,
And awfully the long contention clos'd.
Full o'er their heads, with terrible furprize,
A fudden whirlwind blackened all the fkies:
(They faw, and trembled * !) From the darknefs broke
A dreadful voice, and thus th' Almighty fpoke.

   Who gives his tongue a loofe fo bold and vain,
Cenfures my conduct, and reproves my reign?

---

* The book of *Job* is well known to be dramatic, and, like the tragedies of old *Greece*, is fiction built on truth. Probably this moft noble part of it, the Almighty fpeaking out of the whirlwind (fo fuitable to the after-practice of the *Greek* ftage, when there happened *dignus vindice nodus*) is fictitious; but is a fiction more agreeable to the time in which *Job* lived, than to any fince. Frequent before the Law were the appearances of the Almighty after this manner, *Exod.* c. xix. *Ezek.* c. i. &c. Hence is He faid to *dwell in thick darknefs: And have his way in the whirlwind.*

Lifts up his thoughts againſt me from the duſt,
And tells the World's Creator what is juſt ?
Of late ſo brave, now lift a dauntleſs eye,
Face my demand, and give it a reply :
Where did'ſt Thou dwell at nature's early birth ?
Who laid foundations for the ſpacious *earth* ?
Who on its ſurface did extend the line,
Its form determine, and its bulk confine ?
Who fix'd the corner-ſtone ? What hand, declare,
Hung it on nought, and faſten'd it on air ;
When the bright morning ſtars in concert ſung,
When heav'ns high arch with loud hoſannas rung ;
When ſhouting ſons of God the triumph crown'd,
And the wide concave thunder'd with the ſound ?
Earth's num'rous *kingdoms*, haſt Thou view'd them all ?
And can thy ſpan of knowledge graſp the ball ?
Who heav'd the *mountain*, which ſublimely ſtands,
And caſts its ſhadow into diſtant lands ?

   Who, ſtretching forth his ſceptre o'er the *deep*,
Can that wide world in due ſubjection keep ?
I broke the globe, I ſcoop'd its hollow'd ſide,
And did a baſon for the floods provide ;
I chain'd them with my word ; the boiling ſea,
Work'd up in tempeſts, hears my great decree ;
" * Thus far, thy floating tide ſhall be convey'd ;
" And here, O main, be thy proud billows ſtay'd."

* There is a very great air in all that precedes, but this is ſignally
ſublime. We are ſtruck with admiration to ſee the vaſt and ungo-
vernable ocean receiving commands, and punctually obeying them ;
to find it like a managed horſe, raging, toſſing, and foaming, but
by the rule and direction of its maſter. This paſſage yields in ſubli-
mity to that of *Let there be light*, &c. ſo much only, as the abſolute
government of nature yields to the creation of it.

   The like ſpirit in theſe two paſſages is no bad concurrent argu-
ment, that *Moſes* is author of the book of *Job*.

Haſt

Haſt thou explor'd the *ſecrets* of the deep,
Where, ſhut from uſe, uanumber'd treaſures ſleep ?
Where, down a thouſand fathoms from the day,
Springs the great fountain, mother of the ſea ?
Thoſe gloomy paths did thy bold foot e'er tread,
Whole worlds of waters rolling o'er they head ?
  Hath the cleft *centre* open'd wide to Thee ?
Death's inmoſt chambers didſt Thou ever ſee ?
E'er knock at his tremendous gate, and wade
. To the black portal through th' incumbent ſhade ?
Deep are thoſe ſhades ; but ſhades ſtill deeper hide
My counſels from the ken of human pride.
  Where dwells the *light ?* In what refulgent dome ?
And where has *darkneſs* made her diſmal home ?
Thou know'ſt, no doubt, ſince thy large heart is fraught
With ripen'd wiſdom, through long ages brought ;
Since nature was call'd forth when Thou waſt by,
And into being roſe beneath thine eye !
  Are *miſts* begotten ? Who their father knew ?
From whom deſcend the pearly drops of dew ?
To bind the ſtream by night, what hand can boaſt,
Or whiten morning with the hoary *froſt ?*
Whoſe pow'rful breath, from northern regions blown,
Touches the ſea, and turns it into ſtone ?
A ſudden deſart ſpreads o'er realms defac'd,
And lays one half of the creation waſte ?
  Thou know'ſt Me not ; Thy blindneſs cannot ſee
How vaſt a diſtance parts thy God from Thee.
Canſt Thou in *whirlwinds* mount aloft ? Canſt Thou
In clouds and darkneſs wrap thy awful brow ?
And, when day triumphs in meridian light,
Put forth thy hand, and ſhade the world with night ?
  Who launch'd the *clouds* in air, and bid them roll
Suſpended ſeas aloft, from pole to pole ?

Who

Who can refresh the burning sandy plain,
And quench the summer with a waste of rain?
Who, in rough desarts, far from human toil,
Made rocks bring forth, and desolation smile?
There blooms the rose, where human face ne'er shone,
And spreads its beauties to the sun alone.

   To check the show'r, who lifts his hand on high,
And shuts the sluices of th' exhausted sky,
When earth no longer mourns her gaping veins,
Her naked mountains, and her russet plains;
But, new in life, a chearful prospect yields
Of shining rivers, and of verdant fields;
When groves and forests lavish all their bloom,
And earth and heav'n are fill'd with rich perfume?
 Hast Thou e'er scal'd my wintry skies, and seen
Of *hail* and *snows* my northern magazine?
These the dread treasures of mine anger are,
My funds of vengeance for the day of war,
When clouds rain death, and storms, at my command,
Rage through the world, or waste a guilty land.

   Who taught the rapid *winds* to fly so fast,
Or shakes the centre with his eastern blast?
Who from the skies can a whole deluge pour?
Who strikes through nature with the solemn roar
Of dreadful *thunder*, points it where to fall,
And in fierce *lightning* wraps the flying ball?
Not he who trembles at the darted fires,
Falls at the sound, and in the flash expires.

   Who drew the *comet* out to such a size,
And pour'd his flaming train o'er half the skies?
Did Thy resentment hang him out? Does he
Glare on the nations, and denounce, from Thee?

   Who on low earth can moderate the rein,
That guides the *stars* along th' ethereal plain?

Appoint

Appoint their feafons, and direct their courfe,
Their luftre brighten, and fupply their force?
Canft Thou the fkies benevolence reftrain,
And caufe the *Pleiades* to fhine in vain?
Or, when *Orion* fparkles from his fphere,
Thaw the cold feafon, and unbind the year?
Bid *Mazzaroth* his deftin'd ftation know,
And teach the bright *Arcturus* where to glow?
Mine is the *night*, with all her ftars; I pour
Myriads, and myriads I referve in ftore.

Doft Thou pronounce where day-light fhall be born,
And draw the purple curtain of the morn;
Awake the *fun*, and bid him come away,
And glad *thy* world with his obfequious ray?
Haft Thou, inthron'd in flaming glory, driv'n
Triumphant round the fpacious ring of heav'n?
That pomp of light, what hand fo far difplays,
That diftant earth lies bafking in the blaze?

Who did the *foul* with her rich powers inveft,
And light up reafon in the human breaft?
To fhine, with frefh increafe of luftre, bright,
When ftars and fun are fet in endlefs night?
To thefe my various queftions make reply.
Th' Almighty fpoke; and, fpeaking, fhook the fky.

What then, *Chaldæan* Sire, was thy furprize!
Thus Thou, with trembling heart, and down-caft eyes:
" Once and again, which I in groans deplore,
" My tongue has err'd; but fhall prefume no more.
" My voice is in eternal filence bound,
" And all my foul falls proftrate to the ground."

He ceas'd: When, lo! again th' Almighty fpoke;
The fame dread voice from the black whirlwind broke.

Can that arm meafure with an arm divine?
And canft thou thunder with a voice like Mine?

Or in the hollow of thy hand contain
The bulk of waters, the wide-spreading main,
When, mad with tempests, all the billows rise
In all their rage, and dash the distant skies?

   Come forth, in beauty's excellence array'd;
And be the grandeur of thy pow'r display'd;
Put on omnipotence, and, frowning, make
The spacious round of the creation shake;
Dispatch thy vengeance, bid it overthrow
Triumphant vice, lay lofty tyrants low,
And crumble them to dust. When This is done,
I grant thy safety lodg'd in Thee alone;
Of Thee Thou art, and may'st undaunted stand
Behind the buckler of thine own right-hand.

   Fond man! the vision of a moment made!
Dream of a dream! and shadow of a shade!
What worlds hast Thou produc'd, what creatures fram'd;
What insects cherish'd, that thy God is blam'd?
When * pain'd with hunger, the wild *Raven's* brood
Loud calls on God, importunate for food,
Who hears their cry, who grants their hoarse request,
And stills the clamour of the craving nest?

   Who in the stupid *Ostrich* † has subdu'd
A parent's care, and fond inquietude?

While

---

* Another argument that *Moses* was the author, is, that most of the creatures here mentioned are *Egyptian*. The reason given why the raven is particularly mentioned as an object of the care of Providence, is, because by her clamorous and importunate voice, she particularly seems always calling upon it; thence *κοράσσω a κόρεξ,* Ælian. l. ii. c. 48. is *to ask earnestly.* And since there were ravens on the bank of the *Nile* more clamorous than the rest of that species, those probably are meant in that place.

  † There are many instances of this bird's stupidity: Let two
suffice.

While far she flies, her scatter'd eggs are found,
Without an owner, on the sandy ground;
Cast out on fortune, they at mercy lie,
And borrow life from an indulgent sky:
Adopted by the sun, in blaze of day,
They ripen under his prolific ray.
Unmindful she, that some unhappy tread
May crush her young in their neglected bed.
* What time she skims along the field with speed,
† She scorns the rider, and pursuing steed.

How

suffice. *First*, it covers its head in the reeds, and thinks itself all
out of sight,

 – – – – – – – – *Stat lumine clauso*
Ridendum revoluta caput, creditque latere
Quæ non ipsa videt – – – – – – – – – Claud.

Secondly, They that go in pursuit of them, draw the skin of an
Ostrich's neck on one hand, which proves a sufficient lure to take
them with the other.

They have so little brain, that *Heliogabalus* had six hundred heads
for his supper.

Here we may observe, that our judicious as well as sublime au_
thor, just touches the great points of distinction in each creature,
and then hastens to another. A description is exact when you can_
not *add*, but what is common to another thing; nor *withdraw*, but
something peculiarly belonging to the thing described. A *likeness* is
lost in too much description, as a *meaning* often in too much
illustration.

* Here is marked another *peculiar* quality of this creature, which
neither flies nor runs directly, but has a motion composed of both,
and using its wings as sails, makes great speed.

 Vasta velut Libyæ venantûm vocibus ales
 Cum premitur, calidas cursu trassmittit arenas,
 Inque modum veli sinuatis flamine pennis
 Pulverulenta volat – – – – – – Claud. in Eutr.

† *Xenophon* says, *Cyrus* had horses that could overtake the goat and

the

How rich the *Peacock!* * what bright glories run
From plume to plume, and vary in the fun!
He proudly fpreads them, to the golden ray
Gives all his colours, and adorns the day;
With confcious ftate the fpacious round difplays,
And flowly moves amid the waving blaze.

    Who taught the *Hawk* to find, in feafons wife,
Perpetual fummer, and a change of fkies?
When clouds deform the year, fhe mounts the wind,
Shoots to the fouth, nor fears the ftorm behind;
The fun returning, fhe returns again,
Lives in his beams, and leaves ill days to men.

    Tho' ftrong the *Hawk* †, tho' practis'd well to fly,
An *Eagle* drops her in a lower fky;
An *Eagle*, when, deferting human fight,
She feeks the fun in her unweary'd flight:
Did thy command her yellow pinion lift
So high in air, and fet her on the clift,
Where far above *thy* world fhe dwells alone,
And proudly makes the ftrength of rocks her own;

the wild afs; but none that could reach this creature. A thoufand
golden ducats, or a hundred camels, was the ftated price of a horfe
that could equal their fpeed.

    * Though this bird is but juft mentioned in my author, I could
not forbear going a little farther, and fpreading thofe beautiful
plumes (which are there fhut up) in half a dozen lines. The cir-
cumftance I have marked of his opening his plumes to the fun is
true: *Expandit colores adverfo maxime fole, quia fic fulgentius radiant.*
Plin. l. x. c. 20.

    † *Thyanus (de Re Accip.)* mentions a hawk that flew from *Paris* to
London in a night.

    And the *Egyptians*, in regard to its fwiftnefs, made it their fym-
bol for the wind; for which reafon we may fuppofe the hawk, as
well as the crow *above*, to have been a bird of note in *Egypt*.

Thence

* Thence wide o'er nature takes her dread furvey,
And with a glance predeftinates her prey?
She feafts her young with blood; and, hov'ring o'er
Th' unflaughter'd hoft, enjoys the *pramis'd* gore.

† Know'ft Thou how many moons, by Me affign'd,
Roll o'er the mountain *Goat*, and foreft *Hind*,
While pregnant they a mother's load fuftain?
They bend in anguifh, and caft forth their pain.
Hale are their young, from human frailties freed;
Walk unfuftain'd, and unaffifted feed;
They live at once; forfake the dam's warm fide;
Take the wide world, with nature for their guide;
Bound o'er the lawn, or feek the diftant glade;
And find a home in each delightful fhade.

Will the tall *Reem*, which knows no Lord but Me,
Low at the crib, and afk an alms of thee;
Submit his unworn fhoulder to the yoke,
Break the ftiff clod, and o'er thy furrow fmoke?
Since great his ftrength, go truft him, void of care;
Lay on his neck the toil of all the year;

---

* The eagle is faid to be of fo acute a fight, that when fhe is fo high in air that man cannot fee her, fhe can difcern the fmalleft fifh under water. My author accurately undeiftood the nature of the creatures he defcribes, and feems to have been a Naturalift as well as a Poet, which the next note will confirm.

† The meaning of this queftion is, Knoweft thou the *time and cu-cumftances* of their bringing forth? For to know the time only was eafy, and had nothing extraordinary in it; but the circumftances had fomething peculiarly expreffive of God's Providence, which makes the queftion proper in this place. *Pliny* obfervcs, that the hind with young is by inftinct directed to a certain herb called *Sefehs*, which facilitates the birth. Thunder alfo (which looks like the more im- mediate hand of Providence) has the fame effect. *Pf.* xxix. In fo early an age to obferve thefe things, may ftile our author a Naturalift.

Bid

Bid him bring home the feafons to thy doors,
And caft his load among thy gather'd ftores.
　　Didft thou from fervice the *Wild-Afs* difcharge,
And break his bonds, and bid him live at large,
Through the wide wafte, his ample manfion, roam,
And lofe himfelf in his unbounded home ?
By nature's hand magnificently fed,
His meal is on the range of mountains fpread ,
As in pure air aloft he bounds along,
He fees in diftant fmoke the city throng ;
Confcious of freedom, fcorns the fmother'd train,
The threat'ning driver, and the fervile rein.
　　Survey the warlike *Horfe!* didft Thou inveft
With thunder, his robuft diftended cheft ?
No fenfe of fear his dauntlefs foul allays ;
'Tis dreadful to behold his noftrils blaze ;
To paw the vale he proudly takes delight,
And triumphs in the fulnefs of his might ;
High-rais'd he fnuffs the battle from afar,
And burns to plunge amid the raging war ;
And mocks at death, and throws his foam around,
And in a ftorm of fury fhakes the ground.
How does his firm, his rifing heart, advance
Full on the brandifh'd fword, and fhaken lance ;
While his fix'd eye-balls meet the dazzling fhield,
Gaze, and return the lightning of the field !
He finks the fenfe of pain in gen'rous pride,
Nor feels the fhaft that trembles in his fide ;
But neighs to the fhrill trumpet's dreadful blaft
Till death ; and when he groans, he groans his laft.
　　But, fiercer ftill, the lordly *Lion* ftalks,
Grimly majeftic in his lonely walks ;
When round he glares, all living creatures fly ;
He clears the defart with his rolling eye.

3

Say,

Say, mortal, does he rouse at thy command,
And roar to 'Thee, and live upon thy hand?
Doft thou for him in forefts bend thy bow,
And to his gloomy den the morfel throw,
Where bent on death lie hid his tawny brood,
And, couch'd in dreadful ambufh, pant for blood;
Or, ftretch'd on broken limbs, confume the day,
In darknefs wrapt, and flumber o'er their prey?
* By the pale moon they take their deftin'd round,
And lafh their fides, and furious tear the ground.
Now fhrieks, and dying groans, the defart fill;
They rage, they rend; their rav'nous jaws diftil
With crimfon foam; and, when the banquet's o'er,
They ftride away, and paint their fteps with gore;
In flight alone the fhepherd puts his truft,
And fhudders at the talon in the duft.

Mild is my *Behemoth*, though large his frame;
Smooth is his temper, and repreft his flame,
While unprovok'd. This native of the flood
Lifts his broad foot, and puts afhore for food;
Earth finks beneath him, as he moves along
To feek the herbs, and mingle with the throng.
See with what ftrength his harden'd loins are bound,
All over proof and fhut againft a wound.
How like a mountain cedar moves his tail!
Nor can his complicated finews fail.
Built high and wide, his folid bones furpafs
The bars of fteel; his ribs are ribs of brafs;
His port majeftic, and his armed jaw,
Give the wide foreft, and the mountain, law.

* Purfuing their prey by night is true of moft wild beafts, parti-
cularly the lion. *Pf.* cvi. 20. The *Arabians* have one among their
500 names for the lion, which fignifies *the hunter by moonfhine.*

The

The mountains feed him; there the beasts admire
The mighty stranger, and in dread retire;
At length his greatness nearer they survey,
Graze in his shadow, and his eye obey,
The fens and marshes are his cool retreat,
His noontide shelter from the burning heat;
Their sedgy bosoms his wide couch are made,
And groves of willows give him all their shade.

 His eye drinks *Jordan* up, when fir'd with drought,
He trusts to turn its current down his throat;
In lessen'd waves it creeps along the plain:
* He sinks a river, and he thirsts again.

 † Go to the *Nile*, and, from its fruitful side,
Cast forth thy line into the swelling tide:
With slender hair *Leviathan* command,
And stretch his vastness on the loaded strand.
Will he become Thy servant? Will he own
Thy lordly nod, and tremble at Thy frown?
Or with his sport amuse thy leisure day,
And, bound in silk, with thy soft maidens play?

 Shall pompous banquets swell with such a prize?
And the bowl journey round his ample size?

---

* *Cephei glaciale caput quo suetus anhelam*
 Ferre sitim Python, amnemque avertere ponto.
        Stat. Theb. v. 349.
 Qui spiris tegeret montes, hauriret hiatu
 Flumina, &c.   Claud. Pref. in Ruf.

Let not then this hyperbole seem too much for an eastern poet, though some commentators of name strain hard in this place for a new construction, through fear of it.

 † The taking the crocodile is most difficult. *Diodorus* says, they are not to be taken but by iron nets. When *Augustus* conquered *Egypt*, he struck a medal, the impress of which was a crocodile chained to a palm-tree, with this inscription, *Nemo antea religavit.*

                Or

Or the debating merchants share the prey,
And various limbs to various marts convey ?
Thro' his firm skull what steel its way can win ?
What forceful engine can subdue his skin ?
Fly far, and live; tempt not his matchless might :
The bravest shrink to cowards in his sight;
* The rashest dare not rouse him up : Who then
Shall turn on Me, among the sons of men ?

   Am I a debtor ? Hast thou ever heard
Whence come the gifts that are on Me conferr'd ?
My lavish fruit a thousand vallies fills,
And Mine the herds, that graze a thousand hills :
Earth, sea, and air, All nature is my own ;
And stars and sun are dust beneath my throne.
And dar'st Thou with the World's great Father vie,
Thou, who dost tremble at my creature's eye ?

   At full my huge *Leviathan* shall rise,
Boast all his strength, and spread his wond'rous size.
Who, great in arms, e'er stripp'd his shining mail,
Or crown'd his triumph with a single scale ?
Whose heart sustains him to draw near ? † Behold,
Destruction yawns; his spacious jaws unfold,
And, marshal'd round the wide expanse, disclose
Teeth edg'd with death, and crowding rows on rows :
What hideous fangs on either side arise !
And what a deep abyss between them lies !

---

  * This alludes to a custom of this creature, which is, when sated
with fish, to come ashore and sleep among the reeds.

  † The crocodile's mouth is exceeding wide. When he gapes,
says *Pliny, sit totum os. Martial* says to his old woman,

        Cùm comparata rictibus tuis ora
        Nihacus habet crocodilus angusta.

So that the expression there is barely just.

Mete with thy lance, 'and with thy plummet found,
The one how long, the other how. profound.

His bulk is charg'd with such a furious soul,
That clouds of smoke from his spread nostrils roll,
As from a furnace ; and, when rous'd his ire,
  * Fate issues from his jaws in streams of fire.
The rage of tempests, and the roar of seas,
Thy terror, this thy great Superior please ;
Strength on his ample shoulder sits in state ;
His well-join'd limbs are dreadfully complete ;
His flakes of solid flesh are slow to part ;
As steel his nerves, as adamant his heart.

When, late awak'd, he rears him from the floods,
And, stretching forth his stature to the clouds,
Writhes in the sun aloft his scaly height,
And strikes the distant hills with transient light,
Far round are fatal damps of terror spread,
The Mighty fear, nor blush to own their dread.

  † Large is his front ; and, when his burnish'd eyes
Lift their broad lids, the morning seems to rise.

                              In

---

* This too is nearer truth than at first view may be imagined.
The crocodile, say the naturalists, lying long under water, and being
there forced to hold its breath, when it emerges, the breath long
represt is hot, and bursts out so violently, that it resembles fire and
smoke. The horse suppresses not his breath by any means so long,
neither is he so fierce and animated ; yet the most correct of poets
ventures to use the same metaphor concerning him.

    Collectumque premens *volvit sub naribus* ignem.

By this and the foregoing note I would caution against a false opi-
nion of the eastern boldness, from passages in them ill under-
stood.

  † *His eyes are like the eye-lids of the morning.* I think this gives us as
great an image of the thing it would express, as can enter the
                                   thought

In vain may death in various shapes invade,
The swift-wing'd arrow, the descending blade;
His naked breast their impotence defies;
The dart rebounds, the brittle fauchion flies.
Shut in himself, the war without he hears,
Safe in the tempest of their rattling spears;
The cumber'd strand their wasted vollies strow;
His sport, the rage and labour of the foe.

His pastimes like a cauldron boil the flood,
And blacken ocean with the rising mud;
The billows feel him, as he works his way;
His hoary footsteps shine along the sea;
The foam high-wrought, with white divides the green,
And distant sailors point where death has been.

thought of man. It is not improbable that the *Egyptians* stole their hieroglyphic for the morning, which is the crocodile's eye, from this passage, though no commentator, I have seen, mentions it. It is easy to conceive how the *Egyptians* should be both readers and admirers of the writings of *Moses*, whom I suppose the author of this poem.

I have observed already that three or four of the creatures here described are *Egyptian*; the two last are notoriously so, they are the river-horse and the crocodile, those celebrated inhabitants of the *Nile*; and on these two it is that our author chiefly dwells. It would have been expected from an author more remote from that river than *Moses*, in a catalogue of creatures produced to magnify their Creator, to have dwelt on the two largest works of his hand, *viz.* the elephant and the whale. This is so natural an expectation, that some commentators have rendered *behemoth* and *leviathan*, the elephant and whale, though the descriptions in our author will not admit of it; but *Moses* being, as we may well suppose, under an immediate terror of the *hippopotamos* and crocodile, from their daily mischiefs and ravages around him, it is very accountable why he should permit them to take place.

His

. His like earth bears not on her ſpacious face:
Alone in nature ſtands his dauntleſs race,
For utter ignorance of fear renown'd,
In wrath he rolls his baleful eye around:
Makes ev'ry ſwoln, diſdainful heart, ſubſide,
And holds dominion o'er the ſons of pride.

 Then the *Chaldæan* eas'd his lab'ring breaſt,
With full conviction of his crime oppreſt.

 " Thou can'ſt accompliſh All things, Lord of Might:
" And ev'ry thought is naked to Thy ſight.
" But, oh! Thy ways are wonderful, and lie
" Beyond the deepeſt reach of mortal eye.
" Oft have I heard of Thine Almighty Pow'r;
" But never ſaw Thee till this dreadful hour.
" O'erwhelm'd with ſhame, the Lord of life I ſee,
" Abhor myſelf, and give my ſoul to Thee.
" Nor ſhall my weakneſs tempt Thine anger more:
" Man is not made to *queſtion*, but *adore*."

OCEAN.

O C E A N,

A N

O D E.

O C E A N.

A N

O D E.

Let the sea make a noise, let the floods clap their hands.
Psal. xcviii.

I.

SWEET rural scene!
Of *flocks* and *green!*
At careless ease my limbs are spread;
All nature still,
But yonder rill;
And list'ning pines nod o'er my head:

II.

In prospect wide,
The boundless *tide!*
Waves cease to foam, and winds to roar;
Without a breeze,
The curling seas
Dance on, in *measure* to the shore.

III. Who

III.

Who fings the *fource*
Of *wealth* and *force* ?
Vaft field of commerce, and big *war,*
Where *wonders* dwell !
Where *terrors* fwell !
And *Neptune* thunders from his car ?

IV.

Where ? Where are they,
Whom *Pæan*'s ray
Has touch'd, and bid divinely rave ?——
What ! none afpire ?
I fnatch the lyre,
And plunge into the foaming wave.

V.

The wave refounds !
The rock rebounds !
The *Nereids* to my fong reply !
I lead the choir,
And they confpire,
With voice and fhell, to lift it high.

VI.

They fpread in air
Their bofoms fair,
Their verdant treffes pour behind :
The billows beat
With nimble feet,
With notes triumphant fwell the wind.

VII. Who

VII.

Who love the fhore,
Let thofe adore
The God *Apollo,* and his *Nine,*
Parnaffus' hill,
And *Orpheus'* fkill;
But let *Arion's* harp be mine.

VIII.

The main! the main!
Is *Britain's* reign;
Her ftrength, her glory, is her *fleet:*
The main! the main!
Be *Britain's* ftrain;
As *Tritons* ftrong, as *Syrens* fweet.

IX.

Thro' nature wide
Is nought defcry'd
So rich in pleafure or furprize;
When all-ferene,
How *fweet* the fcene!
How *dreadful,* when the billows rife;

X.

And ftorms deface
The fluid glafs,
In which ere-while *Britannia* fair
Look'd down with pride,
Like *Ocean's* bride,
Adjufting her majeftic air!

XI.

When tempefts ceafe,
And, hufh'd in peace,
The flatten'd furges fmoothly fpread,
Deep filence keep,
And feem to fleep
Recumbent on their oozy bed;

XII.

With what a trance,
The level glance,
Unbroken, fhoots along the feas!
Which tempt from fhore
The painted oar;
And every canvas courts the breeze!

XIII.

When rufhes forth
The frowning *north*
On black'ning billows, with what dread
My fhuddering foul
Beholds them roll,
And hears their roarings o'er my head!

XIV.

With terror, mark
Yon flying *bark!*
Now center-deep defcend the brave;
Now, tofs'd on high,
It takes the fky,
A feather on the tow'ring wave!

XV. Now

XV.

Now spins around
In whirls profound:
Now whelm'd; now pendant near the clouds;
Now stunn'd, it reels
Midst thunders peals:
And now fierce lightning fires the shrouds.

XVI.

All Ether burns!
Chaos returns!
And blends, once more, the seas and skies:
No space between
Thy bosom green,
O deep! and the blue concave, lies.

XVII.

The northern blast,
The shatter'd mast,
The syrt, the whirlpool, and the rock,
The breaking spout,
The stars gone out,
The boiling streight, the monsters shock,

XVIII.

Let others fear;
To *Britain* dear
Whate'er promotes her daring claim;
Those terrors charm,
Which keep her warm
In chace of honest gain, or fame.

XIX.

The ſtars are bright
To chear the night,
And ſhed, thro' ſhadows, temper'd fire;
And *Phœbus'* flames,
With burniſh'd beams,
Which ſome *adore,* and all *admire.*

XX.

Are then the ſeas
Outſhone by *theſe?*
Bright *Thetis!* thou art not outſhone;
With kinder beams,
And ſofter gleams,
Thy boſom wears them as thy own.

XXI.

There, ſet in *green,*
Gold-ſtars are ſeen,
A mantle rich! thy charms to wrap;
And when the ſun
His race has run,
He falls enamour'd in thy lap.

XXII.

Thoſe *clouds,* whoſe dyes
Adorn the ſkies,
That ſilver *ſnow,* that pearly *rain,*
Has *Phœbus* ſtole
To grace the pole,
The plunder of th' invaded main!

XXIII. The

XXIII.

The gaudy *bow*,
Whofe colours glow,
Whofe arch with fo much fkill is bent,
To *Phœbus'* ray,
Which paints fo gay,
By thee the wat'ry woof was lent.

XXIV.

In chambers deep,
Where waters fleep,
What unknown treafures pave the floor!
The *pearl*, in rows,
Pale luftre throws;
The *wealth* immenfe, which ftorms devour.

XXV.

From *Indian* mines,
With proud defigns,
The merchant, fwoln, digs golden ore;
The tempefts rife,
And feize the prize,
And tofs him breathlefs on the fhore.

XXVI.

His fon complains
In pious ftrains,
" Ah cruel thirft of gold !" he cries;
Then ploughs the main,
In zeal for gain,
The tears yet fwelling in his eyes.

P 3   XXVII. Thou

XXVII.

Thou wat'ry vaſt !
What mounds are caſt
To bar thy dreadful flowings o'er !
Thy proudeſt foam
Muſt know its home;
But rage of gold diſdains a ſhore.

XXVIII.

Gold *pleaſure* buys ;
But pleaſure dies,
Too ſoon the groſs fruition cloys;
Tho' *raptures* court,
The *ſenſe* is ſhort;
But virtue kindles living joys;

XXIX.

Joys felt *alone !*
Joys aſk'd of none !
Which time's and fortune's arrows miſs !
Joys that ſubſiſt,
Tho' fates reſiſt,
An unprecarious, endleſs bliſs !

XXX.

The ſoul *refin'd*
Is moſt inclin'd
To every *moral* excellence;
All vice is dull,
A knave's a fool ;
And *virtue* is the child of *ſenſe.*

XXXI. The

XXXI.

The virtuous mind,
Nor *wave*, nor *wind*,
Nor civil rage, nor tyrant's frown,
The shaken ball,
Nor planet's fall,
From its firm basis can dethrone.

XXXII.

This *Britain* knows,
And therefore glows
With gen'rous passions, and expends
Her *wealth* and *zeal*
On public weal,
And brightens both by god-like ends.

XXXIII.

What end so great
As that which late
Awoke the genius of the *main*;
Which tow'ring rose
With GEORGE to close,
And rival great ELIZA's reign?

XXXIV.

A voice has flown
From *Britain*'s throne
To re-inflame a grand design;
That voice shall rear
Yon * *fabric fair*,
As nature's rose at the *divine*.

* A new fund for *Greenwich* hospital, recommended from the throne.

XXXV.

When nature fprung,
Bleft angels fung,
And fhouted o'er the rifing ball;
For ftrains as high
As man's can fly,
Thefe fea-devoted honours call.

XXXVI.

From boift'rous feas,
The lap of eafe
Receives our *wounded*, and our *old;*
High *domes* afcend!
Stretch'd *arches* bend!
Proud *columns* fwell! wide *gates* unfold!

XXXVII.

Here, foft-reclin'd,
From wave, from wind,
And fortune's tempeft fafe afhore,
To cheat their care,
Of former war
They talk the pleafing *fhadows* o'er.

XXXVIII.

In lengthen'd tales,
Our fleet prevails;
In tales the lenitives of *age ?*
And o'er the bowl,
They fire the foul
Of lift'ning *youth*, to martial rage.

XXXIX. Unhappy

XXXIX.

Unhappy they !
And falfly gay !
Who bafk for ever in fuccefs ;
A conftant feaft
Quite palls the tafte,
And long *enjoyment* is *diftrefs.*

· XL.

When, after toil,
His native foil
The panting *mariner* regains,
What *tranfport* flows
From bare *repofe !*
We reap our pleafure from our pains.

XLI.

Ye warlike flain !
Beneath the main,
Wrapt in a wat'ry winding fheet ;
Who bought with blood
Your country's good,
Your country's * *full-blown glory* greet.

XLII.

What pow'rful charm
Can death difarm ?
Your long, your iron flumbers break ?
By *Jove,* by *Fame,*
By GEORGE's name,
Awake ! awake ! awake ! awake !

* Written foon after King George the firft's acceffion.

XLIII. With

XLIII.

With fpiral fhell,
Full blafted, tell,
That all your wat'ry realms fhould ring;
Your *pearl*-alcoves,
Your *coral*-groves,
Should echo *theirs*, and *Britain's* king.

XLIV.

As long as ftars
Guide mariners,
As CAROLINA's virtues pleafe,
Or funs invite
The ravifh'd fight,
The *British* flag fhall fweep the feas.

XLV.

Peculiar both!
Our foil's *ftrong growth*,
And our bold natives' *hardy mind*;
Sure heaven befpoke
Our *hearts* and *oak*,
To give a mafter to mankind.

XLVI.

That nobleft birth
Of teeming earth,
Of forefts fair, that daughter proud,
To foreign coafts
Our grandeur boafts,
And *Britain's* pleafure fpeaks aloud:

XLVII.

Now big with *war,*
Sends fate from far,
If rebel realms their fate demand;
Now, fumptuous fpoils
Of foreign *foils*
Pours in the bofom of our land.

XLVIII.

Hence, Britain lays
In fcales, and weighs
The fate of kingdoms, and of kings;
And as fhe frowns,
Or fmiles, on crowns
A night, or day of *glory,* fprings.

XLIX.

'Thus *Ocean* fwells
The ftreams and rills,
And to their borders lifts them high;
Or elfe withdraws
The mighty caufe,
And leaves their famifh'd channels dry.

SEA-PIECE:

SEA-PIECE:

THE

DEDICATION.

TO

MR. VOLTAIRE.

I.

MY mufe, a bird of paffage, flies.
From frozen climes to milder fkies;
From chilling blafts fhe feeks thy chearing beam,
A beam of favour, *here* deny'd;
Confcious of faults, her blufhing pride
Hopes an afylum in fo great a name.

II.

* To dive full deep in *antient days,*
The *warrior's* ardent deeds to raife,
And *monarchs* aggrandize;—the glory, Thine;
Thine is the *drama,* how renown'd!
Thine, *Epic's* loftier trump to found;——
But let ARION's fea-ftrung harp be Mine:

* Annals of the emperor CHARLES XII, Lewis XIV.

III. But

III.

But where's his *dolphin?* Know'ft thou, where?——
May that be found in Thee, VOLTAIRE!
Save thou from harm my plunge into the wave:
How will thy name illuftrious raife
My finking fong! Mere *mortal* lays,
So patroniz'd, are refcu'd from the grave.

IV.

" Tell me," fay'ft thou, " who courts my fmile?
" What ftranger ftray'd from yonder ifle?"——
No ftranger, Sir! though born in foreign climes;
On *Dorfet* downs, when MILTON's page,
With *Sin* and *Death*, provok'd thy rage,
Thy rage provok'd, *who* footh'd with gentle rhymes?

V.

Who kindly couch'd thy cenfure's eye,
And gave thee clearly to defcry
Sound judgment giving law to fancy ftrong?
Who half inclin'd thee to confefs,
Nor could thy modefty do lefs,
That MILTON's blindnefs lay not in his fong?

VI.

But fuch debates long fince are flown;
For ever fet the funs that fhone
On airy paftimes, ere our brows were grey:
How fhortly fhall we Both forget,
To thee my patron, I my debt,
And thou to thine, for *Pruffia's* golden key.

3   VII. The

VII.

The present, in oblivion caft,
Full foon fhall fleep, as fleeps the paft;
Full foon the wide diftinction die between
The frowns, and favours of the great;
High-flufh'd fuccefs, and pale defeat;
The Gallic gaiety, and British fpleen.

VIII.

Ye wing'd, ye rapid moments! ftay:——
Oh friend! as deaf as rapid, they;
Life's little drama done, the curtain falls!——
Doft thou not hear it? I can hear,
Though nothing ftrikes the liftening ear;
Time groans his laft! ETERNAL loudly calls!

IX.

Nor calls in vain; the call infpires
Far other counfels, and defires,
Than once prevail'd; we ftand on higher ground:
What fcenes we fee!——Exalted aim!
With ardors new, our fpirits flame;
Ambition bleft! with more than laurels crown'd.

A

SEA-PIECE.

ODE THE FIRST.

THE BRITISH SAILOR'S EXULTATION.

I.

IN lofty founds let thofe delight,
 Who brave the foe, but fear the fight;
And bold in word, of arms decline the ftroke:
 'Tis mean to boaft; but great to lend
 To foes the counfel of a friend,
And warn them of the vengeance they provoke.

II.

 From whence arife thefe loud alarms?
 Why gleams the *fouth* with brandifh'd arms?
War, bath'd in blood, from curft ambition fprings:
 Ambition, mean! ignoble pride!
 Perhaps their ardors may fubfide,
When weigh'd the wonders *Britain*'s failor fings.

III. Hear,

III.

Hear, and revere.—At *Britain*'s nod,
From each enchanted grove and wood,
Haftes the huge *oak*, or fhadelefs foreft leaves;
The mountain *pines* affume new forms,
Spread canvas-wings, and fly through ftorms,
And ride o'er rocks, and dance on foaming waves.

IV.

She *nods* again: The labouring earth
Difclofes a tremendous birth;
In fmoaking rivers runs her molten ore;
Thence, monfters of enormous fize,
And hideous afpect, threat'ning rife,
Flame from the deck, from trembling baftions roar.

V.

Thefe minifters of fate fulfil,
On empires wide, an *ifland*'s will,
When thrones unjuft wake vengeance: Know, ye pow'rs!
In fudden night, and ponderous balls,
And floods of flame, the tempeft falls,
When brav'd *Britannia*'s awful fenate low'rs.

VI.

In her * grand council fhe furveys,
In patriot picture, what may raife,
Of infolent attempts, a warm difdain;
From hope's triumphant fummit thrown,
Like darted lightning, fwiftly down
The wealth of *Ind*, and confidence of *Spain*.

* Houfe of Lords.

Q 2

VII. *Bri-*

VII.

Britannia sheaths her courage keen,
And spares her nitrous magazine;
Her *cannon* slumber, till the proud aspire,
And leave all law below them; then *they* blaze!
They thunder from resounding seas,
Touch'd by their injur'd master's soul of fire.

VIII.

Then furies rise! the battle raves!
And rends the skies! and warms the waves!
And calls a tempest from the peaceful deep,
In spite of nature, spite of JOVE,
While all-serene, and hush'd above,
Tumultuous winds in azure chambers sleep.

IX.

A thousand deaths the bursting bomb
Hurls from her disembowel'd womb;
Chain'd, glowing globes, in dread alliance, join'd,
Red-wing'd by strong, sulphureous blasts,
Sweep, in black whirlwinds, men and masts;
And leave sing'd, naked, blood-drown'd, decks behind.

X.

Dwarf laurels rise in tented fields;
The wreath immortal *ocean* yields;
There war's whole sting is shot, whole fire is spent,
Whole glory blooms: How pale, how tame,
How lambent is BELLONA's flame;
How her storms languish on the continent!

XI. From

XI.

From the dread front of *antient* war
Lefs terror frown'd; her fcythed car,
Her caftled elephant, and batt'ring beam,
Stoop to thofe engines which deny
Superior terrors to the fky,
And boaft their clouds, their thunder, and their flame.

XII.

The flame, the thunder, and the cloud,
The night by day, the fea of blood,
Hofts whirl'd in air, the yell of finking throngs,
The gravelefs dead, an *ocean* warm'd,
A firmament by mortals ftorm'd,
To patient *Britain*'s angry brow belongs.

XIII.

Or do I dream? Or do I rave?
Or fee I.Vulcan's footy cave,
Where Jove's red bolts the giant brothers frame?
Thofe fwarthy gods of *toil* and *heat*,
Loud peals on mountain anvils beat,
And panting tempefts rouze the roaring flame.

XIV.

Ye fons of *Ætna!* hear my call;
Unfinifh'd let thofe baubles fall,
Yon fhield of Mars, Minerva's helmet blue:
Your ftrokes fufpend, ye brawny throng!
Charm'd by the magic of my fong,
Drop the feign'd thunder, and attempt the true.

Q 3   XV. Begin:

XV.

Begin : * And, firſt, take rapid *flight*,
　　Fierce *flame*, and clouds of thickeſt *night*,
And ghaſtly *terror*, paler than the dead ;
　　Then, borrow from the north his *roar*,
　　Mix *groans*, and *deaths* ; one *phial* pour
Of wrong'd *Britannia*'s wrath ; and it is made ;
Gaul ſtarts, and trembles,—at your dreadful trade.

* Alluding to VIRGIL's deſcription of thunder.

ODE

ODE THE SECOND.

IN WHICH IS

THE SAILOR'S *PRAYER* BEFORE ENGAGEMENT.

I.

SO form'd the bolt, ordain'd to break
    Gaul's haughty plan, and *Bourbon* shake;
If *Britain*'s crimes support not *Britain*'s foes,
    And edge their swords: O Pow'r Divine!
    If blest by Thee the bold design,
Embattled hosts a single arm o'erthrows.

II.

Ye warlike dead, who fell of old
    In *Britain*'s cause, by fame enroll'd
In deathless annal! deathless deeds inspire;
    From oozy beds, for *Britain*'s sake,
    Awake, illustrious chiefs! awake;
And kindle in your sons paternal fire.

III.

The day commission'd from Above,
    Our worth to weigh, our hearts to prove,
If war's full shock too *feeble* to sustain;
    Or *firm* to stand its final blow,
    When vital streams of blood shall flow,
And turn to crimson the discolour'd main;

Q 4   IV. *That*

IV.

That day's arriv'd, that fatal hour !———
" Hear us, O hear, Almighty Pow'r !
" Our guide in counsel, and our strength in fight !
" Now war's important die is thrown,
" If left the day to man alone,
" How blind is wisdom, and how weak is might !

V.

" Let prostrate hearts, and awful fear,
" And deep remorse, and sighs sincere
" For *Britain's* guilt, the wrath divine appease ;
" A wrath, more formidable far
" Than angry nature's wasteful war,
" The whirl of tempests, and the roar of seas.

VI.

" From out the deep, to Thee we cry,
" To Thee, at nature's helm on high !
" Steer Thou our conduct, dread OMNIPOTENCE !
" To Thee for succour we resort ;
" Thy favour is our only port ;
" Our only rock of safety, thy defence.

VII.

" O Thou, to whom the lions roar,
" And, not unheard, thy boon implore !
" Thy throne our bursts of cannon loud invoke :
" Thou canst arrest the flying ball ;
" Or send it back, and bid it fall
" On those, from whose proud deck the thunder broke.

VIII. " *Britain,*

VIII.

" *Britain*, in vain, extends her care
" To climes * remote, for aids in war;
" Still farther muſt it ſtretch to cruſh the foe;
" There's one alliance, one alone,
" Can crown her arms, or fix her throne;
" And that alliance is not found below.

IX.

" ALLY SUPREME ! we turn to Thee;
" We learn obedience from the ſea;
" With ſeas, and winds, henceforth, thy laws fulfil;
" 'Tis Thine our blood to freeze, or warm;
" To rouze, or huſh, the martial ſtorm;
" And turn the tide of conqueſt, at thy will.

X.

" 'Tis Thine to beam ſublime renown,
" Or quench the glories of a crown;
" 'Tis Thine to doom, 'tis Thine from death to free;
" To turn aſide his levell'd dart,
" Or pluck it from the bleeding heart:——
" *There* we caſt anchor, we confide in THEE.

XI.

" THOU, who haſt taught the *north* to roar,
" And ſtreaming † lights nocturnal pour
" Of frightful aſpect ! when proud foes invade,
" Their blaſted pride with dread to ſeize,
" Bid *Britain's* flags, as meteors, blaze;
" And GEORGE depute to thunder in thy ſtead.

* Ruſſia.   † Aurora Borealis.

XII. " The

XII.

" The *right* alone is bold, and strong;
" Black, hovering clouds appall the *wrong*
' With dread of vengeance: Nature's awful Sire!
" Less than one moment shouldst Thou frown,
" Where is puissance, and renown?
' Thrones tremble, empires sink, or worlds expire.

XIII.

" Let GEORGE the just chastise the vain:
" THOU, who dost curb the rebel main,
" To mount the shore when boiling billows rave!
" Bid GEORGE repel a bolder tide,
" The boundless swell of *Gallic* pride;
" And check *ambition's* overwhelming wave.

XIV.

" And when (all milder means withstood)
" *Ambition,* tam'd by loss of blood,
" Regains her reason; then, on angels wings,
" Let *peace* descend, and shouting greet,
" With peals of joy, *Britannia's* fleet,
" How richly freighted! It, triumphant, brings
" The poise of kingdoms, and the fate of kings."

BUSIRIS,

B U S I R I S,

KING OF EGYPT.

A

T R A G E D Y.

ACTED AT THE

THEATRE-ROYAL IN DRURY-LANE.

1 7 1 9.

O triſte planè acerbumque funus ! O morte ipſâ mortis tem-
pus indignius ! Jam deſtinata erat egregio juveni, jam
electus nuptiarum dies ; quod gaudium, quo mœrore muta-
tum eſt ?　　　　　　　　　　　　　　PLIN. Epiſt.

PROLOGUE.

BY A FRIEND.

SPOKEN BY MR. BOOTH.

LONG have you seen the Greek *and* Roman *names,*
   Affifted by the mufe, renew their fame,
While yet unfung thofe heroes fleep, from whom
Greece *form'd her* Plato's, *and her* Cæfars Rome.
   Such, Egypt, *were thy fons ! divinely great*
In arts, in arms, in wifdom, and in ftate.
Her early monarchs gave fuch glories birth,
Their ruins are the wonders of the earth.
Structures fo vaft by thofe great kings defign'd,
Are but faint fketches of their boundlefs mind :
Yet ne'er has Albion's *fcene, though long renown'd,*
With the ftern tyrants of the Nile *been crown'd.*
   The tragic mufe in grandeur fhould excel,
Her figure blazes, and her numbers fwell.
The proudeft monarch of the proudeft age,
From Egypt *comes to tread the* Britifh *ftage:*

Old

Old Homer's *heroes, moderns are to those*
Whom this night's venerable scenes disclose.
   Here pomp and splender serves but to prepare:
To touch the soul is our peculiar care;
By just distress soft pity to impart,
And mend your nature, while we move your heart;
Nor would these scenes in empty words abound,
Or overlay the sentiment with sound.
When passion rages, eloquence is mean;
Gestures and looks best speak the moving scene.
   Ye shining Fair! when tender woes invite
To pleasing anguish and severe delight,
By your affliction you compute your gain,
And rise in pleasure as you rise in pain.
If then just objects of concern are shown,
And your hearts heave with sorrows not your own,
Let not the gen'rous impulse be withstood,
Strive not with nature; blush not to be good:
Sighs only from a nobler temper rise,
And 'tis your virtue swells into your eyes.

D R A M A T I S

DRAMATIS PERSONÆ.

M E N.

BUSIRIS, King of *Egypt*,	Mr. ELRINGTON.
MYRON, the Prince,	Mr. BOOTH.
NICANOR, Father of *Mandane*,	Mr. MILLS.
MEMNON,	Mr. WILKS.
RAMESES, Conspirators,	Mr. WALKER.
SYPHOCES,	Mr. THURMOND.
PHERON,	Mr. WILLIAMS.
AULETES, a Courtier,	Mr. W. MILLS.

W O M E N.

MYRIS, Queen of *Egypt*,	Mrs. THURMOND.
MANDANE,	Mrs. OLDFIELD.

SCENE, a Temple at MEMPHIS, in *Old Egypt*.

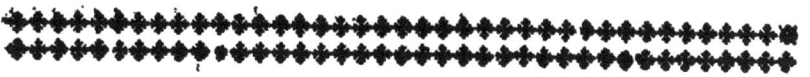

BUSIRIS,

KING OF EGYPT.

ACT I.   SCENE I.

Enter PHERON *and* SYPHOCES.

SYPHOCES.

IF glorious ſtructures, and immortal deeds,
  Enlarge the thought, and ſet our ſouls on fire,
My tongue has been too cold in *Egypt*'s praiſe,
The queen of nations, and the boaſt of times,
Mother of ſcience, and the houſe of gods !
Scarce can I open wide my lab'ring mind
To comprehend the vaſt idea, big
With arts and arms, ſo boundleſs in their fame.

PHERON.

Thrice happy land ! did not her dreadful king,
Far-fam'd *Buſiris,* whom the world reveres,
Lay all his ſhining wonders in diſgrace,
By cruelty and pride ?

SYPHOCES.

SYPHOCES.

By pride indeed ;

He calls himself The *Proud*, and glories in it,
Nor would exchange for *Jupiter's Almighty*.
Have we not seen him shake his silver reins
O'er harness'd monarchs to his chariot yok'd?
In sullen majesty they stalk along,
With eyes of indignation and despair,
While he aloft displays his impious state,
With half their rifled kingdoms o'er his brow,
Blazing to heaven in diamonds and gold.

PHERON.

Nor less the tyrant's cruelty than pride ;
His horrid altars stream with human blood,
And piety is murder in his hands.   [*A great shout.*

SYPHOCES.

There rose the voice of twice two hundred thousand,
And broke the clouds, and clear'd the face of day ;
The king, who from his temple's airy height,
With heart dilated, that great work surveys,
Who shall proclaim what can be done by man,
Has struck his purple streamer, and descends.

PHERON.

Twice ten long years have seen that haughty pile,
Which nations with united toil advance,
Gain on the skies, and labour up to heaven.

SYPHOCES.

The king——or prostrate fall, or disappear.   [*Exeunt.*

Enter BUSIRIS, *attended.*

BUSIRIS.

This antient city, *Memphis* the renown'd,
Almost coæval with the Sun himself,
And boasting strength scarce sooner to decay,

How

How wanton fits fhe amid nature's fmiles;
Nor from her higheft turret has to view,
But golden landfcapes and luxuriant fcenes;
A wafte of wealth, the ftorehoufe of the world !
Here, fruitful vales, far-ftretching, fly the fight;
There, fails unnumber'd whiten all the ftream;
While from the banks full twenty thoufand cities
Survey their pride, and fee their gilded towers
Float on the waves, and break againft the fhore :
To crown the whole, this rifing pyramid

.[*Shews the plan.*

Lengthens in air, and ends among the ftars;
While every other object fhrinks beneath
Its mighty fhade, and leffens to the view,
As kings compar'd with me.

Enter AULETES. *He falls proftrate.*

AULETES.
O live for ever,

Bufiris, firft of men !

BUSIRIS.
Auletes, rife.

AULETES.
Embaffadors from various climes arrive,
To view your wonders, and to greet your fame;
Each loaden with the gifts his country yields,
Of which the meaneft rife to gold and pearl;
The rich *Arabian* fills his ample vafe
With facred incenfe ; *Ethiopia* fends
A thoufand courfers fleeter than the wind;
And their black riders darken all the plain :
Camels and elephants from other realms,
Bending beneath a weight of luxury,

VOL. I.   R   Bring

Bring the beft feafons of their various years,
And leave their monarchs poor.

BUSIRIS.

What from the *Perfian?*

AULETES.

He bends before your throne, and far outweighs
The reft in tribute, and outfhines in ftate.

BUSIRIS.

Away; he fees me not; I know his purpofe;
A fpy upon my greatnefs, and no friend:
Take his Embaffador, and fhew him *Egypt;*
In *Memphis* fhew him various nations met,
As in a fea, yet not confin'd in fpace,
But ftreaming freely through the fpacious ftreet,
Which fend forth millions at each brazen gate,
Whene'er the trumpet calls; high over-head
On the broad walls the chariots bound along,
And leave in air a thunder of my own:
Jove too has pour'd the *Nile* into my hand,
The prince of rivers, Ocean's eldeft fon:
Rich of myfelf, I make the fruitful year,
Nor afk precarious plenty from the fky——
Throw all my glories open to his view,
Then tell him, in return for trifles offer'd,
I give him *this,* and when a *Perfian* arm

[Gives him a bow.

Can thus with vigour its reluctance bend,
And to the nerve its ftubborn force fubdue;
Then let his mafter think of arms—but bring
More men than yet e'er pour'd into the field;
Mean time, thank heaven, our tide of conqueft drives
A different way, and leaves him ftill a king:
This to the *Perfian.*——I receive the reft.

And

And give the world an anſwer.   [*Exit* Buſiris.

MANDANE, *attended by prieſts and her virgins, is ſeen*
ſacrificing at a diſtance.

An hymn to ISIS *is ſung. The prieſts go out.*

MANDANE, *attended by her maids, advances.*
MANDANE.

My morning duty to the gods is over,
Yet ſtill this terror hangs upon my ſoul,
And ſaddens every thought——I ſtill behold
The dreadful image ; ſtill the threat'ning ſword
Points at my breaſt, and glitters in mine eye. ——
But 'twas a dream ; no more.   My virgins, leave me:
And thou, great Ruler of the World, be preſent !
O kindly ſhine on this important hour !
This hour determines all my future life,
And gives it up to miſery or joy.   [*She advances,*
Theſe lonely walks, this deep and ſolemn gloom,
Where noon-day ſuns but glimmer to the view,
This houſe of tears, and manſion of the dead,
For ever hides him from the hated light,
And gives him leave to groan.

Back ſcene draws, and ſhews MEMNON *leaning on his*
father's tomb.

                                   Was ever ſcene
So mournful ! If, my lord, the dead alone
Are all your care, life is no more a bleſſing.
How could you ſhun me for this diſmal ſhade,
And ſeek from love a refuge in deſpair ?
MEMNON.
Why haſt thou brought thoſe eyes to this ſad place,
Where darkneſs dwells, and grief would ſigh ſecure

In welcome horrors and beloved night ?
Thy beauties drive thy friendly fhades before them,
And light up day e'en here.   Retire, my love ;
Each joyful moment I would fhare with thee,
My virtuous maid, but I would mourn alone.

MANDANE.

What have you found in me fo mean, to hope
That while you figh, my heart can be at peace ?
Your forrows flow from your *Mandane*'s eyes.

MEMNON.

O my *Mandane* !

MANDANE.

Wherefore turn you from me ?
Have I offended, or are you unkind ? ——
Ah me !. a fight as ftrange, as pitiful !
From this big heart, o'ercharg'd with gen'rous forrow,
See the tide working upward to his eye,
And ftealing from him in large filent drops,
Without his leave !—can thofe tears flow in vain ?

MEMNON.

Why will you double my diftrefs, and make
My grief my crime, by difcompofing you.——
And yet I can't forbear ! Alas, my father !
That name excufes all ; what is not due
To that great name, which life or death can pay ?

MANDANE.

Speak on, and eafe your lab'ring breaft : It fwells
And finks again ; and then it fwells fo high,
It looks as it would break.   I know 'tis big
With fomething you would utter.   Oft in vain
I have prefum'd to afk your mournful ftory ;
But ever have been anfwered with a frown.

MEMNON.

O my *Mandane* ! did my tale concern

3

· Myfelf

Myfelf alone, it would not lie conceal'd;
But 'tis wrapt up in guilt, in royal guilt,
And therefore 'tis unfafe to touch upon it:
To tell my tale is to blow off the afhes
From fleeping embers, which will rife in flames
At the leaft breath, and fpread deftruction round.
But thou art faithful, and my other felf;
And, O! my heart this moment is fo full,
It burfts with its complaints; and I muft fpeak.
  Myris, the prefent queen, was only fifter
Of great *Artaxes*, our late royal lord:
Bufiris, who now reigns, was firft of males
In lineal blood, to which this crown defcends.
Not with long circumftance to load my ftory,
Ambitious *Myris* fir'd his daring foul,
And turn'd his fword againft her brother's life:
Then mounting to the tyrant's bed and throne,
Enjoy'd her fhame, and triumph'd in her guilt.

MANDANE.

So black a ftory well might fhun the day.

MEMNON.

Artaxes' friends (a virtuous multitude)
Were fwept away by banifhment or death,
In throngs, and fated the devouring grave.
My father!——Think, *Mandane*, on your own,
And pardon me!——   [*Weeps.*
The tyrant took me, then of tender years,
And rear'd me with a fon (a fon fince dead).
He vainly hop'd, by fhews of guilty kindnefs,
To wear away the blacknefs of his crime,
And reconcile me to my father's fate;
Hence have I long been forc'd to ftay my vengeance
To fmooth my brow with fmiles, and curb my tongue,
While the big woe lies throbbing at my heart.——

Enter PHERON *at a distance.*

PHERON. [*Aside.*]

So close! so loving!—Here I stand unseen,
And watch my rival's fate.

MEMNON.

But thou, my fair;
Thou art my peace in tumult, life in death;
Thou yet canst make me bless'd,

MANDANE.

As how, my lord?

MEMNON,

Ah! why wilt thou insult me?

MANDANE.

Memnon————

MEMNON.

Speak!

MANDANE.

Nature forbids; and when I would begin,
She stifles all my spirits, and I faint:
My heart is breaking, but I cannot speak.
O let me fly.——

MEMNON.

You pierce me to the soul. [*Holding her.*

MANDANE.

O! spare me for a moment, till my heart
Regains its wonted force, and I will speak——
Pheron, you know, is daily urgent with me,
Breaks through restraints, and will not be refused.

[Pheron *shews a great concern.*

Yet more: The prince, the young impetuous prince,
Before his father sent him forth to war,
And gave the *Mede* to his destructive sword,
Has often taught his tongue a silken tale,

Descended

Defcended from himfelf, and talk'd of love.
Since laft I faw thee, his licentious paffion
Has haunted all my dreams————
This day the court fhines forth in all its luftre,
To welcome her returning warrior home;
Alas, the malice of our ftars!

MEMNON.

To place it
Beyond the power of fate to part our loves;
Be this our bridal night, my life!—my foul!   [*Embrace.*

PHERON.

Perdition feize them both! and have I lov'd
So long, to catch her in another's arms!
Another's arms for ever! O the pang!
Heart-piercing fight!—but rage fhall take its turn—
It fhall be fo—and let the crime be his
Who drives me to the black extremity;
I fear no farther hell than that I feel.   [*Exit.*

MEMNON.

Trembling I grafp thee, and my anxious heart
Is ftill in doubt if I may call thee mine.
O blifs too great! O painful ecftafy!
I know not what to utter.

MANDANE.

Ah, my lord!
What means this damp that comes athwart my joy,
Chaftifing thus the lightnefs of my heart?——
I have a father, and a father too,
Tender as nature ever fram'd.   His will
Should be confulted.   Should I touch his peace,
I fhould be wretched in my *Memnon*'s arms.

MEMNON.

Talk not of wretchednefs.

MANDANE.

                      Alas! this day
First gave me birth, and (which is strange to tell)
The fates e'er since, as watching its return,
Have caught it as it flew, and mark'd it deep
With something great; extremes of good or ill.

MEMNON.

Why should we bode misfortune to our loves?
No; I receive thee from the gods, in lieu
Of all that happiness they ravish'd from me;
Fame, freedom, father, all return in thee.
Had not the gods *Mandane* to bestow,
They never would have pour'd such vengeance on me;
They meant me thee, and could not be severe.
Soon as night's favourable shades descend,
The holy priest shall join our hands for ever,
And life shall prove but one long bridal-day.
Till then, in scenes of pleasure lose thy grief,
Or strike the lute, or smile among the flowers,
They'll sweeter smell, and fairer bloom for thee.—
Alas! I'm torn from this dear tender side,
By weighty reasons, and important calls;
Nay, e'en by love itself—I quit thee now,
But to deserve thee more.   [*They embrace.*

MANDANE.

        Your friends are here.   [*Exit* Mand.

MEMNON. ·

Excellent creature! how my soul pants for thee!
But other passions now begin their claim;
Doubt, and disdain, and sorrow, and revenge,
With mingling tumult, tear up all my breast:
O how unlike the softnesses of love!

                                 Enter

Enter SYPHOCES.

SYPHOCES.

Hail, worthy *Memnon*.

MEMNON.

Welcome, my *Sophoces*.
And much I hope thou bring'ſt a bleeding heart;
A heart that bleeds for others miſeries,
Bravely regardleſs of its own, though great;
That firſt of characters.

SYPHOCES.

And there's a ſecond,
Not far behind; to reſcue the diſtreſs'd,
Or die.

MEMNON.

Yes, die; and viſit thoſe brave men,
Who, from the firſt of time, have bath'd their hands
In tyrants' blood, and graſp'd their honeſt ſwords
As part of their own being, when the cauſe,
The public cauſe demanded. O my friend!
How long ſhall *Egypt* groan in chains? How long
Shall her ſons fall in heaps without a foe?
No war, plague, famine, nothing but *Buſiris*,
His people's father! and the ſtate's defence!
Yet but a remnant of the land ſurvives.

SYPHOCES.

What havock have I ſeen? Have we not known
A multitude become a morning's prey,
When troubled reſt, or a debauch, has ſour'd
The monſter's temper? Then 'tis inſtant death;
Then fall the brave and good, like ripen'd corn
Before the ſweeping ſcythe; not the poor mercy
To ſtarve and pine at leiſure in their chains.——
But what freſh hope, that we receive your ſummons
To meet you here this morning?

MEMNON.

MEMNON.

　　　　　　Know, *Syphoces*,
'Twas on this day my warlike father's blood,
So often lavish'd in his country's cause,
And greatly sold for conquest and renown;
'Twas on this execrable day it flow'd
On his own pavement, in a peaceful hour,
Smok'd in the dust, and wash'd a ruffian's feet.
This guilty day returning, rouses all
My smother'd rage, and blows it to a flame.
Where are our friends?

SYPHOCES.

　　　　　　At hand. *Ramesès*,
Last night, when gentle rest o'er nature spread
Her still command, and care alone was waking,
Like a dum, lonely, discontented, ghost,
Enter'd my chamber, and approach'd my bed:
With bursts of passion, and a peal of groans,
He recollects his godlike brother's fate,
The drunken banquet, and the midnight murder,
And urges vengeance on the guilty prince.
Such was the fellness of his boiling rage,
Methought the night grew darker as he frown'd.

MEMNON.

I know he bears the prince most deadly hate;
But this will enter deeper in his soul;　　[*Shews a letter.*
And rouse up passions, which till now have slept:
Murder will look like innocence to this.

SYPHOCES.

How, *Memnon?*

MEMNON.

　　　　　　This reminds me of thy fate;
The queen has courted thee with proffer'd realms,
And sought by threats to bend thee to her will;

　　3　　　　　　　　　　　　　　　　　　She

She languishes, she burns, she wastes away
In fruitless hopes, and dies upon thy name.

SYPHOCES.

O fatal love! which, stung by jealousy,
Expell'd a life far dearer than my own,
By cursed poison.—Ah divine *Apame*!
And could the murd'ress hope she should inherit
This heart, and fill thy place within these arms?—
But grief shall yield—Revenge, I'm wholly thine!

MEMNON.

The tyrant too is wanton in his age,
He shews that all his thoughts are not in blood;
Love claims its share; he envies poor *Rameses*
The softness of his bed; and thinks *Amelia*
A mistress worthy of a monarch's arms.

SYPHOCES.

But see, *Rameses* comes; a sullen gloom
Scowls on his brow, and marks him through the dusk.

Enter RAMESES, PHERON, *and other conspirators.*

MEMNON.

To what, my friend, shall *Memnon* bid you welcome?
To tombs, and melancholy scenes of death?
I have no costly banquets, such as spread
Prince *Myron's* table, when your brother fell.

[*To* Rameses.

I have no gilded roof, no gay apartment,
Such as the queen prepar'd for thee, *Syphoces*.
Yet be not discontent, my valiant friends,
Busiris reigns, and 'tis not out of season
To look on aught may mind us of our fate:
His sword is ever drawn, and furious *Myris*
Thinks the day lost that is not mark'd with blood.

RAMESES.

RAMESES.

And have we felt a tyrant twenty years,
Felt him as the raw wound the burning steel;
And are we murmuring out our midnight curses,
Drying our tears in corners, and complaining?
Our hands are forfeited—Gods! strike them off.
No hands we need to fasten our own chains,
Our masters will do that; and we want souls
To raise them to an use more worthy men.

MEMNON.

Ruffles your temper at offences past?
Here then, to sting thee into madness.

[*Gives the Letter.* Rameses *reads.*]

RAMESES.

                    Oh!

SYPHOCES.

See how the struggling passions shake his frame!

RAMESES.

My bosom joy, that crowns my happy bed
With tender pledges of our mutual love,
Far dearer than my soul! and shall my wife,
The mother of my little innocents,
Be taken from us! Torn from me, from mine,
Who live but on her sight! And shall I hear
Her cries for succour, and not rush upon him?
My infant hanging at the neck upbraids me,
And struggles with his little arms to save her.—
These veins have still some gen'rous blood in store,
The dregs of those rich streams his wars have drain'd;
I'll giv't in dowry with her.

PHERON.

                    Well resolv'd:
A tardy vengeance shares the tyrant's guilt.

RAMESES.

RAMESES.

Let me embrace thee, *Pheron*; thou art brave,
And doſt diſdain the coldneſs of delay.
Curſe on the man that calls *Rameſes* friend,
And keeps his temper at a tale like this;
When rage and rancour are the proper virtues,
And loſs of reaſon is the mark of men.

MEMNON.

Thus I've determin'd: When the midnight hour
Lulls this proud city, and her monarch dreams
Of humbler foes, or his new miſtreſs' love,
Then we will ruſh at once, let looſe the terrors
Of rage pent in, and ſtruggling twenty years
To find a vent, and at one dreadful blow
Begin and end the war.
A more auſpicious junĉture could not happen..
The *Perſian*, who for years has join'd our counſels,
Stirr'd up the love of freedom, and in private
Long nurs'd that glorious appetite with gold,
This morn with tranſport ſnatch'd the wiſh'd occaſion
Of throwing his reſentment wide, and now
He frowns in arms, and gives th' event to fate.

RAMESES.

This hand ſhall drag the tyrant from the throne,
And ſtab the royal viĉtim on this altar.

[Pointing to the tomb.

MEMNON.

O juſtly thought! Friends, caſt your eyes around;
All that moſt awful is, or great in nature,
This ſolemn ſcene preſents; the gods are here,
And here our fam'd forefathers' ſacred tombs;
Who never brook'd a tyrant in this land.
Let us not aĉt beneath the grand aſſembly!
The ſlighted altars tremble, and theſe tombs

Send

Send forth a peal of groans to urge us on.
Come then, furround my father's monument,
And call his fhade to witnefs to your vows.

RAMESES.

Nor his alone. O all ye mighty dead !
Illuftrious fhades ! who nightly ftalk around
The tyrant's couch, and fhake his guilty foul ;
Whether already you converfe with gods,
Or ftray below in melancholy glooms,
From earth, from air, from heav'n, and even hell,
Come, I conjure you, by the pris'ner's chain,
The widow's fighing, and the orphan's tears,
The virgin's fhrieks, the hero's fpouting veins,
By gods blafphem'd, and free-born men enflav'd.

MEMNON.

Hear, *Jove !* and you moft injur'd heroes, hear,
While we o'er this thrice-hallow'd monument
Thus join our hands, and, kneeling to the gods,
Faft bind our fouls to great revenge !

ALL.

We fwear——

MEMNON.

This night the tyrant and his minions bleed.

PHERON. [*Afide.*]

So, now my foe is taken in the toil,
And I've a fecond caft for this proud maid——
It is an oath well fpent, a perjury
Of good account in vengeance, and in love.

MEMNON.

We wrong the mighty dead, if we permit
Our eyes alone to count this grand affembly :
A thoufand unfeen heroes walk among us ;
My father rifes from his tomb; his wounds
Bleed all afrefh, and confecrate the day :

He

He waves his arm, and chides our tardy vengeance:
More than this world shall thank us.   O my friends!
Such our condition, we have nought to lose;
   And great may be our gain, if this be great,
   To crush a Tyrant, and preserve a State;
   To still the clamours of our fathers blood,
   To fix the basis of the Public good,
   To leave a fame eternal; then to soar,
   Mix with the gods, and bid the world adore.

A C T

A C T II.

S C E N E I.

The Palace.

*A magnificent throne difcovered, and feveral courtiers walk-
ing to and fro.*

Enter SYPHOCES *and* RAMESES. *Shouts at a diflance.*

RAMESES.

WHAT means this duft and tumult in the court,
 Thefe ftreamers fooling in the wind, thefe fhouts,
The tyrant blazing in full infolence,
And all his gaudy courtiers bafking round him,
Like pois'nous vermin in a dog-day fun ?
SYPHOCES.
Your father and prince *Myron* are arriv'd,
And with one peal of joy the nation rings.
RAMESES.
Long has my father ferv'd this tyrant king,
With zeal well worthy of a better caufe.
Though with his helm he hides a hoary brow,
Long vers'd in death, the father of the field,
At the fhrill trumpet he throws off the weight
Of fourfcore years, and fprings upon the foe.
The tranfport danger gives him, conquers nature,
And a fhort youth boils up within his veins.
SYPHOCES.
Behold this way they pafs to meet the king.

MYRON

MYRON *and* NICANOR *paſs the ſtage with attendants.*

RAMESES. [*Looking on* Myron.]

What pity 'tis that one ſo loſt in guilt,
Should thus engage the fight with manly charms,
And make vice lovely!

SYPHOCES.

Pardon me, *Rameſes :*

Though to my *foe,* I muſt be ever juſt.
He's gen'rous, grateful, affable, and brave :
But then he knows no limit to his paſſion ;
The tempeſt beaten bark is not ſo toſs'd
As is his reaſon, when thoſe winds ariſe :
And though he draws a fatal ſword in battle,
And kindles in the warm purſuit of fame,
Pleaſure ſubdues him quite ; the ſparkling eye,
And gen'rous bowl, bear down his graver mind,
While fiery ſpirits dance along his veins,
And keep a conſtant revel in his heart.

RAMESES.

But here the tyrant comes !—With what exceſs
Of idle pride will he receive his ſon!
How with big words will he ſwell out this conqueſt,
And into grandeur puff his little tales !

Enter KING, *and aſcends the throne ; on the other ſide,*
Enter MYRON *and* NICANOR.

KING.

Welcome, my ſon ; great partner of my fame ;
I thank thee for th' encreaſe of my dominions,
That now moie mountains riſe, more rivers flow,
And more ſtars ſhine in my ſtill-growing empire.
The ſun himſelf ſurveys it not at once,
But travels for the view, whilſt far disjoin'd
My ſubjects live unheard-of by each other ;

VOL. I.   S   Theſe

These wrapt in shades, whilst those enjoy the light;
Their day is various, but their king the same.

MYRON.

Here, Sir, your thanks are due; to this old arm,
Whose nerve not threescore winter camps unbend,
You owe your victory, and I my life.
When my fierce courser, with a jav'lin stung,
First rear'd in air, then tearing with a bound
The trembling earth, plung'd deep amidst the foe;
And now a thousand deaths from ev'ry side,
Had but one mark, and on my buckler rung;
Through the throng'd legions, like a tempest, rush'd
This friend, o'er gasping heroes, rolling steeds,
And snatch'd me from my fate.

BUSIRIS.

I thank thee, general;
Thou hast a heart that swells with loyalty,
And throws off the infection of these times;
But thy degenerate boy——

NICANOR.

No more my son;
I cut him off; my guilt, my punishment.
Look not, dread Sir, on me, through his offence;
O let not that discolour all my service,
And ruin those who blame him for his crimes.

BUSIRIS.

Old man, I will not wear the crown in vain;
Subjects shall work my will, or feel my pow'r;
Their disobedience shall not be my guilt.
Who is their welfare, glory, and defence?
The land that yields them food, and ev'ry stream
That slakes their thirst, the air they breathe, is mine.
And is concurrence to their own enjoyment
By due submission, a too great return?

Death

Death and deftruction are within my call——
But thou fhalt flourifh in thy mafter's fmile.
A faithful minifter adorns my crown,
And throws a brighter glory round my brow.

NICANOR.

Take but one more, one fmall one, to your favour,
And then my foul's at peace—I have a daughter,
An only daughter, now an only child,
Since her loft brother's folly; fhe deferves
The moft a father can for fo much goodnefs:
Her mother's dead, and we are left alone;
We two are the whole houfe; nor are we two;
In her I live, the comfort of my age;
And if the king extend his grace fo far,
And take that tender bloffom into fhelter,
Then I have all my monarch can beftow,
Or heav'n itfelf; but this, that I may wear
My life's poor remnant out in your command;
Stretch forth my being to the laft in duty,
And, when the fates fhall fummon, die for you.

BUSIRIS.

Nicanor, know, thy daughter is our care.

MYRON.

O, Sir, be greatly kind, exert your pow'r,
And with the monarch furnifh out the friend!——
Art thou not he, that gallant-minded chief,   [To Nic.
Who would not ftoop to give me lefs than life?
And fhall I prove ungrateful? Shocking thought!
He that's ungrateful, has no guilt but one;
All other crimes may pafs for virtues in him.

NICANOR.

What joy my daughter's promis'd welfare gives me,
My lips I need not open to difcover——
Thus humbly let me thank you.

BUSIRIS.

Dry thy tears,
And follow us; thy daughter's near our queen,
And longs, no doubt, to see thee: Bless the maid,
And then attend us on affairs of state.——
I hear, there's treason near us: Though the slaves
Fall off from their obedience, and deny
That I'm their monarch, I'm *Busiris* still:
  Collected in myself, I'll stand alone,
  And hurl my thunder, though I shake my throne:
  Like death, a solitary king I'll reign
  O'er silent subjects, and a desart plain;
  Ere brook their pride, I'll spread a gen'ral doom,
  And ev'ry step shall be from tomb to tomb.   [*Exit.*
            [Myr. *and* Aul. *who talk'd aside, advance.*

MYRON.

Her absent beauties glow'd upon my mind,
And sparkled in each thought.   She never left me—
Would'st thou believe it? In the field of battle,
In the mid terror, and the flame of fight.
Mandane, thou hast stol'n away my soul,
And left my fame in danger.—My rais'd arm
Has hung in air, forgetful to descend,
And, for a moment, spar'd the prostrate foe—
O that her birth rose equal to my own!
Then I might wed with honour, and enjoy
A lawful bliss——And why not now? Methinks
Absence has plac'd her in a fairer light,
Enrich'd the maid, and heighten'd ev'ry charm.

AULETES.

She comes!

MYRON.

That modest grace subdu'd my soul:

                                            That

That chaftity of look, which feem to hang
A veil of pureft light o'er all her beauties,
And by forbidding, moft inflames, defire.

[*Enter* MANDANE.

What tender force ! what dignity divine !
What virtue confecrating ev'ry feature !
Around that.neck, what drofs are gold and pearl !
Mandane ! pow'rful being, whofe firft fight
Gives me a tranfport not to be exprefs'd ;
And with one moment over-pays a year
Of danger, toil, and death, and abfence from thee.

MANDANE.

My lord, I fought my father.

MYRON.

Leave me not ;
I've much to fay ! much more than you conceive ;
Yes, by the gods, much more than I can utter :
My breath is fnatch'd ; I tremble ; I expire.   [*Afide.*
Nay, here I'll offer tender violence—   [*Takes her hand.*
May I not breathe my foul upon this hand ?
When your eyes triumph, and infult my pain,
Permit me here to take a fmall revenge.

MANDANE.

My lord, I am not confcious of my fault.

MYRON.

'Tis falfe—I know the language of thofe eyes ;
They ufe me ill—See my heart beat, *Mandane* ;
Believe not me, but tell yourfelf my paffion—
Is it in art to counterfeit within ?
To drive the fpirits, and inflame the blood ?
Each nerve is pierc'd with light'ning from your eye,
And every pulfe is in the throbs of love.

MANDANE.

My lord my duty calls ; I muft not ftay.

MYRON.

MYRON.

Give me a moment: I have that to ſpeak
Will burſt me, if ſuppreſſ—O heavenly maid!
Thy charms are doubled,—ſo is thy diſdain—
Who is it; tell me, who enjoys thy ſmile?
There is a happy man, I ſwear there is;
I know it by your coldneſs to your friend——
That thought has fix'd a ſcorpion on my heart,
That ſtings to death——And is it poſſible
You ever ſpoke of *Myron* in his abſence,
Or caſt at leiſure a light thought that way?

MANDANE.

I thought of you, my lord, and of my father,
And pray'd for your ſucceſs; nor muſt I now
Neglect to give him joy.

MYRON.

Yet ſtay; you ſhall not go——Ungrateful woman!
I would not wrong your father; but, by heav'n,
His love is hatred, if compar'd with mine.
I underſtand whence this unkindneſs flows;
Your heart reſents ſome licence of my youth,
When love had touch'd my brain.. You may forgive me
Becauſe I never ſhall forgive myſelf;
But that you live, I'd ruſh upon my ſword.
If you forgive me, I ſhall now approach,
Not as a lover only, but a wretch
Redeem'd from baſeneſs to the ways of honour,
And to my paſſion join my gratitude:
Each time I kneel before you, I ſhall riſe,
As well a better, as a happier, man,
Indebted to your virtue, and your love.

MANDANE.

I muſt not hear you.

3

MYRON.

O torment me not!
Hear me you muſt, and more—Your father's valour,
In the late battle, reſcu'd me from death:
And how ſhall I be grateful! Thou'rt a princeſs;—
Think not, *Mandane*, this a ſudden ſtart;
A flaſh of love, that kindles and expires:
Long have I weigh'd it; ſince I parted hence,
No night has paſs'd but this has broke my reſt,
And mix'd with ev'ry dream. My fair, I wed thee
In the matureſt counſel of my ſoul.

MANDANE. [*Aſide.*]

O gods! I tremble at the riſing ſtorm;
Where can this end?

MYRON.

And do you then deſpiſe me?

MANDANE.

My lord, I want the courage to accept
What far tranſcends my merit, and for ever
Muſt ſilently upbraid my little worth.

MYRON.

Have I forſook myſelf, forgone my temper
Headlong to all the gay delights of youth,
And fall'n in love with virtue moſt ſevere;
Turn'd ſuperſtitious, to make thee my friend?
Gods! have I ſtruggled through the pow'rful reaſons
That ſtrongly combated my fond reſolves?
Was wealth o'erlook'd, and glory of no weight;
My parent's crown forgot, and my own conqueſts;
And all to be refus'd to ſooth your pride,
And make my rival ſport?

MANDANE. [*Kneels.*]

With patience hear me—

Nor

Nor let my truſt in *Myron* prove my ruin.

MYRON.

Diſtraction! Art thou marry'd?

MANDANE.

Oh!

MYRON.

My heart foretold it.—Ah my ſoul! *Auletes.* [*Swoons.*

AULETES.

Madam, 'tis prudent in you to withdraw— [*Exit* Mand.

MYRON.

I do not live—I cannot bear the light!
Where is *Mandane?* But I would not know.
She is not mine.—Yet, though not mine in love,
Revenge, my juſt revenge, may overtake her.
O how I hate her! Let me know her faults:
Did the proud maid inſult me in diſtreſs,
And ſmile to ſee me gaſping? Speak, *Auletes.*
Did ſhe not ſigh? Sure ſhe might pity me,
Though all her love is now another's right.

AULETES.

She ſigh'd, and wept; but I remov'd her from you.

MYRON.

It was well done—Yet I could gaze for ever.
And *did* ſhe ſigh? And *did* ſhe drop a tear?
The tears ſhe ſhed for me are ſurely mine;
And ſhall another dry them on thoſe cheeks,
And make them an excuſe for greater fondneſs?
Shall I aſſiſt the villain in his joys?
No; I will tear her from him——
I'd grudge her beauties to the gods that gave them.

AULETES.

My lord, have temper.

MYRON.

And another's paſſion
Warm

Warm on that lip ! another's burning arms
Strain'd round the lovely waift for which I die,
And fhe confenting, wooing, growing to him !
What golden fcenes, when abfent, did I feign !
What lovely pictures did I draw in air !
What luxury of thought ! And fee my fate !
Shall then my flave enjoy her ; and I languifh
In my triumphal car, my foot on purple,
And o'er my head a canopy of gold,
Fate in my nod, and monarchs in my train !
What if I ftab him ? No—She will not wed
His murderer—I never form'd a wifh,
But full fruition taught me to forget it.
And am I leffen'd by my late fuccefs ?
And have I loft my conqueft ? Fly, *Auletes,*
And tell her ———

AULETES.

What, my lord ?

MYRON.

No, bid her ———

AULETES.

Speak !

MYRON.

I know not what—My heart is torn afunder.

AULETES.

Retire, my lord, and re-compofe yourfelf :
The queen approaches—Ha ! her bofom fwells ;

[*Exit* Myron.

Her pale lip trembles ; a diforder'd hafte
Is in her fteps ; her eyes fhoot gloomy fires ——
When *Myris* is in anger, happy they
She calls her friends.

Enter QUEEN.

QUEEN.

Auletes, where's the king ?

AULETES.

AULETES.

At council, madam.

QUEEN.

Let him know I want him.

[*Exit* Auletes.

Bafe ! to forget to whom he owes a crown !
Fool ! to provoke *her* rage, whofe hand is red
In her own brother's blood !'

Enter KING *and* PHERON.

KING.

         Horrid confpiracy !

PHERON.

This night was deftin'd for the bloody deed.

KING.

Miftaken villains ! if they wifh my death,
They fhould in prudence lay their weapons by :
So jealous are the gods of *Egypt*'s glory,
I cannot die whilft flaves are arm'd againft me.
Hafte, *Pheron,* to the dungeon ; plunge them down
Far from the hopes of day ; there let them lie
Banifh'd this world while yet alive, and groan
In darknefs, and in horror—Let double chains
Confume the flefh of *Memnon*'s loaded limbs,
'Till death fhall knock them off—A king's thy friend ;
Nay, more ; *Bufiris.*———Go ; let that fuffice—

[*Exit* Pher.

QUEEN.

My lord, your thought's engag'd.

KING.

         Affairs of ftate
Detain'd me from my queen.

QUEEN.

         The world may wait :
I've a requeft, my lord.

KING.

KING.

Oblige me with it.

QUEEN.

Will you comply?

KING.

My queen, my pow'r is yours.

QUEEN.

Your queen!

KING.

My queen.

QUEEN.

Indeed, it should be so —
Then sign these orders for *Amelia*'s death.———
He starts, turns pale, he's sinking into earth.———
Enough; be gone, and fling thee at her feet;
Doat on my slave, and sue to her for mercy.
Go; pour forth all the folly of thy soul;
But bear in mind, thou giv'st not of thy own:
Thou giv'st that kindness, which I bought with blood,
Nor shall I lose unmov'd.

KING.

I wish, my queen,
This still had slept a secret for thy sake;
But since thy restless jealousy of soul
Has been so studious of its own disquiet,
Support it as you may—I own I've felt
Amelia's charms, and think them worth my love.

QUEEN.

And dar'st thou bravely own it too? O insult!
Forgetful man! 'tis I then owe a crown!
Thou hadst still grovell'd in the lower world,
And view'd a throne at distance, had not I
Told thee, thou wast a man, and (dreadful thought!)
Through my own brother cut thy way to empire;

But

But thou might'ſt well forget a crown beſtow'd;
That gift was ſmall; I liſten'd to thy ſighs,
And rais'd thee to my bed.

KING.

I thank you for it:
The gifts you made me were not caſt away:
I underſtand their worth: Huſband and King
Are names of no mean import; they riſe high
Into dominion, and are big with pow'r.———
Whate'er I was, I now am king of *Egypt*,
And *Myris'* lord.

QUEEN.

I dream: Art thou *Buſiris?*
Buſiris, that has trembled at my feet?
And art thou now my Jove, with clouded brow
Diſpenſing fate, and looking down on *Myris?*
Doſt thou derive thy ſpirit from thy crimes?
'Cauſe thou haſt wrong'd me, therefore doſt thou threaten,
And roll thine eye in anger? Rather bend,
And ſue for pardon!—O deteſtable!
Burn for a ſtranger's bed!

KING.

And what was mine,
When *Myris* firſt vouchſaf'd to ſmile on me?

QUEEN.

Diſtraction! death! upbraided for my love!———
Thou art not only criminal, but baſe:
Mine was a godlike guilt: Ambition in it;
Its foot in hell, its head above the clouds;
For know, I hated when I moſt careſs'd:
'Twas not *Buſiris,* but the crown, that charm'd me,
And ſent its ſparkling glories to my heart:
But thou canſt ſoil thy diadem with ſlaves.

KING.

KING.

Syphoces is a king then.

QUEEN.
Ha!

KING.

Let fair *Amelia* know the king attends her. *[Exit.*

QUEEN.

Go, tyrant, go, and wisely, by thy shame,
Prepare thy way to ruin : I'll o'ertake thee,
   Living or dead; if dead, my ghost shall rise,
   Shriek in thy ears, and stalk before thine eyes :
   In death, I'll triumph o'er my rival's charms,
   And chill thy blood, when clasp'd within her arms;
   Alone to suffer is beneath the Great;
   Tyrant, thy torment shall support my State. *[Exit.*

A C T

A C T III.

S C E N E I.

SCENE, *The General's Houſe.*

Enter the KING.

KING.

HERE dwells my ſtubborn fair: I'll ſooth her pride,
And lay an humbled monarch at her feet:
But let her well conſider; if ſhe's ſlow
To welcome bliſs, and dead to glory's charms,
Then my reſentment riſes in proportion
To this high grace extended to my ſlave,
And turns the force of her own charms againſt her:
Monarchs may court, but cannot be deny'd.

[*Enter the* QUEEN, *veiled.*

Amelia, dry thy tears, and lay aſide
That melancholy veil.——Ha! *Myris!*

QUEEN.

Myris!

A name that ſhould like thunder ſtrike thine ear,
And make thee tremble in this guilty place:
But wherefore doſt thou think I meet thee here?
Not with mean ſighs, and deprecating tears,
To humble me before thee, and increaſe
The number of thy ſlaves, in hope to break
Thy reſolution, and avert thy crime;
But to denounce, if thou ſhalt dare perſiſt,

The

The vengeance due to injur'd heav'n and me:
And by this warning double thy offence:
Think, think of vengeance; 'tis the only joy
Which thou haft left me; I'm no more thy wife,
Nor queen; but know I am a woman ftill.

Enter AULETES.

AULETES.

May all the gods watch o'er your life and empire,
And render omens vain! So fierce the ftorm,
Old *Memphis* from her deep foundations fhakes,
And fuch unheard-of prodigies hang o'er us,
As make the boldeft tremble: See the moon
Robb'd of her light, difcolour'd, without form,
Appears a bloody fign, hung out by *Jove*,
To fpeak peace broken with the fons of men;
The *Nile*, as frighted, fhrinks within its banks;
And as this hour I pafs'd great *Ifis'* temple,
A fudden flood of light'ning ruſh'd upon it,
And laid the ſhrine in aſhes.

KING.

O mighty *Ifis!*
Why all theſe ſigns in nature? Why this tumult
To tell me I am guilty? If my crown
The fates demand, why, let them take it back:
My crown, indeed, I may refign; but O!
Who can awake the dead?———
'Tis hence theſe ſpeƈtres ſhock my midnight thoughts,
And nature's laws are broke to difcompofe me;
'Tis I that whirl theſe hurricanes in air,
And ſhake the earth's foundations with my guilt.
O *Myris!* give me back my innocence.

QUEEN.

I bought it with an empire.

KING.

I would remind thee of my late commands.

AULETES.

Madam, 'tis needlefs to remind your flave—
At dead of night I fet the pris'ners free.

QUEEN.

Yes, fet the pris'ners free—'tis great revenge;
Such as my foul pants after—It becomes me,
O it will gall the tyrant! ftab him home;
And if one fpark of gratitude furvives,
Soften *Syphoces* to my foft defire:

   The tyrant's torment is my only joy;
   Ye gods! or let me perifh, or deftroy;
   Or rather both; for what has life to boaft
   When vice is tafielefs grown, and virtue loft?
   Glory and wealth I call upon in vain,
   Nor wealth, nor glory, can appeafe my pain;
   My every joy upbraids me with my guilt,
   And triumphs tell me facred blood is fpilt.   [*Exit* Qu.

Enter MYRON.

MYRON.

The fhining images of war are fled,
The fainting trumpets languifh in mine ear,
The banners furl'd, and all the fprightly blaze
Of burnifh'd armour, like the fetting fun,
Infenfibly is vanifh'd from my thought:
No battle, fiege, or ftorm, fuftain my foul
In wonted grandeur, and fill out my breaft:
But foftnefs fteals upon me, melting down
My rugged heart in languifhments and fighs,
And pours it out at my *Mandane*'s feet——
I fee her e'en this moment ftand before me,
Too fair for fight, and fatal to behold:
I have her here; I clafp her in my arms;

And in the madneſs of exceſſive love,
Sigh out my heart, and bleed with tenderneſs.

AULETES.

My lord, too much you cheriſh this deluſion:
She is another's.

MYRON.

Do not tell me ſo:
Say rather ſhe is dead: each heav'nly charm
Turn'd into horror! O the pain of pains
Is when the fair one, whom our ſoul is fond of,
Gives tranſport, and receives it from another!
How does my ſoul burn up with ſtrong deſire;
Now ſhrink into itſelf! Now blaze again!
I'll tear and rend the ſtrings that tie me to her:
If I ſtay longer here, I am undone.

As he is going, Enter NICANOR.

NICANOR.

My prince, and, ſince ſuch honours you vouchſafe,
My *friend!* I have preſum'd upon your favour;
This is my daughter's birth-day, and this night
I dedicate to joys, which ever languiſh,
If you refuſe to crown them with your preſence.

MYRON.

Nicanor, I was warm on other thoughts——

NICANOR.

I am ſtill near you in the day of danger,
In toilſome marches, and the bloody field,
When nations againſt nations claſh in arms,
And half a people in one groan expire;
Why am I, with your helmet, thrown aſide,
Caſt off, and uſeleſs, in the hour of peace?

T 2

MYRON.

Since then you prefs it, I muft be your gueft.———
Methinks I labour, as I onward move,   *[Afide.*
As under check of fome controuling pow'r.
What can this mean ? Wine may relieve my thoughts,
And mirth and converfe lift my foul again.   *[Exeunt.*

The back fcene draws, and fhews a banquet.

Enter MANDANE, *richly dreffed.*

MANDANE.

It was this day that gave me life; this day
Should give much more, fhould give me *Memnon* too:
But I am rival'd by his chains; they clafp
The hero round (a cold, unkind, embrace!) ;
And but an earneft of far worfe to come :
While he, my foul, in dungeon darknefs clos'd,
Breathes damp unwholefome fteams, and lives on poifon,
I am compell'd to fuffer ornaments,
To wear the rainbow, and to blaze in gems ;
To put on all the fhining guilt of drefs,
When 'tis almoft a crime that I ftill live :
Thefe eyes, which can't diffemble, pouring forth
The dreadful truth, are honeft to my heart;
Thefe robes, O *Memnon* ! are *Mandane*'s chains,
And load, and gall, and wring, her bleeding heart.
        [Exit Mandane.

Enter MYRON, NICANOR, AULETES, &c. *They take
their places.*

NICANOR.

Sound louder, found, and waft my wifh to heav'n.
Hear me, ye righteous gods, and grant my pray'r ;
For ever fhine propitious on my daughter:

    3   Protect

Protect her, prosper her; and when I'm dead,
Still bless me in *Mandane*'s happiness!

[*The bowl goes round. Music.*

Haste, call my daughter; none can taste of joy
Till she, the mistress of the feast, is with us.

A servant brings NICANOR *a letter: He reads it.*

The king's commands at any hour are welcome.

MYRON.

Not leave us, general?

NICANOR.

Ha! the king here writes me,
The discontented populace, that held,
O'er midnight bowls, their desperate cabals,
Are now in bold defiance to his power:
Amid the terrors of this stormy night,
Ev'n now they deluge all yon western vale,
And form a war, impatient for the day:
The spreading poison too has caught his troops,
And the revolting soldiers stand in arms
Mix'd with seditious citizens.

MYRON,

Your call is great.

Enter MANDANE. MYRON *starts from his seat in disorder.*

MANDANE. [*Aside.*]

O *Memnon!* how shall I become a banquet,
Suppress my sorrows, and comply with joy?
Severest fate! Am I deny'd to grieve?

NICANOR.

Be comforted, my child: I'll soon return.
Why dost thou make me blush? I feel my tears
Run trickling down my cheek.

T 3

MYRON.

MYRON. [*Aside to* Auletes.]

I muſt away:

Her ſmiles were dreadful, but her tears are death.

I can no more: I ſink beneath her charms,

And feel a deadly ſickneſs at my heart.

NICANOR.

Your cheek is pale: I dare not let you part:

You are not well———

MYRON.

A ſmall indiſpoſition:

I ſoon ſhall throw it from me—Farewel, general;

Conqueſt attend your arms.

NICANOR.

You ſhall not leave

Your ſervant's roof; 'tis an unwholeſome air,

And my apartment wants a gueſt.

MYRON.

Nicanor,

If health returns, I ſhall not preſs my couch,

And hear of diſtant conqueſts; but o'ertake thee,

And add new terror to the front of war.

NICANOR.

Mean time, you are a guardian to my child:

Let her not miſs a father in my abſence:

She's all my ſoul holds dear.

BOTH. [*Embracing.*]

Farewel. Farewel.

NICANOR *waits on* MYRON *off the ſtage, and returns.*

NICANOR.

My child, I feel a tenderneſs at heart

I never felt before: Come near, *Mandane;*

Let me gaze on thee, and indulge the father——

Thy dying mother with her clay-cold hand

Preſs'd

Prefs'd mine; then, turning on thee her faint eyes,
Let fall a tear of fondnefs, and expir'd——
I cannot love thee well enough; her grace
Softens thy cheek, and lives within thine eye.
Let me embrace you *both*——My heart o'erflows——
If I fhould fall—Thy mother's monument——
But I fhall kill thy tendernefs—No more:
Nay, do not weep; I fhall return again,
And with my deareft child fit down in peace,
And long enjoy her goodnefs.

MANDANE.

> If the gods

Regard your daughter's fervent vows, you will.

NICANOR.

Farewel, my only care; my foul is with thee;
Regard *yourfelf*, and you remember *me*.   [*Exit.*

Enter MYRON *and* AULETES.

MYRON.

No place can give me eafe; my reftlefs thought,
Like working billows in a troubled fea,
Toffes me to and fro; nor know I whither.
What am I, who, or where?——Ha! where indeed!
But let me paufe, and afk myfelf again,
If I am well awake—Impetuous blifs!
My heart leaps up; my mounting fpirits blaze;
My foul is in a tempeft of delight!

AULETES.

My lord, you tremble, and your eyes betray
Strange tumults in your breaft.

MYRON.

> What hour of night?

AULETES.

My lord, the night's far fpent.

MYRON.

> The gates are barr'd,

T 4

And

And all the houfhold is compos'd to reft.
AULETES.
All: And the great *Nicanor*'s own apartment,
Proud to receive a royal gueft, expects you.
MYRON.
Perdition on thy foul for naming him !
Nicanor ! O I never fhall fleep more !
Defend me ! Whither wander'd my bold thoughts !
Broke loofe from reafon, how did they run mad !
And now they are come home all arm'd with ftings,
And pierce my bleeding heart——
I beg the gods to difappoint my crime ;
Yet almoft wifh them deaf to my defire :
I long, repent ; repent, and long again ;
And ev'ry moment differs from the laft.
I muft no longer parley with deftruction :
Auletes, feize me ; force me to my chamber ;
There chain me down, and guard me from myfelf :
Hell rifes in each thought ; 'tis time to fly.   [*Exeunt.*

Enter MANDANE *and* RAMESES.

RAMESES.
I hope your fears have giv'n a falfe alarm.
MANDANE.
You've heard my frequent vifions of the night ;
You know my father's abfence, *Myron*'s paffion :
Juft now I met him ; at my fight he ftarted ;
Then with fuch ardent-eyes he wander'd o'er me,
And gaz'd with fuch malignity of love,
Sending his foul out to me, in a look
So fiercely kind, I trembled, and retir'd.
RAMESES.
No more ; my friends (which, as I have inform'd you,
The queen to gall the tyrant has fet free)

Are

Are lodg'd within your call: th' appointed fignal,
If danger threatens, brings them to your refcue.

MANDANE.

Where are they?

RAMESES.

      In the hall beneath your chamber:
Memnon alone is wanting; he's providing
For your efcape before the morning dawn:
The reft in vifors, fearing to be known,
Have ventur'd thro' the ftreets for your protection.

MANDANE.

Aufpicious turn! then I again am happy.

RAMESES.

Aufpicious turn indeed! and what compleats
The happinefs, the bafe man that betray'd us
This arm laid low: I watch'd him from the king;
I took him warm, while he, with lifted brow,
Confefs'd high thought, and triumph'd in his mien:
I thank'd him with my dagger in his heart.
'Tis late; refrefh yourfelf with fleep, *Mandane.*

          [*Exit* Mandane.

So, 'tis refolv'd, if *Myron* dares attempt
So black a crime, it juftifies the blow:
He dies; and my poor brother's ghoft fhall fmile.
This way he bends his fteps: I hate his fight;
And fhall till death has made it lovely to me.   [*Exit.*

Enter MYRON *and* AULETES.

MYRON.

O how this paffion, like a whirlpool, drives me,
With giddy, rapid motion, round and round,
I know not where, and draws in all my foul!
I reafon much; but reafon about her;
And where fhe is, all reafon dies before her;

                And

And arguments but tell me I am conquer'd.———
So black the night, as if no star e'er shone
In all the wide expanse; the light'ning's flash
But shews the darkness; and the bursting clouds
With peals of thunder seem to rock the land:
Not beasts of prey dare now from shelter roam,
But howl in dens, and make the forest groan.
What then am I? A monster, yet more fell,
Than haunts the wilds?—I am, and threaten more:
My breast is darker than this dreadful night,
And feels a fiercer tempest rage within.———
I must—I will—This leads me to her chamber—
Did not the raven croak?   [*Starting.*

AULETES.

I hear her not.

MYRON.

By heav'n, methinks earth trembles under me.——
Awake, ye furies, you are wanting to me;
O finish me in ill; O take me whole;
Or gods confirm me good, without allay,
Nor leave me thus at variance with myself;
Let me not thus be dash'd from side to side—
The old man wept at parting, kneel'd before me,
Confided in me, gave her to my care,
Nor long since sav'd my life—And doubt I still?
I'm guilty of the fact; here let me lie,
And rather groan for ever in the dust,
And float the marble pavement with my tears,
Than rise into a monster.   [*Flings himself down.*

MANDANE, *passing at a distance, speaks to a servant.*

MANDANE.

Well, observe me.

Before the rising sun my lord arrives,

To

To feal our vows; the holy prieft is with him:
Watch to receive them at the weftern gate,
And privately conduct them to my chamber.   [*Exit.*

        MYRON. [*Starting up.*]

O torment! racks! and flames! then fhe expects him
With open arms! Am I caft out for ever;
For ever muft defpair, unlefs I fnatch
The prefent moment? She is all prepar'd;
Her wifhes waking, and her heart on fire!
That pow'rful thought fweeps heav'n and hell before it,
And lays all open to the prince of *Egypt*;
Born to enjoy whatever he defires,
And fling fear, anguifh, and remorfe, behind him.
I fee her midnight drefs, her flowing hair,
Her flacken'd bofom, her relenting mien,
All the forbidding forms of day flung off
For yielding foftnefs—O I'm all confufion!
I fhiver in each joint! Ah! fhe was made
To juftify the blackeft crimes, and gild
Ruin and death with her deftructive charms.

        AULETES.

You'll force her then?

        MYRON.

            Thou villain but to think it.
No; I'll folicit her with all my pow'r;
Conqueft and crowns fhall fparkle in her fight:
If fhe confent, thy prince is blefs'd indeed,
Takes wings, and tow'rs above mortality;
If fhe refift, I put an end to pain,
And lay my breathlefs body at her feet.

   MANDANE, *paffing at a diftance to her chamber*, MYRON
              meets her.

        MANDANE.

Is this well done, my lord?

                MYRON.

MYRON.

Condemn me not
Before you hear me: Let this posture tell you,
I'm not so guilty as perhaps your fears,
Your commendable, modest fears, suspect:
Nay, do not go; you know not what you do;
I wou'd receive a favour, not constrain it;
Return, or good *Nicanor*, best of fathers,
Shall charge you with the murder of his friend.

MANDANE.

And dare you then pronounce that sacred name,
And yet persist! Were you his mortal foe,
What could your malice more?

MYRON.

O, fair *Mandane!*
I know my fault; I know your virtue too;
But such the violence of my disorder,
That I dare tempt e'en you: Methinks that guilt
Has something lovely which proclaims your pow'r—
But touch me with your hand, I die with bliss.
Why swells your eye? By heav'n, I'd rather see
All nature mourn, than you let fall a tear.
I own I'm mad; but I am mad of love:
You can't condemn me more, than I myself;
In that we are agreed; Agree in all.
Condemn, but pity me; resent, but yield;
For, O, I burn, I rave, I die, with love!

MANDANE.

O Sir!——

MYRON.

Nay, do not weep so; it will kill me:
This moment, while I speak, my eyes are darken'd;
I cannot see thee; and my trembling limbs

Refuse

Refuse to bear their weight; all left of life
Is that I love : If love was in our pow'r,
The fault were mine; since not, you must comply.
How godlike to bestow more heav'nly joys
Than you can think, and I support, and live !

MANDANE.

O, how can you abuse your sacred reason,
That particle of heav'n, that soul of *Jove*,
To varnish o'er, and paint, so black a crime !
O prince !——

MYRON.

What says *Mandane* ?

MANDANE.

Sir, observe me :
My bursting sighs, and ever-streaming tears,
Your noble nature has with pity seen;
But would they not work deeper in your soul,
Were you convinc'd my sorrows flow for you ?
For you, my lord, they flow ; for I am safe
(I know you are surpriz'd) : They flow for you;
Myron, my *father's friend*, my *prince*, my *guest*—
Myron, my guardian god, attempts my peace,
And need I further reason for these tears ?
Nature affords no object of concern
So great, as to behold a gen'rous mind
Driv'n by a sudden gust, and dash'd on guilt—
'Tis base; you ought not : 'Tis impracticable;
You cannot—Make necessity your choice ;
Nor let one moment of defeated guilt,
Of fruitless baseness, overthrow the glory
Your whole illustrious life has dearly bought,
In toilsome marches, and in fields of blood.

Enter

Enter AULETES, *and servants.*

AULETES.

My lord, your life's beset; the room beneath
Is throng'd with ruffians, which but wait the signal,
To rush and sheath their daggers in your heart.

MYRON.

Betray'd! Curst forceress; it was a plot,
Concerted by them all, to take my life,
And this the bait to tempt me to the toil.
She dies——————

AULETES.

　　　　No; first enjoy, then murder her——
Trust to my conduct, and you still are safe.
They all are mask'd: I have my vizor too;
But time is short: for once confide in me.
You, Sir, for safety, fly to your apartment;

　　　　　　　　　　　　　[*To the prince.*
You bear *Mandane* to her closet——You　　[*To servants.*
Speed to the southern gate, and burst it open.

　　[*As the servants seize* Mandane, *she gives the signal. She
　　is borne off.*

Enter RAMESES *and conspirators, mask'd.*

RAMESES.

The villain fled? Perdition intercept him!
Disperse; fly several ways; let each man bear
A steady point, well levell'd at his heart:
If he escapes us now, success attend him;
May he for ever triumph!

　　[*As they pass the stage in confusion,* AULETES *enters
　　　　mask'd among them.*

AULETES.

Ha! Why halt you!

　　　　　　　　　　　　　　　　Pursue,

Purfue, purfue; e'en now I faw the monfter,
The villain *Myron*, with thefe eyes I faw him,
Bearing his prize fwift to the weftern gate:
There, there, it burft.   [*A noife without.*

ALL.

     Away; purfue!

AULETES. [*Without.*]

     'Tis done;
Advance the maffy bar, and all is fafe:
Stand here, and with your lives defend the pafs.

Enter MYRON.

MYRON.

I fhall at leaft have-time for vengeance on her.
And then I care not if I die. Barbarians!
Their fwords are pointed at my life! 'Tis well!
But I will give them an excufe for murder;
Such, fuch a caufe—Off love, and foft compaffion;
Harden each finew of my heart to fteel:
I'll do, what done will fhock myfelf, and thofe
Whom time fets fartheft from this dreadful hour.

Enter MANDANE, *forc'd in by* AULETES.

MANDANE.

By all the pow'rs that can revenge a falfhood,
I'm innocent from any thoughts of blood.

MYRON.

Why then your champions here in arms? 'Tis falfe.

MANDANE.

Ah! let my life fuffice you for the wrong
You charge upon me! O my royal mafter!
My fafety from all ill! my great defender!
Or did my father but infult my tears,
And give me to your care to fuffer wrong;

Kill

Kill me, but not your friend, but not my father;
He loves us both, and my fevere diſtreſs
Will ſcarce more deeply wound him than your guilt.

[Myron *walks paſſionately at a diſtance.*

MYRON.

Slaves, are you ſworn againſt me ? Stop her voice,
And bear her to my chamber..

MANDANE.

O Sir! O *Myron !*

Behold my tears—Here will I fix for ever—
I'll claſp your feet, and grow into the earth—
O cut me, hew me—give to ev'ry limb
A ſeparate death—but ſpare my ſpotleſs virtue ;—
But ſpare my fame—You wound to diſtant ages—
And thro' all time my memory will bleed.

MYRON. [*As ſervants force in* Mandane.]

Diſtraction ! All the pains of hell are on me !

MANDANE. [*She is borne off.*]

O *Memnon !* O my lord !—my life ! where art thou ?

[Myron *expreſſes ſudden paſſion and ſurprize : Stands*
awhile fix'd in aſtoniſhment ; then ſpeaks.

MYRON.

As many accidents concur to work
My paſſions up to this unheard-of crime,
As if the gods deſign'd it—be it then
Their fault, not mine—*Memnon !* Said ſhe not *Memnon ?*
My heart began to ſtagger ; but 'tis over—
Heav'n blaſt me, if I thought it poſſible
I could be ſtill 'more curſt—That hated dog,
Her lord, her life !—I thank her for my cure
Of all remorſe and pity ; this has left me
Without a check, and thrown the looſen'd reins

On,

On my wild paffion, to run headlong on,
And in her ruin quench a double fire;
The blended rage of vengeance and of love.

  Deftruction full of tranfport! Lo, I come,
  Swift on the wing, to meet my certain doom:
  I know the danger, and I know the fhame;
  But, like our Phœnix, in fo rich a flame
  I plunge triumphant my devoted head,
  And doat on death in that luxurious bed.

A C T   IV.

S C E N E   I.

Enter MYRON *in the utmoſt diſorder, bare-headed, without*
light, &c. Walks diſturbedly before he ſpeaks.

MYRON.

HENCEFORTH let no man truſt the firſt falſe ſtep
Of guilt; it hangs upon a precipice,
Whoſe ſteep deſcent in laſt perdition ends.
How far am I plung'd down beyond all thought
Which I this evening fram'd!——But be it ſo:
Conſummate horror! guilt beyond a name!
Dare not, my ſoul, repent; in thee repentance
Were ſecond guilt, and thou blaſphem'ſt juſt heav'n,
By hoping mercy.   Ah! my pain will ceaſe
When gods want pow'r to puniſh—Ha! the dawn—
Riſe never more, O ſun! let night prevail;
Eternal darkneſs cloſe the world's wide ſcene,
And hide me from *Nicanor* and myſelf!
Who's there?   [*Enter* Auletes.

AULETES.
My lord?

MYRON.
Auletes?

AULETES.
                    Guard your life.
The houſe is rouz'd; the ſervants all alarm'd;
The gilded tapers dart from room to room;

                              Solemn .

Solemn confusion, and a trembling hafte,
Mixt with pale horror, glares on ev'ry face;
The ftrengthen'd foe has rufh'd upon your guard,
And cut their paffage thro' them to the gate;
Implacable *Ramefes* leads them on,
Breathing revenge, and panting for your blood.

MYRON.

Why, let them come; let in the raging torrent:
I wifh the world would rife in arms againft me;
For I muft die; and I would die in ftate.

The doors are burft open. Servants pafs the ftage in tumult:
RAMESES, &c. purfue MYRON's guards over the ftage;
then RAMESES and SYPHOCES enter, meeting.

RAMESES.

Where is the prince?

SYPHOCES.

      The monfter ftands at bay:
We can no more than fhut him from efcape,
Till further force arrive.

RAMESES.

       O my *Syphoces!*

SYPHOCES.

This is a grief; but not for words.
Does fhe ftill live?

RAMESES.

      She lives!—but O how blefs'd
Are they which are no more! By ftealth I faw her,
Caft on the ground in mourning weeds fhe lies;
Her torn and loofen'd treffes fhade her round;
Thro' which her face, all pale, as fhe were dead,
Gleams like a fickly moon; too great her grief
For words or tears! but ever and anon,
After a dreadful, ftill, infidious calm,

      Collecting

Collecting all her breath, long, long suppress'd,
She sobs her soul out in a lengthen'd groan,
So sad, it breaks the heart of all that hear,
And sends her maids in agonies away.

SYPHOCES.

O tale, too mournful to be thought on !

RAMESES.

Hold———

No, let her virgins weep; forbear, Syphoces;
Tear out an eye, but damp not our revenge;
Dispatch your letters; I'll go comfort her.

[A servant speaks aside to Rameses. Exit Syphoces.

And has she then commanded none approach her ?
I'm sorry for it; but I cannot blame her.
Such is the dreadful ill, that it converts
All offer'd cure into a new disease:
It shuns our love, and comfort gives her pain.

Re-enter SYPHOCES.

SYPHOCES.

Your father is return'd; redundant Nile,
Broke from its channel, overswells the pass,
And sends him back to wait the waters fall.

RAMESES.

And is he then return'd ?—I tremble for him.———
I see his white head rolling in the dust :
But haste; it is our duty to receive him.   [Exit.

Enter MYRON.

MYRON.

I feel a pain of which I am not worthy;
A pain, an anguish, which the honest man
Alone deserves.—Is it not wondrous strange,
That I, who stabb'd the very heart of nature,

Should

Should have furviving aught of man about me?
And yet I know not how, of gratitude
And friendfhip ftill the ftubborn fparks furvive;
And poor *Nicanor's* torments pierce my foul.
Confufion! he's return'd—————   [*Starting.*

Enter NICANOR.

NICANOR.   [*Advancing to embrace* Myron.]
                                        My prince—————
MYRON.   [*Turning afide, and hiding his face.*]
                                        My friend——

NICANOR.

I interrupt you, Sir—————
          MYRON.   [*Smiting his breaft.*]
                              I had thee there:
Before thou cam'ft, my thoughts were bent upon thee.
          NICANOR.
O Sir, you are too kind!
              MYRON.   [*Afide.*]
                              Death! tortures! hell!
          NICANOR.
What fays my prince?
              MYRON.
                              A fudden pain,
To which I'm fubject, ftruck acrofs my heart:
'Tis paft: I'm well again.
              NICANOR.
                              Heav'n guard your health!
          MYRON.
Doft thou then wifh it?
              NICANOR.
                              Am I then diftrufted?
Then, when I fav'd your life, I did the leaft
I e'er wou'd do to ferve you.
                              U 3   MYRON.

MYRON.

Barbarous man !

NICANOR.

What have I done, my prince ? which way offended ?
Has not my life, my soul, been yours ?

MYRON.

Oh !—oh !—

NICANOR. [*Takes him by the hand.*]

By heav'n, I'm wrong'd ! speak, and I'll clear myself.

MYRON.

I'm poison and deftruction ; curfe thy gods ;
I'll kill thee in compaffion.———O my brain !
Away, away, away !   [*Shoves him from him, going.*

NICANOR.

Do, kill me, prince———

You fhall not go ;—I do demand the caufe,
Which has put forth thy hand againft thy father !
For, thus provok'd, I'll do myfelf the juftice,
To tell thee, youth, that I deferve that name ;
Nor have thy parents lov'd thee more than I.

MYRON.

I hear them ; they are on me—Loofe thy hold,
Or I will plant my dagger in thy breaft.

NICANOR.

Your dagger's needlefs ! O ungrateful boy !

MYRON. [*Embrace.*]

Forgive me, father ! O my foul bleeds for thee !

[*As he is going out,* Auletes *meets him, and fpeaks to him
afide.*

What, no efcape ? on ev'ry fide inclos'd ?
Then I refolve to perifh by his hand ;
'Tis juft I fhou'd ; and meaner death I fcorn :
But how to work him to my fate, to fting
His paffion up fo high, will be a tafk

5

To me fevere; as difficult as ftrange.

Support me, cruel heart; it muft be done. [*Afide.*

NICANOR.

Now, from my very foul, I cannot tell—

But 'tis enchantment all; for things fo ftrange

Have happen'd, I might well diftruft my fenfe;

But, if mine eyes are true, I plainly read

A heart in anguifh; and, I muft confefs,

Your grief is juft—It was inhuman in you—

But tell the caufe; unravel, from the bottom,

The myftery that has embroil'd our loves

(For ftill, my prince, I love, fince you repent):

What accident depriv'd me of my friend,

And loft you to yourfelf?

MYRON.

A traitor's fight!

NICANOR.

Beneath my roof?

MYRON.

Beneath thy very helmet:

Thou art a traitor. Guard thyfelf. [*Draws.*

NICANOR.

Diftraction!

Traitor!———For ftanding by your father's throne;

And ftemming the wild ftream, that roars againft it,

Of rebel fubjects, and of foreign foes?

For training thee to glory and to war?

For taking thee from out thy mother's arms

A mortal child, and kindling in thy foul

The noble ardors of a future god?

Farewel; I dare not truft my temper more.

MYRON.

Grey-headed, venerable, traitor!

U 4

Enter

Enter RAMESES.

RAMESES.

Ha!

Turn, turn, blafphemer, and reprefs thy taunts;
All provocation's needlefs, but thy fight.

[*He affaults the prince :* Nicanor *binders him.*

NICANOR.

Forbear, my fon.

RAMESES.

Forbear ?

NICANOR.

If I am calm,

Your rage fhould ceafe.

RAMESES.

No; 'tis my own revenge;

Unlefs, Sir, you difown me for your fon,

NICANOR.

Thy fword againft thy prince ?

RAMESES.

A villain !

NICANOR.

Hold !

RAMESES.

The worft of villains !

NICANOR.

'Tis too much.

RAMESES.

O father !——

NICANOR.

What would'ft thou ?

RAMESES.

Sir, your daughter——

NICANOR.

Rightly thought;

She

She beſt can comfort me in all my ſorrow:
Call, call *Mandane :* To behold my child
Wou'd cheer me in the agonies of death:
Call her, *Rameſes.*——Am I diſobey'd?

RAMESES.

O Sir!——

NICANOR.

What mean thoſe tranſports of concern?

RAMESES.

Though I'm an outcaſt from your love, I weep
To open your black ſcene of miſery.

NICANOR.

Where will this end?—O my foreboding heart!

RAMESES.

Should he, to whom, as to a god, at parting,
You gave, with ſtreaming eyes, your ſoul's delight,
While yet your laſt embrace was warm about him,
Gloomy and dreadful as this ſtormy night,
Ruſh on your child, your comfort, your *Mandane,*
All ſweet and lovely as the bluſhing morn,
Seize her by force, now trembling, breathleſs, pale,
Proſtrate in anguiſh, tearing up the earth,
Imploring, ſhrieking, to the gods and you——
O hold my brain!—Look there, and think the reſt.

*The back ſcene opens. A darken'd chamber, a bed, and the
curtains drawn. Women paſs out, weeping, &c. NICANOR
falls back on RAMESES.*

NICANOR.

Is't poſſible—my child! my only daughter!
The growth of my own life! that ſweeten'd age
And pain!—O nature bleeds within me.

MANDANE.

Weep not, my virgins; ceaſe your uſeleſs tears;

Kindneſs

Kindnefs is thrown away upon defpair,
And but provokes the forrow it would eafe.

NICANOR.

Affift me forwards.

MANDANE.

                    Moft unwelcome news !
Is he return'd ? The gods fupport my father.
I now begin to wifh he lov'd me lefs.

NICANOR.

There, there, fhe pierc'd the very tend'reft nerve:
She pities me, dear babe ; fhe pities me :
Through all the raging tortures of her foul,
She feels my pain ! But hold, my heart, to thank her ;
Then burft at once, and let the pangs of death
Put *Myron* from my thought.   [*Goes to her.*

MANDANE.

                    Severeft fate
Has done its worft—I've drawn my father's tears.——

NICANOR.

Forbear to call me by that tender name ;
Since I can't help thee, I would fain forget
Thou art a part of me—It only fharpens
Thofe pangs, which, if a ftranger, I fhould feel——
O fpare me, my *Mandane !* To behold thee
In fuch excefs of forrow, quite deftroys me,
And I fhall die, and leave thee, unreveng'd.

MANDANE.

O Sir ! there are misfortunes moft fevere,
Which yet can bear the light, and, well fuftain'd,
Adorn the fufferer.—But this affliction
Has made defpair a virtue, and demands
Utter extinction, and eternal night,
As height of happinefs.   [*Scene fhuts on them.*
                                              Enter

Enter SYPHOCES.

RAMESES.

O my *Syphoces!*

SYPHOCES.

And does this move you? does this melt you down,
And pour you out in forrow? Then fly far,
Ere *Memnon* comes; he comes with flufhing cheek,
And beating heart, to bear a bride away,
And blefs his fate: How dreadfully deceiv'd!

RAMESES.

The melancholy fcene at length begins.

Enter MEMNON.

MEMNON.

O give me leave to yield to nature,
And indulge my joy————
My friend! my brother! O the ecftafy
That fires my veins, and dances at my heart!
You love me not, if you refufe to join
In all the juft extravagance and flight
Of boundlefs tranfport on this happy hour.
Where is my foul, my blifs, my lovely bride?
Call, call her forth: O hafte; the prieft expects us,
And ev'ry moment is a crime to love.

RAMESES. [*To* Syphoces.]

Speak to him:—Pr'ythee fpeak.

SYPHOCES.

By heav'n I cannot.

MEMNON.

What can this mean?

RAMESES.

Syphoces.

SYPHOCES.

Nay; *Ramefes.*

MEMNON.

By all the gods, they ftruggle with their forrows,
And fwallow down their tears to hide them from me:
By friendfhip's facred name, I charge you, fpeak.

[*They look on him with the utmoft concern, and go out on
different fides of the ftage.*]

Was ever man thus left to dreadful thought,
And all the horrors of a black furmife !
What woe is this, too big to be exprefs'd ?
O my fad heart ! Why bod'ft thou fo feverely ?
Mandane's life's in danger ! There indeed;
Fortune, I fear thee ftill; her beauties arm thee;
Her virtues make thee dreadful to my thought;
But for my love, how I could laugh at fate !

Enter a fervant, and gives him a paper. He reads.

Enter RAMESES, MEMNON *fwoons, and falls on RA-*
MESES.

RAMESES.

'Twere happy if his foul wou'd ne'er return:
The gods may ftill be merciful in this.———
His lips begin to rife.—How fares my friend ?

MEMNON.

Did *Myron* feel my pangs, you'd pity him.

Enter SYPHOCES.

SYPHOCES.

Fainting beneath th' oppreffion of her grief,
This way *Mandane* feeks the frefher air:
Let us withdraw; 'twill pain her to be feen,
And moft of all by you.

MEMNON.

By my own heart
I judge, and am convinc'd.—I dare not fee her:
The fight would ftrike me dead.———

[*As*

[*As* Memnon *is going,* Mandane *meets him: Both start back: She shrieks.* Memnon *recovers himself, and falls at her knees, embracing them: She tries to disengage: He not permitting, she raises him: He takes her passionately in his arms: They continue speechless and motionless for some time.*

RAMESES.

Was ever mournful interview like this?
See how they writhe with anguish! hear them groan!
See the large silent dew run trickling down,
As from the weeping marble; passion choaks
Their words, and they're the statues of despair!

MEMNON.

O my *Mandane!*
        [*At this she violently breaks from him, and exit.*
                        But one moment more.
    As Memnon *is following,* Rameses *holds him.*

RAMESES.

Brother——

MEMNON.

    Forgive me.——

RAMESES.

            You're to blame———

MEMNON.   [*Pointing after her.*]

                        Look there.

My heart is bursting.

RAMESES.
    With Revenge?

MEMNON.

                        And Love,

RAMESES.

Revenge!

MEMNON.
One dear embrace; 'twill edge my sword.
                        SYPHOCES.

Syphoces.

No, *Memnon*; if our fwords now want an edge,
They'll want for ever; to this fpot I charm thee,
By the dread words, Revenge and Liberty!
This is the crifis of our fates; this moment
The guardian gods of *Egypt* hover o'er us;
They watch to fee us act like prudent men,
And out of ills extract our happinefs.
My friends, thefe dire calamities, like poifon,
May have their wholefome ufe: This fad occafion,
If manag'd artfully, revives our hopes;
It gives *Nicanor* to our finking faction,
And ftill the tyrant fhakes.

Rameses.

                              My father comes;
Or fnatch this moment, or defpair for ever:
While paffions glow, the heart, like heated fteel,
Takes each impreffion, and is work'd at pleafure.

Enter Nicanor.

Nicanor.

Why have the gods chofe out my weakeft hours
To fet their terrors in array againft me?
This wou'd beat down the vigour of my youth,
Much more grey hairs, and life worn down fo low,
Vain man! to be fo fond of breathing long,
And fpinning out a thread of mifery:
The longer life, the greater choice of evil;
The happieft man is but a wretched thing,
That fteals poor comfort from comparifons;
What then am I? Here will I fit me down,
Brood o'er my cares, and *think* myfelf to death.
Draw near, *Ramefes*; I was rafh erewhile,
And chid thee without caufe—How many years
Have I been cas'd in fteel?

                                        Rameses.

RAMESES.

Full threefcore years
Have chang'd the feafons o'er your crefted brow,
And feen your faulchion dy'd in hoftile blood.

NICANOR.

How many triumphs fince the king has reign'd?

RAMESES.

They number juft your battles, one for one.

NICANOR.

True; I have follow'd the rough trade of war
With fome fuccefs, and can without a blufh
Review the fhaken fort, and fanguine plain.
I have thought pain a pleafure, thirft and toil
Bleft objects of ambition. I remember
(Nor do my foes forget that bloody day)
When the barb'd arrow from my gaping thigh
Was wrench'd with labour, I difdain'd the groan,
Becaufe I fuffer'd for *Bufiris'* fake.

RAMESES.

The king is not to blame.

NICANOR.

Is not the prince his fon?

RAMESES.

But in himfelf——

NICANOR. [*Rifing in paffion.*]

And has he loft his guilt,
'Caufe he has injur'd me? Erewhile thy blood
Was kindled at his name.—Didft thou not tell me
A fhameful black defign on poor *Amelia?*
O *Memnon!* what a glorious race is this,
To make the gods a party in our caufe,
And draw down bleffings on us!

MEMNON.

MEMNON.

               He that fupports them
In fuch black crimes, is fharer of their guilt.

NICANOR.

Point out the man, and, with thefe wither'd hands,
I'd fly upon his throat, though he were lodg'd
Within the circle of *Bufiris'* arms.

RAMESES.

He that prevents it not when in his power,
Supports them in their courfe of flaming guilt;
And you are he.

NICANOR.

Thou rav'ft.

SYPHOCES.

               The army's yours:
I've founded every chief; but wave your finger,
Thoufands fall off the tyrant's fide, and leave him
Naked of help, and open to deftruction:
But fweep his minions, cut a pander's throat,
Or lop a fycophant, the work is done.

NICANOR. [*Starting.*]

What would you have me do?

MEMNON.

               Let not your heart
Fly off from your own thought; be truly great;
Refent your country's. fufferings as your own:
A generous foul is not confin'd at home,
But fpreads itfelf abroad o'er all the public,
And *feels* for every member of the land.
What have we feen for twenty rolling years,
But one long tract of blood! or, what is worfe,
Throng'd dungeons pouring forth perpetual groans;
And free-born men opprefs'd! Shall half mankind
Be doom'd to curfe the moment of their birth?

5

Shall all the mother's fondnefs be employ'd
To rear them up to bondage, give them ftrength
To bear afflictions, and fupport their chains?

SYPHOCES. [*Kneeling.*]

To you the valiant youth moft humbly bend,
And beg that nature's gifts, the vigorous nerve,
And graceful port defign'd to blefs the world,
And take your great example in the field,
May not be forc'd by lewdnefs in high place,
To other toils, to labour for difeafe,
To wither in a loath'd embrace, and die
At an inglorious diftance from the foe.

RAMESES. [*Kneeling.*]

To you *Amelia* lifts her hands for fafety.

MEMNON. [*Burfting into tears.*]

To you—To you—

NICANOR.

By heav'n he cannot fpeak.—I underftand thee:
Rife—Rife—my fon: Rife all; your work is done;
They perifh all; thefe creatures of my fword.
Have I not feen whole armies vaulted o'er
With flying jav'lins, which fhut out the day,
And fell in rattling ftorms at my command,
To flay, and bury, proud *Bufiris'* foe?
He lives and reigns; for I have been his friend:
But I'll unmake him, and plough up the ground
Where his proud palace ftands.   [*Exit.*

MEMNON.

O my *Mandane!*
The gods by dreadful means beftow fuccefs,
And in their vengeance moft feverely blefs:
From thy bright ftreaming eyes our triumphs flow,
The tyrant falls, *Mandane* ftrikes the blow:

VOL. I.   X   So

So the fair moon, when feas fwell high, and pour
A wafteful deluge on the trembling fhore,
Infpires the tumult from her clouded throne,
Where filent, penfive, pale, fhe fits alone,
And all the diftant ruin is her own.

ACT

A C T V.

SCENE I.

The Field.

Enter BUSIRIS *and* AULETES. *An alarum at a diftance.*

BUSIRIS.

WELCOME the voice of war! Tho' loud the found,
It faintly fpeaks the language of my heart;
It whifpers what I mean. But fay, *Auletes*,
What urge thefe forlorn rebels in excufe
For choofing ruin?

AULETES.
Various their complaints:
But fome are loud, that while your heavy hand
Preffes whole millions with inceffant toil
(Toils fitter far for beafts than human creatures)
In building wonders for the world to gaze at,
Weeds are their food, their cup the muddy *Nile*.

BUSIRIS.
Do they not build for me? Let that reward them.
Yes, I will build more wonders to be gaz'd at,
And temper all my cement with their blood.
Whofe pains and art reform'd the puzzled year,
Thus drawing down the fun to human ufe,
And making him their fervant? Who pufh'd off

X 2

With

With mountain dams the broad redundant *Nile*,
Defcended from the moon, and bid it wander
A ftranger ftream in unaccuftom'd fhores ?
Who from the *Ganges* to the *Danube* reigns ?
But virtues are forgot.—Away—To arms !
I call to mind my glorious anceftry,
Which, for ten thoufand rolling years renown'd,
Shines up into eternity itfelf,
And ends among the gods.   .   [*An alarum.*

Enter MEMNON.

AULETES.

     The rebel braves us.

BUSIRIS.

Hold ! let our weapons thirft one moment longer ;
And death ftand ftill 'till he receives my nod.——
Whom meet I in the midft of my own realm,
With bold defiance on his brow ?

MEMNON.

       The flave,
Whom dread *Bufiris* lately laid in chains ;
An emblem of his country.   -

BUSIRIS.

     Is it thus
You thank my royal bounty ?

MEMNON.

       Thus you thank'd
The good *Artaxes* ; thus you thank'd my father.

BUSIRIS.

What I have done, conclude moft right and juft ;
For I have done it ; and the gods alone
Shall afk me Why : Thou liv'ft, altho' they fell ;
And, if they fell unjuftly, greater thanks
Are due from Thee, whom e'en injuftice fpar'd.

MEMNON.

MEMNON.

Thy kindneffes are wrongs; they mean to footh
My injur'd foul, and fteal it from revenge.

BUSIRIS.

Turn back thine eye; behold thy troops are thin,
Thy men are rarely fprinkled o'er the field,
And yet thou carrieft millions on thy tongue.

MEMNON.

All thy blood-thirfty fword has laid in duft
Are on my fide; they come in bloody fwarms,
And throng my banners: Thy unequall'd crimes
Have made thee weak, and rob my victory——

BUSIRIS.

Ha!

MEMNON.

Nay, ftamp not, tyrant; I can ftamp as loud,
And raife as many dæmons at the found.

BUSIRIS.

I wear a diadem.

MEMNON.

And I a fword.

BUSIRIS.

Yet, yet fubmit, I give thee life.

MEMNON.

Secure your own:
No more, *Bufiris*; bid the fun farewel.

BUSIRIS.

Bufiris and the fun fhould fet together:
If this day's angry gods ordain my fate,
Know thou, I fall like fome vaft pyramid;
I bury thoufands in my great deftruction,
And thou the firft.——Slave! in the front of battle;
There thou fhalt find me.

X 3

MEMNON.

MEMNON.

                         Thou shalt find me there,
And have well paid that gratitude I owe.

                                    [*Exeunt.*

A continued alarum.
Enter MYRON *and* NICANOR, *meeting.*

NICANOR.

Does not mine eye strike terror through thy soul,
And shake the weapon from thy trembling arm?
Base boy! the foulness of thy guilt secures thee
From my reproach; I dare not name thy crime.

MYRON.

Old man, didst thou stand up in thy own cause,
I then should be afraid of fourscore years,
And tremble at grey hairs; but since thy frenzy
Has lent those venerable locks to cast
A gloss of virtue on the blackest crime,
Accurst rebellion! this gives back my heart,
With all its rage, and I'm a man again.

NICANOR.

Come on, and use that force of arms I taught thee;
I'll now resume the life I gave so late.

MYRON.

I grieve thou hast but half a life to lose,
And dost defraud my vengeance—At my touch,
Thou moulder'st into dust, and art forgotten:

            [*Preparing to fight,* Myron *stops short.*

Ah, no, I cannot fight with thee; begone,
And shake elsewhere; thou canst not want a death
In such a field, though I refuse it to thee:
Ramses, Memnon, give them to my sword,
Sustain'd by thousands; but to fly from thee,

                                    From

From thee, moſt injur'd man', ſhall be my praiſe,
And riſe above the conqueſt of my foes.

NICANOR.

'Tis not old age, th' avenging gods purſue thee !
[*He retires before* Nicanor *off the ſtage.* *A loud alarum.*

Enter BUSIRIS *and* AULETES, *in purſuit.*

BUSIRIS.

'Tis well; I like this madneſs of the field :
Let heighten'd horrors, and a waſte of death,
Inform the world, *Buſiris* is in arms :
But then I grudge the glory of my ſword
To ſlaves and rebels ; while they die by me,
They cheat my vengeance, and ſurvive in fame.

AULETES.

I panted after in the paths of death,
And could not but from far behold your plume
O'erſhadow ſlaughter'd heaps, while your bright helm
Struck a diſtinguiſh'd terror through the field,
The diſtant legions trembling as it blaz'd.

BUSIRIS.

Think not a crown alone lights up my name ;
My hand is deep in fight.   Forbid it, *Iſis !*
That whilſt *Buſiris* treads the ſanguine field,
The foremoſt ſpirit of his hoſt ſhould conquer
But by example, and beneath the ſhade,
Of this high-brandiſh'd arm.   Did'ſt thou e'er fear ?
Sure 'tis an art ; I know not how to fear ;
'Tis one of the few things beyond my power ;
And if death muſt be fear'd before 'tis felt,
Thy maſter is immortal, O *Auletes.*——
But while I ſpeak, they live !
　　Where fall the ſounding cataracts of *Nile,*
　　The mountains tremble, and the waters boil ;

X 4　　　　　　　Like

Like them, I'll rush; like them my fury pour,
And give the future world one wonder more.

[*Exeunt.*

Enter MYRON, *engaged with a party: His plume is smitten
off: He drives the foe, and returns.*

MYRON.

When death's so near, but dares not venture on us,
'Tis heaven's regard, a kind of salutation,
Which to ourselves our own importance shews :—
Faint as I am, and almost sick of blood,
There is one cordial would revive me still ;
The sight of *Memnon* ; place that fiend before me.—

[*Exit.*

Enter MEMNON.

MEMNON.

Where, where's the prince ? O give him to my sword !
His tall white plume, which, like a high-wrought foam,
Floated on the tempestuous stream of fight,
Shew'd where he swept the field; I follow'd swift,
But my approach has turn'd him into air.———

[*Enter* MYRON.

The fight but now begins !

MYRON.

Why, who art thou?

MEMNON.

Prince, I am—

MYRON.   [*Disdainfully.*]

Memnon !

MEMNON.

No—I'm *Mandane.*

MYRON.

Ha !

MEMNON.

MEMNON. [*Striking his own head and breast.*]
She's here, she's here, she's all : Her wrongs and virtues !
Virtues and wrongs ! Thou worse than murderer !

MYRON.
I charge thee name her not ; forbear the croak
With that ill-omen'd note.

MEMNON.
Mandane !

MYRON.

Be it so.
When I reflect on her mean love for thee,
And plot against my life, my pain is less.

MEMNON.
'Tis false ; she meant, she knew it not ; *Ramefes,*
He, only he, was conscious of the thought.

MYRON.
Then I'm a wretch indeed !

MEMNON.

As such I'll use thee :
I'll crush thee like some poison on the earth ;
Then haste and cleanse me in the blood of men.

MYRON.
I thank thee, for this spirit which exalts thee
Into a foe I need not blush to meet :
Now, from my soul, it joys me thou art found ;
And found alive : By heav'n, so much I hate thee,
I fear'd that thou wast dead, and hadst escap'd me :
I'll drench my sword in thy detested blood,
Or soon make thee immortal by my own.
Villain !

MEMNON.
Myron !

MYRON.
Rebel !

MEMNON.

MEMNON.

  Myron!   *[They fight.*

MYRON.

    Hell!

MEMNON.

Mandane!

   MYRON. [*Falls.*]

Juſt the blow, and juſter ſtill,
Becauſe imbitter'd to me by that hand
I moſt deteſt; which gives my ſoul an earneſt
Of vaſt unfathomable woes to come;
That dreadful dowry for my dreadful love.
I leave the world my miſery's example;
If us'd aright, no trivial legacy.   *[Dies.*

   Enter SYPHOCES.

    SYPHOCES.

My lord, I bring you moſt unwelcome news:
As poor *Mandane* wander'd near the field,
In hope to ſee her injuries reveng'd,
Thoughtleſs of any ſufferings but the paſt,
A party of the foe ſaw, ſeiz'd, and bore her off.

    MEMNON.

Vengeance and conqueſt now are trivial things;
Love made their prize. 'Tis impious in my ſoul
To entertain a thought but of her reſcue:
Now, now, I plunge into the thickeſt war,
As ſome bold diver, from a precipice
Into mid ocean, to regain a gem
Whoſe loſs impoveriſh'd kings; to bring it back,
Or ſee the day no more.   *[Exeunt.*

   Enter MANDANE, *priſoner.*

    MANDANE.

A gen'rous foe will hear his captive ſpeak;

      A benefit

A benefit thus, kneeling, I implore :
Let one of all thofe fwords that glitter round me,
Vouchfafe to hide its point within my breaft.

Enter MEMNON.

MEMNON.

Ah villains ! curfed Atheifts ! Can you bear
That pofture from that form ? What, what are numbers,
When I behold thofe eyes ! Not mine the glory,
That fingly thus I quell a hoft of foes.
Inhuman robbers ! O bring back my foul !
  [*They force her off. He rufhes in upon them, and is taken.*
Poor comfort to mankind, that they can lofe
Their lives but once—But, oh ! a thoufand times
Be torn from what they love.

Enter RAMESES.

RAMESES.

Far have I waded in the bloody field,
Laborious through the ftubborn ranks of war,
And trac'd thee in a labyrinth of death ;
But thus to find thee !—Better find thee dead !
Thefe flaves will ufe thee ill.

MEMNON.

　　　　　　Of that no more :
Myron is dead, and by this arm.

RAMESES.

　　　　　　I thank thee :
All my few fpirits left exult with joy ;
I'll chafe and fcourge him through the lower world.

MEMNON.

Alas, thou bleed'ft !

RAMESES.

　　Curfe on the tyrant's fword ;

　　　　　　　　　　I bleed

I bleed to death : But could not leave the world
Without a laſt embrace.   Juſt now I met
The poor *Mandane.*

                    MEMNON.

          Quickly ſpeak.   What ſaid ſhe ?
          RAMESES.

Nothing of comfort ; ceaſe to aſk me farther :
If you meet more, your meeting will be ſad.—
Your arm ! I faint.—Ah ! what is human life ?
How, like the dial's tardy-moving ſhade,
Day after day ſlides from us unperceiv'd !
The cunning fugitive is ſwift by ſtealth ;
Too ſubtle is the movement to be ſeen ;
Yet ſoon the hour is up—and we are gone.
Farewel : I pity thee.   [*Dies.*

                    MEMNON.

                    Farewel, brave friend !
Would I could bear thee company to reſt ;
But life in all its terrors ſtands before me,
And ſhuts the gates of peace againſt my wiſhes.—
Do I not hear a peal of diſtant thunder ?
And ſee, a ſudden darkneſs ſhuts the day,
And quite blots out the ſun !—But what to me
The colour of the ſky ? A death-cold dew
Hangs on my brow, and all my ſlacken'd joints
Are ſhook without a cauſe.—A groan ! From whence ?
Again ! And no one near me ? Vain deluſion !—
I fear not vain ! I fear ſome ill is tow'rds me,
More dreadful ſure than all that's paſt.—*Mandane ?*
I hop'd ſhe was at peace, and paſt the reach
Of this ill news ; but ſuch my wayward fate,
I cannot aſk a curſe, but 'tis deny'd me :
And could I wiſh I ne'er could ſee her more ?

                                             Enter

Enter MANDANE, *guarded.*

MANDANE.

This is my brother: A fhort privacy
Is a fmall favour you may grant a foe.

GUARD.

Let it be fhort; we may not wait your leifure.

MEMNON.

'Tis wond'rous ftrange; there's fomething holds me from her,
And keeps this foot faft rooted to the ground.
This is the laft time I fhall ever pray.   [*Kneeling.*
To me, ye gods, confine your threaten'd vengeance,
And I will blefs your mercies while I fuffer!

[Memnon *and* Mandane *advance flowly*
to the front of the ftage.

MANDANE.

What didft thou pray for?

MEMNON.

For thy peace.

MANDANE.

'Twas kind.

But oh! thofe hands in bonds deny the blefling,
For which they earneftly were rais'd to heav'n——

MEMNON.

I fear fo too: What we have yet to do
Muft be foon done: This meeting is our laft.
How fhall we ufe it?

MANDANE.

How! Confult thy chains,
And my calamities.

MEMNON.

Sad counfellors,
And cruel their advice—Are there no other?

MANDANE.

MANDANE.

I look around—and find no glimpfe of hope ;
A perfect night of horror and defpair.

MEMNON.

Of horror and defpair indeed, *Mandane :*
Canft thou believe me ? Nay can I believe
Myfelf? The laft thing that I wifh'd for was—'Tis falfe !
The weight of my misfortunes hurts my mind.

MANDANE.

Was what ?

MEMNON.

I dare not think ; to think is to look down
A precipice ten thoufand fathom deep,
That turns my brain !—Oh ! Oh !

MANDANE.

                   Memnon, no more :
That filence, and thofe tears, need no explaining ;
And it is kind, with fuch fevere reluctance,
To think upon my death—though neceffary.

MEMNON.

Ah hold ! You plant a thoufand daggers here :
Talk not of dying—I difown the thought ;
Right is not right, and reafon is not reafon ;
All is diftraction, when I look on thee.
O all ye pitying gods ! dafh out from nature
Your ftars, your fun, but let *Mandane* live.

MANDANE.

No; death long fince was my confirm'd refolve.

MEMNON.

Myron is dead.

MANDANE.

          What joy a heart like mine
Can feel, it feels———Had he been never born,
I might have liv'd—'tis now impoffible.

MEMNON.

MEMNON.

This even to my miseries I owe,
That it discovers greater virtues still,
In her my soul adores.———O my *Mandane*!
O glorious maid! then thou wilt be at peace—
        [Memnon *walks thoughtfully, then returns.*
Must I survive, and change thy tenderness
For a stern master, and perpetual chains?
Long I may groan on earth to sate their malice,
Then through slow torments linger into death,
No steel to stab, no wall to dash my brain!

MANDANE.

Ha!

MEMNON.

    Why thus fix'd in thought? What mighty birth
Is lab'ring in your soul? Your eyes speak wonders—

MANDANE.

Will not the blood-hounds be content with life?

MEMNON.

Alas, *Mandane*! No; they study nature,
To find out all her secret seats of pain,
And carry killing to a dreadful art:
A simple death in *Egypt* is for friends.

MANDANE.

O then it must be so!—and yet it cannot!—

MEMNON.

What means this sudden paleness?

    MANDANE.   [*Feeling in her bosom, she swoons.*]
                        Heav'n assist me!

MEMNON.

My love! *Mandane*! hear me, my espous'd!
My dearest heart! the infant of my bosom!
Whom I would foster with my vital blood.

    2   MANDANE.

MANDANE. [*Shews a dagger.*]
'Tis well; and in return, I give thee—This.
MEMNON.
Millions of thanks, thou refuge in defpair.
MANDANE.
Terrible kindnefs! Horrid mercy! Oh!
I cannot give it thee.
MEMNON.
Full well I know
Thy tender foul, and I muft fo ce it from thee.
[*As he is ftruggling with her for the dagger, fhe fpeaks.*
MANDANE.
My lord! my foul! myfelf! you tear my heart:
Art thou not dearer to my eyes than light?
Doft thou not circulate through all my veins;
Mingle with life, and form my very foul?
MEMNON.
Now, monfters, I defy you: Fate forbids
A long farewel: My guard may interpofe,
And make your favour vain—Thus, only thus. [*Embrace.*
And now—[*Going to ftab himfelf.*]
MANDANE. [*Holds his arm.*]
Ah no! Since laft I faw thee, thrice I rais'd
My trembling arm, and thrice I let it fall.—
If you refufe compaffion to my fex,
Memnon betrays me, and is *Myron's* friend.——
As I a poniard, you fupply an arm,
And I fhall ftill be happy in your love.
[*After a paufe of aftonifhment, he finks gently on the earth.*
MEMNON.
From dreadful to more dreadful I am plung'd,
And find in deepeft anguifh deeper ftill: ·
I can't complain in common with mankind——
But am a wretched fpecies all alone:

Muft

Muſt I not only loſe thee, but be curs'd
To ſprinkle my own hands with thy life blood?

MANDANE.

It cannot be avoided.

MEMNON.
Nor perform'd.
Lift up my hand againſt thee as a foe!
I who ſhould ſave thee from thy very father,
And teach thy deareſt friends to uſe thee well,
Make kindneſs kind, and ſoften all their ſmiles?
O, my *Mandane!* think how I have lov'd!
O, my *Mandane!* think upon thy pow'r!
How often haſt thou ſeen me pale with joy,
And trembling at a ſmile? And ſhall I——

MANDANE.

Myron!——
[*At that* MEMNON *ſtarts up ſuddenly.*

MEMNON.

Ah hold! I charge thee hold! One glance that way
Awakes my hell, and blows up all its flames:——
The world turns round; my heart is ſick to death!
O my diſtraction! perfect loſs of thought!

MANDANE.

Why ſtand you like a ſtatue? Are you dead?
What do you fold ſo faſt within your arms?
Why, with fix'd eye-balls, do you pierce the ground?
Why ſhift your place, as if you trod on fire?
Why gnaw your lip, and groan ſo dreadfully?
My lord, if I have ſpent whole live-long nights
In tears, and ſigh'd away the day in private,
Only oppreſs'd with an exceſs of love,
O turn, and ſpeak to me.

MEMNON.
And theſe, no doubt,

VOL. I. Y Are

Are arguments that I fhould draw thy blood.—
No child was ever lull'd upon the breaft
With half that tendernefs has melted from thee,
And fell like balm upon my wounded foul!
And fhall I murder thee? Yes, thus—thus—thus;—

        - [*Embracing fome time.*

MANDANE.

Alas! my lord forgets we are to die.

    [Memnon *gazes with wonder on the dagger.*

MEMNON.

By heav'n I had; my foul had took her flight
In blifs—Why, is not this our bridal day?

MANDANE.

That way diftraction lies.

MEMNON.
    Indeed it does.

BOTH.

Oh! Oh!

MANDANE.

Thy fighs and groans are fharper than thy fteel.
The guard is on us.

MEMNON.
    Then it muft be done.
Sun, hide thy face, and put the world in mourning.
Though blood ftart out for tears, 'tis done—But one,
One laft embrace. [*As he embraces her, fhe burfts into tears.*
    Let me not fee a tear—I could as foon
Stab at the face of heav'n, as kill thee weeping.

MANDANE.

'Tis paft; I am compos'd.

MEMNON.
    And now—and now.

MANDANE.

MANDANE.

Be not fo fearful; 'tis the fecond blow
Will pain my heart—indeed this will not hurt me.

MEMNON.

O thou haft ftung my foul quite through and through,
With thofe kind words: I had juft fteel'd my breaft,

[*Dafhing down the dagger.*

And thou undo'ft it all——I could not bear
To raze thy fkin to fave the world from ruin.

MANDANE. [*Stabs herfelf.*]

If you're a woman, I'll be fomething more,——
I fhall not tafte of heaven till you arrive. [*Dies.*

MEMNON.

Struck home—and in her heart—She's dead already;
And now with me all nature is expir'd.————
My lovely bride, now we again are happy, [*Stabs himfelf.*
And better worlds prepare our nuptial bow'r.——
Now every fplendid object of ambition,
Which lately, with their various gloffes, play'd
Upon my brain, and fool'd my idle heart,
Are taken from me by a little mift,
And all the world is vanifh'd. [*Dies.*

A march founded. Enter NICANOR *and* SYPHOCES, *vic-*
torious.

The guards, which are advancing to the bodies, fly.

NICANOR.

The day's our own; the *Perfian's* angry pow'rs
Have well repaid this morning infolence,
And turn'd the defperate fortune of the field,
By fure, though late, relief.

SYPHOCES.

Nicanor, friend,

I from

I from the city bring you welcome news :
My guilty letter from the amorous queen
I fpread amongft the multitude; while yet
Their blood was warm with reading the black fcroll,
Myris, to view the fortune of the fight,
Leaving her palace for the weftern tow'r,
Was feiz'd, torn, fcatter'd, on the guilty fpot,
Where her great brother fell,

NICANOR.

The gods are juft.

SYPHOCES.

See where *Bufiris* comes ; your royal captive,
In his misfortune great ; an awful ruin !
And dreadful to the conqueror !

NICANOR. [*Advancing, fees the bodies.*]

Sad fight !
A fight that teaches triumph how to mourn,
And more than juftifies thefe ftreaming tears,
Even on the moment that my country's fav'd
From fore oppreffion, and inglorious chains.

[*He falls on his attendants,*

A great fhout. Enter BUSIRIS, *wounded.*

BUSIRIS.

Conquer'd ? 'Tis falfe ; I am your mafter ftill ;
Your mafter, though in bonds : You ftand aghaft
At your good fate, and, trembling, can't enjoy.
Now, from my foul, I hug thefe welcome chains
Which fhew you all *Bufiris,* and declare
Crowns and fuccefs fuperfluous to my fame.——
You think this ftreaming blood will lower my thought ;
No, ye miftaken men, I fmile at death ;
For living here, is living all alone ;
To me a real folitude, amid

5

A throng

A throng of little beings groveling round me;
Which yet ufurp one common fhape and name.
I thank thefe wounds, thefe raging pains, which promife
An interview with equals foon elfewhere.

[*He fees* Memnon.]

Ha! dead? 'Tis well: He rofe not to my fword;
I only wifh'd his fate, and there he lies.
Some, when they die, die all; their mould'ring clay
Is but an emblem of their memories;
The fpace quite clofes up thro' which they pafs'd:
That I have liv'd, I leave a mark behind,
Shall pluck the fhining age from vulgar time,
And give it whole to late pofterity:
My name is writ in mighty characters,
Triumphant columns, and eternal domes,
Whofe fplendor heighten our *Egyptian* day,
Whofe ftrength fhall laugh at time, till their great bafis,
Old earth itfelf, fhall fail: In after-ages,
Who war or build, fhall build or war from me;
Grow great in each as my example fires:
'Tis I of art the future wonders raife;
I fight the future battles of the world. ———
Great *Jove*, I come! *Egypt*, thou art forfaken; [*Sinks.*
Afia's impoverifh'd by my finking glories;
And the world leffens, when *Bufiris* falls.   [*Dies.*

SYPHOCES.

Bear the dead monarch to his pyramid;
And for what ufe foe'er it was defign'd
By that high-minded, but miftaken, man,
There let him lie magnificent in death;
Great was his life, great be his monument;
And on *Bufiris*' nephew, young *Arfaces*,
Of gentler fpirit, let the crown devolve.

From

From this day's vengeance, let the nations know,
Jove lays the pride of haughtieſt monarchs low ;
And they, who, kindled with ambitious fire,
In arts and arms with moſt ſucceſs aſpire,
If void of virtue, but provoke their doom,
Graſp at their fate, and build themſelves a tomb.

EPILOGUE,

EPILOGUE,

BY A FRIEND.

SPOKEN BY MRS. OLDFIELD.

*T*HE race of critics, dull, judicious rogues,
 To mournful plays deny brisk Epilogues :
Each gentle swain, and tender nymph, say they,
From a sad tale should go in tears away ;
From hence quite home should streams of sorrow shed,
And, drown'd in grief, steal supperless to bed.
 This doctrine is so grave the Sparks won't bear it ;
They love to go in humour to their claret.
The Cit, who owns a little fun worth buying,
Holds half-a-crown too much to pay for crying :
Besides, who knows, without these healing arts,
But Love might turn your heads, and break your hearts ;
And the poor Author, by imagin'd woes,
Might people Beth'lem with our Belles and Beaux ?
 Hence I, who lately bid adieu to pleasure,
Robb'd of my spouse, and my dear virgin treasure ;
I, whom you saw, despairing, breathe my last,
Am free and easy, as if nought had past ;
Again put on my airs, and play my fan,
And fear no more that dreadful creature, Man.

          —But

—But whence does this malicious mirth begin ?
I know, ye beasts, you reckon it no sin.
   'Tis strange that crimes the same, in diff'rent plays,
Should move our horror, and our laughter raise.
Love's Jove secure the comic Actor tries ;
But, if he's wicked, in blank verse he dies.
The farce, where wives prove frail, still makes the best ;
And the poor cuckold is a standing jest :
But our brave bard, a virtuous son of Isis,
Counts a bold stroke in Love among the vices ;
In blood and wounds a guilty land he dips ye,
And wastes an empire for one ravish'd gypsy.
   What musty morals fill an Oxford head,
To notions of pedantic virtue bred !
There each stiff Don at gallantry exclaims,
And calls fine men and ladies filthy names ;
They tell you Rakes and Jilts corrupt a nation ;
—Such is the prejudice of education !
   You, who know better things, will sure approve
These scenes, that shew the boundless power of Love.
Let, when they will, th' Italian Things appear,
This play, we trust, shall throng an audience here.
Bold Myron's passion, up to phrenzy wrought,
Would ill be warbled through an Eunuch's throat :
His part, at least, his part requires a Man ;
Let Nicolani act it, if he can.